CHARLIE WALKER is an adventurer, writer, and public speaker. He has travelled over 50,000 miles by human power. Between adventures he lives in London, where he rides a bicycle daily.

THROUGH
SAND & SNOW

A forty-thousand mile journey to
adulthood via the ends of the earth

by

CHARLIE
WALKER

For my father

MAPS

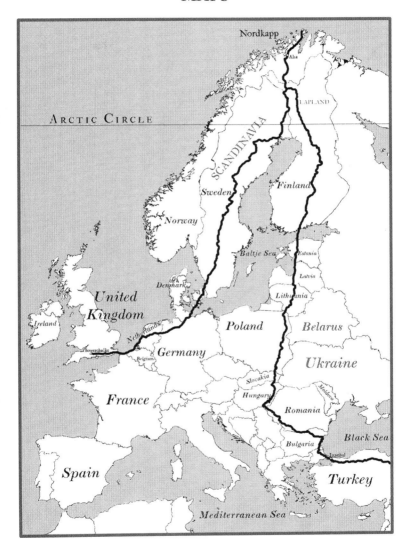

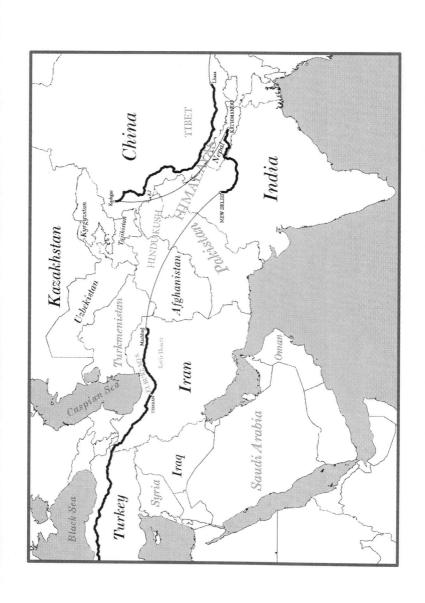

PROLOGUE

There are basically two types of men in the world.
Those who stay at home, and those who don't.
- Rudyard Kipling

30 January 2011

I neared the checkpoint in the late afternoon. Stopping at a steep spur which jutted into the heart of the valley, I hid the bicycle behind a crumbling mud wall, fished another coat and a third pair of gloves from my bags and fumbled them on. The day was a cruel, sunless grey and the temperature hovered around -20°C. Video camera in my pocket, I scrambled up and slumped prostrate on the snow just behind the ridge.

The checkpoint was notoriously well guarded, but getting into Tibet had become a burning obsession. Maybe it marked the point at which I would move from bicycle tourist to grizzled explorer. I'd gorged on books by Sven Hedin and Heinrich Harrer, daring heroes from a different age. I knew that foreign travellers had been turned away, time and time again, from the mysterious mountain kingdom, and not much had changed since the Chinese took control.

I also knew that, if I made it, I would find little but brutal weather and loneliness. I was poorly equipped and would face genuine danger from the cold. However, I was only six months into my adventure. If I stumbled at this early hurdle then I might as well fly home and be done with it.

I used the camera's zoom to search for a way past the collection of squat, whitewashed barracks. The road ran straight through the base, punctuated by three manned barriers. A few bare-branched poplars thrust skyward from the frozen earth and patchy snow. Beyond the perimeter, a handful of sheds and mud-walled cottages comprised the village of Kudi.

At the centre of the base stood a three-storey guard tower. A tall fence on its left ran down to a partially frozen river overlooked by another, smaller tower. Walking along the river seemed a risky option, as I'd be unable to test the thickness of the ice. To the right, another fence climbed the valley's impossibly steep scree wall. Dragging a heavy bicycle around it would require Herculean strength and make too much noise. My only option was to walk straight through the middle.

As terrified as I was exhilarated, I pitched my tent behind the mud wall and set my alarm for 4 a.m.

The hut door opened and I froze, mid-stride, on the faintly starlit road. I could taste the adrenalin in the back of my throat and my numb fingers throbbed. I could feel my heart beating.

Three Chinese soldiers stepped out of the guard hut and paused, adjusting to the bitterly cold night air. They didn't speak. Not ten yards away, I stood stock-still and eyed the silhouettes of their rifles. I held my breath, fearing they'd see the billowing condensation.

The shortest of the three hawked and spat on the frozen ground then walked over to a rusting white car. The other two stayed where they were, staring silently into the night, stamping their feet and breathing into their ungloved hands.

Have they heard me? Are they looking for me? Perhaps a villager spied me creeping along the road and reported me? What will they do to me if I'm discovered? Arrest? Deportation? Worse?

The western gateway to Tibet was strictly off-limits to foreigners, and I was carrying a camera with footage of their base. *I shouldn't be here. Why did I come?*

The driver took three or four attempts to coax his vehicle into life. I dragged my bicycle to one side, using the cough of the ignition to mask the sound. Thankful for my dark clothes and the tape over my panniers' reflective surfaces, I crouched between its frame and a wall of wooden planks. The engine sputtered. Headlights flickered on, and the beam washed over me as the car swung across the middle of the road. I bowed my head and held my breath, awaiting capture.

But it never came.

The other two soldiers climbed in and all three drove away.

I breathed out at last.

Edging around the red-and-white-striped barrier, I left the guard hut behind. But it was too early to celebrate. I wheeled my bike deeper into the base, keeping close to the unlit buildings.

I soon saw four more soldiers, perched on footstools, in bulky winter coats and hats, next to an open-backed truck. Hugging themselves for warmth, they huddled around a small fire in a metal bucket with crude ventilation holes punched in its side. Their snub-nosed rifles stood together, muzzles pointed skyward, propped against a wheel. Just beyond them lay the second barrier. A temperamental floodlight buzzed nearby.

Abandoning my bicycle, I crept closer. Then another soldier exited a building thirty yards behind me and started walking towards the fire. Caught in the middle, I flitted forward, threw myself flat on the ground and rolled underneath the truck. I wormed further, then crouched behind one of the wheels. The men, their guns and the fire were no more than a yard from me. A whiff of diesel cut through the earthy smell of burning coal. I breathed as lightly as possible into the crook of my elbow, trying not to cough.

The approaching soldier barked an order. One of the four got up and walked back to the building with him, boots squeaking with each step. After a few moments of silence, the remaining three started telling jokes. As their laughter became louder and more boisterous, I built up the courage to slip back the way I'd come.

Having retrieved the bike, I delved down a narrow alley, strewn with discarded plastic bags and animal droppings, which led away from the base. I winced each time an ice puddle cracked beneath my feet.

With a low growl, a vast Tibetan mastiff leapt at me from the rear of one of the buildings. It was stopped short by its chain, but came close enough for the heat of its shit-eating breath to blast me full in the face. Desperate to silence the frenzied barking, I swung my boot and clapped the brute clean across the muzzle. The dog retreated with a whimper and I continued towards the boundary fence.

The bottom wire was rusted thin and broken in several places. Feeling like James Bond, I took a pair of folding pliers from my pocket, cut three wires, bent back the sharp ends as far as I could, and crawled through, dragging the bike behind me. I moved on as quickly and quietly as possible, hoping it would snow before morning to cover my tracks.

Thirty minutes later, I had cleared Kudi and rejoined the road. I mounted up, high on the stupidity of what I had just done, against all the odds – successfully, and very illegally, entered Tibet.

ONE

BEGINNING

I was excited, vain-glorious, knowing I had far to go; but not,
as yet, how far. As I left home that morning and walked
away from the sleeping village, it never occurred to me
that others had done this before me.
- Laurie Lee

1 July 2010

My father cried most as I left. We had a small family farewell on a bright summer's morning in the Wiltshire village I had called home for all of my twenty-two years. As I straddled the old bicycle, my sister tied freshly picked lavender to the basket. She said it would make the headwinds smell sweet. My mother hugged me tightly before turning her flooding face into my father's shoulder. My uncle seemed the only person present, myself included, able to see the excitement of my adventure. With a high-pitched chuckle, he told me to have fun. My grandmother stood a little apart in a tweed skirt and waved gravely, both arms raised above her stooped figure of eighty-eight years.

There were plenty of tears, but none escaped my eyes as I pedalled off down the lane, shaven-headed and confused. I should have been sad, or perhaps happy, or at least excited. However, I felt nothing but emptiness.

The village road was overhung with branches of riotous green. The recently strimmed verges tinged the air with a cocktail of two-stroke and cut grass. I glimpsed people I had vaguely known my whole life but rarely spoken to. They were going about their lives, ambling to the post box or pottering in front gardens, oblivious to the fact that I was turning my life upside down.

Sweat soon trickled from under my cheap helmet,

running down my face and salting my taste buds. I was very unfit. Preparations had been rushed, with very little planning and no time for training. Knowing only where I was heading in the grand scheme of things, I would follow road signs to the ferry port in Dover. Once in France, I could work out which route to take according to whim – I could just steer north towards the Arctic.

When deciding where my trip would take me, I chose the furthest point from home on each of Europe, Asia and Africa: the continents that could be reached without crossing an ocean. I reasoned that, if a mountaineer deals in the vertical and aims for the highest point, a cyclist, who deals in the horizontal, should aim for the furthest point. Nordkapp in Europe was the first target. The most distant place in Asia was Singapore, some six thousand miles away as the crow flies. The third goal, in Africa, was Cape Town. It was another six thousand crow miles from Singapore, but I would have to take the long way around the Indian Ocean, back through Asia and down Africa's eastern flank. From Cape Town I would steer my handlebars homeward. That was it. From home to home via Nordkapp, Singapore and Cape Town.

The specifics didn't really matter to me. I was just eager for adventure, wanting to follow in the footsteps of great explorers: to do something brave, difficult and dangerous. I wanted to visit remote places, meet remote peoples, and be absent from England long enough for an air of mystique to develop around me in the eyes of those I knew. The three goals were really just a concept clumsily crowbarred into a non-specific journey I longed to make, a way of justifying something that I had no good excuse to do. Why would I choose a life of uncertainty and physical hardship when I could have settled deeper into the journalism job I was lucky to have? People wouldn't accept that without a reason. I needed a something to pin my odyssey on.

Staring at a small world map, I tried to work out how

long I might be gone. On that map the length of Britain was roughly the same as the breadth of my thumb. I decided that riding a thumb's breadth might take a month on average and so started planting my thumbs, one beside the other, across continents. After forty-eight thumbs, I landed back in Britain. Four years it would take. Perhaps around forty thousand miles.

'Mum, Dad, I've had an idea. I'm going away on my bicycle for a while...'

After forty fast miles the expected pangs of parting still hadn't hit and I was flagging on the uphills in unusually hot weather. Taking off the itchy helmet for the first and last time, I slumped onto a shaded verge. My pale feet looked soft and weak in their new sandals, like those of a middle-aged tourist on a self-drive holiday. Pulling my video camera from a pannier and holding it at arm's length, I self-consciously began to talk into the lens for the first time.

'Here I am, halfway through my first day of, um, four years' cycling, um, about forty thousand miles around Europe, Asia and Africa.

'I left home this morning. I left my family, my parents and, er, it was hard.' My voice rose an octave and caught in my throat. 'They were crying as I left, which wasn't easy to see, but, um...'

My lips buckled, and I switched the camera off as the hot tears began. The enormity of what I'd set myself finally swept over me and I curled into a foetal ball among the dandelions, sobbing pathetically into the long grass. All the questions and doubts that other people had voiced on my behalf suddenly became my own: Why on earth are you going so far? Four years is too long. What are you running from? You're going to be lonely. You're not strong enough. You'll be back in a year.

I was terrified. *What the hell* am *I doing?* I asked myself. *This is crazy! What right do I have to put my family through this?*

They'll worry themselves sick. Will Grandma live to see me return? Will the cat? Why am I doing this? What am I trying to prove?

The questions hung, unanswered, but the crying was cathartic. After five minutes of snivelling and guttural choking noises, I became embarrassed in front of myself and stopped. I'd let out what had gradually coiled tighter and deeper in my mind for almost a year. The emotional jack-in-the-box was sprung, and I was able to turn to the task at hand: getting to the port in time for my ferry. The other concerns could wait.

That first day was a gruelling ninety-five-miles through the tightly packed hills of southern England. Thick boughs of foliage draped over every fence, and the warm smell of summer swirled in the air. My hundred-pound, secondhand bicycle, named 'Old Geoff' after an aged teacher I'd been fond of, felt cumbersome. The temperature was 30°C and I'd never ridden that far in a day before. In fact, I hadn't ridden so much as a mile for two months.

Stopping on the green in a sleepy market town, I asked an elderly lady minding a stall to watch Old Geoff while I waddled stiffly into a dark, ancient pub to ask for water. The sour note of stale, spilled beer was familiar and comforting. While the bored young barman filled my bottles, I leant on the sticky counter and blurted out that I was just a few hours into a four-year bicycle journey that would cross mountains, deserts and continents.

'Why do you want to do that?' he asked disinterestedly. I opened my mouth to answer but found no words. His question had stumped me. I defensively gabbled something about wanting to see the world and scuttled out into the fresh air.

Why do I want to do this? What could I have told him? That I have pretensions of being a heroic explorer? No, that won't cut it. The great age of exploration is surely over anyway. That I think it will make me more attractive to women? No, I can't admit that to anyone but myself. That a sizeable dollop of ego was among the ingredients that cooked up this plan? That I want to prove something to myself but don't know precisely what? That I'm simply bored of my lovely, unchallenging life and need to do something, anything to shake a gnawing sense of lethargy?

All of the reasons that sprang to mind felt embarrassing and self-indulgent. I was a young man wanting to slay dragons, but I'd grown up swaddled and in a post-dragon world. I had never faced any real challenge. My twenty-two years had been eased by circumstance and privilege. I was white, straight, privately educated and part of a loving family. If I was honest with myself, I knew that I wasn't bad looking and had a pretty decent mind. Throughout my life I'd slipped from one pleasant and unchallenging situation to another. Boarding school had been fun and a bit of a cruise. I didn't work particularly hard and yet got acceptable grades. I got on with people and was adequate at sports. I ruffled few feathers and was made head boy for the final year, despite being caught drinking the previous term. During final exams I was found stoned on the roof and effectively expelled, but I was still allowed back to collect the Head of School award at prizegiving.

University didn't stretch me much either; I enjoyed what I did of my studies, made good friends and became more confident with women. Within days of completing a journalism postgraduate diploma I was working on a national newspaper in London and could have climbed that ladder if I'd stuck at it.

There had been nothing to rail against. My life had been charmed, and it had been boring. It's only a short hop from complacency to arrogance – both are terrible things. I needed to make some road bumps for myself. Samuel Johnson's Prince Rasselas leaves the luxurious palace he grew up in, saying, 'I fly from pleasure…because pleasure has ceased to please'. I too wanted to know what existed outside my bubble. I wanted hardship and pain.

Outside the pub, the old lady looked up from her table of miscellaneous trinkets. With her hands slung in stretched cardigan pockets, she had a face worn by years, not cares. Perched in the sunshine, birdlike, on a low wall in her parochial hometown, she seemed utterly content.

'Where on earth are you going on that bicycle with all that stuff?' she clucked in a pleasant West Country brogue.

I mentally rifled through the countries ahead and picked one for dramatic effect.

'China! I'm cycling to China.' I relished the exotic sound of it.

'Awww! That's nice,' she returned in an endearing, if condescending, coo. I would have elicited more of a response if I'd said London. China seemed beyond her fathom.

Halfway to Dover, I stayed in the home of a friend's family. Sitting in a bathtub with ice cubes bobbing in the water, I sipped a beer and watched the goose pimples rise on my aching legs. We ate a barbecued dinner on a sweeping lawn in the late midsummer light. The neat stripes mown into the grass reminded me of my parents' home, where they were probably sitting with white wine, wondering when they'd next see me. The family excitedly asked questions about my trip, many of which I'd never considered. One question stuck with me as I pedalled away in the morning: why are you doing this *alone*? The obvious answer was that it would be difficult to find someone willing to do it with me. But there was more to it than that. I had travelled alone before and, while I knew that I preferred company, I had some notion that I would 'grow' somehow if I spent long tracts of time by myself. The word 'introspection' floated through my mind. I tried to dismiss it, shying away from the phrase 'to find myself'. It sounded clichéd, self-indulgent and something people use as an excuse to get drunk on Southeast Asian beaches. However, as I was venturing outside my cosy life to see *what* I found, then I could expect to also find who 'I' was when measured in the real world where ease isn't a birthright.

In the afternoon I stopped in a lay-by and asked a man in a sandwich van to fill my water bottle. A lorry driver asked in a gruff voice where I was going. Too tired to choose an evocative sounding country, I replied simply. 'Dover.'

'Well, you better have a bacon butty then, to help you on your way. It's on me,' he said.

Mick had thick-rimmed glasses and a couple of small cuts on his cheek from shaving that morning. A soft whiff of recently smoked tobacco hung about him. He told me about the longest queue of lorries he had ever waited in at Dover port. Nodding along, I ate the sandwich, trying not to get ketchup on my clean white vest.

Struggling to find somewhere to pitch my tent that evening, I asked the landlady of a Kentish pub if I could sleep in the beer garden. She said it was fine and introduced me to an outdoor table of her regulars. They were six heavy-set labourers with crudely tattooed forearms, beer bellies stretching their t-shirts, and accents that made me sound like a snotty prince. They plied me with drinks and made generous online donations to the charities I was supporting. After several pints of beer, and having watched Uruguay nudge past Ghana on penalties in the World Cup quarter finals, I fumbled my tent up in the garden and tumbled gracelessly inside.

Waking at 6 a.m. with a pulsing hangover, I sprinted for the port along a busy road closed to cyclists. Drivers honked angrily, but I was running late. If I missed the free crossing given by a kind press officer at P&O then I'd have to pay for one myself, and my shoestring budget wouldn't appreciate that. With two minutes to spare, I pedalled up the ramp, left Old Geoff on the car deck, and headed to the Club Lounge, courtesy of my free ticket. Well-dressed, middle-aged holidaymakers sat on the sofas around me drinking complimentary champagne and firing glances at my yellow swimming shorts and clinging school athletics vest. It was the only clothing I had, but I didn't care. I'd made it off the island. I clambered up to the helipad and inhaled the salt air deeply while looking back at the white cliffs, an iconic sight to travellers for centuries more usually seen as a sign of homecoming. Taken by the idea of symbolism, I hurled my old mobile phone into the water. I wouldn't be needing it and felt a surge of freedom as it slotted into the foaming wake without a splash.

TWO

SUMMER

*I was a pebble in a catapult, pulled back to breaking point, about to
be sent hurtling towards whatever destiny had in store. Total freedom.
At that moment I wouldn't have changed places with anyone.*
- Jonny Bealby, *Running With the Moon*

3 July 2010

Disembarking in Calais, I was soon lost, overwhelmed
by the massiveness, the untold potential, of the
Eurasian landmass spread before me. In my eagerness to
be moving, I failed to read road signs and took the wrong
route out of town. A bald, spherical man with lively grey
eyebrows set me right, and I began tracing the coast.

The evening was cool and the twilight long, so I rode
until dark, crossing into Belgium. I looked for somewhere
to camp for a long time but there were regular farm
buildings along the road. I felt insecure about sleeping too
close to buildings in case I was found and told to piss off.

Eventually I gave up on finding a secluded spot and
followed a dirt track towards a bright floodlight. A lean
poultry farmer answered my knock at the farmhouse door.
He wore rubber boots and baggy blue overalls with several
neatly stitched denim patches. The farmer walked me
down an aisle between two chicken enclosures and allowed
me to camp in a tiny garden next to a child's swing. The
place was enveloped in the stench of chicken shit. I was
too tired to eat and drifted off to the cooing and chooking
of 85,000 chickens. My first three days on the road had
been haphazard and I was yet to 'stealth camp' without
permission – something I would have to do for the vast
majority of the next few years. I had a lot to learn about
life on a bicycle.

I drifted into Bruges, plucking strawberries from a punnet in Old Geoff's basket. The soft July weather had lured flocks of tourists to the city centre. Sitting on the cobblestones in the market square, I ate roughly carved chunks of sweating salami from my pannier. A young boy with a pudding-bowl haircut stared scornfully at me while melted ice-cream crawled over each of his knuckles one by one and dripped onto his red-buckled sandals.

I watched the crowds milling before the twelfth century belfry: knots of friends, families or lovers. I was an oddity and, with my freshly shorn head, looked thuggish. A little St. George's cross flew from the back of my bike, and I wondered if people related the flag to English football hooligans, who had been in the news again recently. I pulled off the little flag and dropped it in a bin. People avoided catching my eye and I felt lonely, isolated among the crowds. My self-consciousness was still acute. I needed to prove to myself that I was strong and self-reliant, that I could survive on my own. It was important to learn the difference between loneliness and aloneness.

I need to get used to being happily alone, I thought to myself. *Surely that's one of the reasons for this journey? It won't be easy. Until I master that, progress can be my distraction. Just keep moving.*

I looked at my still-crisp map and fixed on a nearby village as the place to ask for directions to. When I looked up, my breath caught in my throat. Banquo's ghost was staring straight at me, beckoning with a thin finger.

The old man stood in shadow across the street, his grey face untouched by the whir of activity and light all around him. He must have been staring for some time, waiting until I glimpsed him through the onslaught of tourists. He approached, wheeling a bicycle as old as himself. 'Where do you want to go?' His English was thickly accented.

'Dammé.'

'The village of the Dammé, this way,' he said ominously, before vanishing into the melee of other cyclists rattling over cobblestones on antiquated bicycles. I followed behind, wondering if he'd said *Dammé* or *damned,* until the crowds thinned and I came up beside him. We chatted as we rode along a few miles of a canal path. An enviably energetic eighty-year-old, Luc told me he cycled everywhere to keep busy and healthy in his old age. Dammé looked like a village from a Belgian chocolate box and nothing like the Village of the Damned, despite all the well-heeled blonde children. In an outdoor bar, Luc ordered Trappist beers and insisted I try the *maatjes* (soused herring), a Flemish specialty. The briny fish challenged my tastebuds while Luc reminisced about growing up in Nazi-occupied Belgium.

The narrative of the Second World War in Britain is one of fighting and loss and horror and heroism. However, Luc's stories of that time were fascinating precisely for their *lack* of those things. 'For a school child in Brugge,' he said, 'with no fighting or bombing, nothing was very different during the war. Belgium was quickly taken by the Nazis and life went on. Except, of course, for Jews or the minority involved in the resistance.

'People from England will find it strange, but I remember the German soldiers being much more polite and better behaved to us Belgians than the allied soldiers were after liberation in forty-four. When I think about it now, our 'liberators' seemed to feel a sense of entitlement. Many just helped themselves to things that they wanted.'

We sat together for a couple of hours and Luc told me about his life. He'd been one of the first foreigners to work in China after it opened to the West in the seventies. 'If you left the cities you were quickly in a medieval world. They were still using ploughs made of wood and pulled by buffalo. Their clothes were rags. The word peasant doesn't really describe how simple and poor they were.'

Luc seemed glad of my company and the conversation. I guessed he was often lonely. A solitary, feline character, he had never married but had spent his life on the move. He still travelled every year to a small farm he'd bought in northern Thailand. It was run by a Thai woman who lived with the son she'd had by Luc. His words hinted at an interesting story, but I didn't probe deeply. The sun was setting and I needed to find somewhere to camp.

I left Luc with a sense of sadness, realising that this condensed relay of pleasure in company and regret at parting would repeat itself countless times as I travelled. I would have to satisfy myself with fleeting friendships, scratching the surface but struggling to dig much deeper. As I pitched my tent in the garden of a half-built house, I wondered what countless other stories Luc must have. Had so much travel made it difficult for him to settle? Was he happy? What did he regret? He invited me to stay with him when I pedalled back through Europe in four years time. I said I would be delighted but caught myself doubting I would ever get that far.

Continuing into the Netherlands, I kept a fast pace, pedalling pangs of loneliness into submission. Striving to embrace the transience of my experiences, I began to spot novel things, smile, and simply move on. Impressions were formed cheaply and cheerfully. I knew I wasn't being 'intrepid'. I was barrelling north, sprinting towards Nordkapp. Forests and fields and streams and spires blurred fleetingly in my periphery. Old Geoff was the only constant: a simple secondhand bicycle, no suspension or fancy features. Steel frame, tough leather saddle, brakes, gears, and a couple of pannier racks. He'd cost only a hundred pounds.

One night in an Amsterdam backpackers' hostel was enough to swear me off staying in cities. I paid twenty-five euros that I couldn't afford to share a dormitory with several over-sexed American teenagers, legally drunk for the first time. The Netherlands nudged past Uruguay to reach the World Cup final that night. The city was a riot of neon orange Afro wigs and honking vuvuzelas. Mobs of burly men marched the streets, clapping hands above heads and barking jingoistic chants. The fug of alcohol and sweat draped itself over the warm night.

Swept out of the city the next morning on a somnolent tide of Dutch commuters stoically embracing their hangovers, I followed cycle paths northward. I covered many miles each day and yet had time to read, eat slowly and take glorious afternoon naps under trees. I acclimatised to my new lifestyle and developed good routines: waking up with slow breakfasts in the sunshine, packing each possession into its designated place, saddling up, and hitting the road. The first half hour of cycling was always spent trying to ignore the pain in my nether regions and the stiffness in my thighs. Some things would evidently take longer to adjust to.

The heat rose in northwest Germany. Hazy, stagnant air choked the land and, desperate to cool myself, I plunged into every lake I passed. The swelter finally broke with a terrific thunderstorm that I watched from a bus shelter with a bottle of *erdbeerwein* (strawberry wine) given to me that morning by a smiling shirtless farmer in denim dungarees.

A short ferry ride landed me in Denmark, where I met a man cycling down a country lane. He looked like a thick-set Michael Palin, and his nose was smeared with the white zinc sunblock that cricketers sometimes use. His faded panniers had various items of kit strapped on with decaying bungee cords. We continued along the road together. A sixty-year-old Australian on his umpteenth cycle tour, Bruce spoke in a very matter-of-fact way with an accent thick as molasses. He didn't seem interested in getting to know me but instead gave helpful tips on bicycle maintenance and how to stealth camp close to settlements.

Camped in a fir forest that evening, Bruce taught me to replace spokes, as my first had broken that afternoon. 'Yer see, if yer tie a liddle scrap of plastic onta the new spoke, then yer know which one ta tight'n or loos'n when "trueing" the wheel and yer 'void buggering about with all th'other ones and makin' things wurse…'

I learned that Bruce *sees* a country, *really* sees it. His route through Denmark formed a wiggly line all over his tattered map, constantly doubling back on itself, thoroughly probing the land and all its nooks. My route so far was as close to a straight line from Calais as I could make it. I knew instinctively that I should slow down, enjoy the unique textures of the places I was passing though, and generally savour the journey as Bruce did. However, I wanted to get Europe out of the way and breach the more exotic lands that lay ahead in Asia. I mentioned this to Bruce and he replied simply, 'You're on yours an' I'm on mine. Every adventure's different, mate. There's more'n one way t' skin a cat.'

In the morning we parted at a fork in the road. Bruce laid a hairy, brown hand on my shoulder and looked me in the eye. 'Things'll offen get tough on yer ride, mate. But just yer remember, it was *your* decision to make this journey. Naabody else. *Yours!* Yer took a long hard think and decided that yer *wanted* to do it, that yer had the courage fer it, and that yer was up fer it. When yer think yer wanna quit, just yer remember that. Good luck to yers.'

I stood at the junction watching him ride away, his sun-bleached trousers tucked into his long socks and his helmeted head turning from side to side, looking at the fields of cows.

Half a day in Copenhagen was enough to fall in love. In an uncharacteristic bout of romanticism, I decided that if I grow lonely and old, I'll move to Copenhagen in summer and marry the city. The wide streets were lined with ornate buildings prettily painted in pastel colours, and the picturesque waterways were dotted with people strolling in the evening sun. I cooked supper on a beach in the northern suburbs, where at 9 p.m. people still swam and played volleyball in the rich, slanting sunlight. The Danish were statuesque and beautiful. Oozing self-assurance, the girls wore skimpy bikinis while the blond, bare-chested boys moved easily, their sculpted sinews shifting beneath sun-burnished skin.

After eating, I decided to ask someone if I could camp in their garden that night. The suburb was affluent and the first house I tried had an expansive lawn. I rang the doorbell and put on a face that I hoped was simultaneously vulnerable, friendly and unassuming. A bald man opened the door six inches and confirmed that he did indeed speak English. Oozing English charm (or so I hoped) I asked for permission and received a 'no' and a closed door. Undeterred, I knocked at the next house. The kitchen window was thrust open and a Botox-fixed face appeared. The mask looked me up and down before launching into a Danish rant. I patiently waited until she finished.

'I'm sorry. I don't understand,' I said. 'Do you speak English?' She paused a moment and then repeated the tirade in English. The gist was: 'No! You're not welcome here. Go away!' I hadn't yet asked for anything.

The third house was similar to the first, with a grand, rolling garden. The excuse given was that they had a valuable statue in the garden that they feared might be damaged or stolen.

'We're very sorry but we simply can't risk it,' said the handsome middle-aged man in boat shoes and a polo shirt. 'It's really worth a lot of money, you know.'

As I wheeled down the long driveway, I glimpsed the statue – a life-sized bronze sculpture of a leaping dolphin. *How was I supposed to steal that bloody great thing on a bicycle?* I thought later while pitching my tent in a mosquito-infested wood.

Over the coming months, I would be invited into dozens of homes by people, often with almost nothing to their names. I was struck by the irony that having something material to protect seems to isolate people from the world they live in.

THREE

MIDNIGHT SUN

*I wondered why it was that places are so much
lovelier when one is alone.*
- Daphne du Maurier

19 July 2010

I woke to a soft rustling outside the tent. Dawn had already broken so I guessed it to be about 3 a.m. Careful not to make a sound, I raised my head from a pillow of bundled clothes and looked through the open tent flap. Two yards away stood a reindeer with magnificent, many-pointed antlers spanning three feet. He was sniffing a pannier on Old Geoff, who lay plonked down beside the tent. His broad face, somewhere between a cow and an antelope, nodded at the end of a long, muscular neck as he began scratching it on the pannier. A curtain of white hair sprouted from his throat. I smelled a faint mixture of dung and urine, soft enough to not be unpleasant.

Propped up on one elbow, I watched, staying completely still for as long as I could, while the reindeer casually snuffled around, tearing scattered clumps of grass from the forest floor. The glade was suffused with a soft emerald light and distant birdsong welcomed the Nordic summer morning. The scene was ethereal. After a while, my eyes fixed on a spot among the pines and crossed slightly, staring into space. I didn't refocus. I couldn't; I didn't want to. I could hear the reindeer, and smell him, and sense him in my periphery. Just knowing he was there was enough. I remained still and unblinking, transfixed, wishing the moment would last forever.

Eventually I moved to relieve an aching shoulder and the world shifted back into focus. The reindeer looked sharply in my direction and we locked eyes for a moment before he cantered away, weaving through the trees. I gazed after him for a while before climbing out into the cool morning and gathering some blueberries for breakfast. Walking barefoot among the trees was a daily pleasure. My feet sank slowly into the thick, spongy carpet of moss. I greedily inhaled the sweet scent of pinesap, and marvelled at the enormity of the forest. The day before, a Swedish villager told me proudly that the Boreal forest covers eleven per cent of Earth's land, stretching across Scandinavia, Siberia and Canada with only the Bering Strait to break its continuity.

I continued northwards along the spine of Sweden on gravel backroads. I rarely covered ten miles without encountering a pristine lake mirroring the surrounding pine forest: a green infinity of silent, matchstick sentinels serrating the crests of the hills.

The settlements simplified, becoming ever scarcer, usually centred around small sawmills. The tiny groups of wooden houses were painted a maroon which glowed a regal red in the late evening light. Sunset came later and later until, eventually, as I entered the Arctic Circle, darkness stopped coming. A simple evening routine emerged: find a lake, swim and wash in the bracing water, pitch my tent on the cushioned forest floor, eat a late supper, pull a bandana over my eyes and sleep.

One morning I spotted a man sitting serenely under a roadside tree, gazing into the middle distance. An absurdly over-loaded bicycle stood beside him. I approached. He looked to be in his mid-fifties and had scarred stumps where his thumbs had once been. His clothes were dirty, faded and threadbare. On closer inspection, his baggage was mostly sacks of empty drinks cans and bottles. I opened with the standard cycle tourist question.

'Hi! Where are you headed?'

'Nowhere really. It's shummer and I'm already far enough nord to make a living so I'm jusht relaxing. I'm

Derek.' He didn't offer his hand but pointed at the ground beside him, so I sat down. In his thick Dutch accent, Derek told me how he made his living.

'I'm homeless. I don't mind saying that. I see no problem with it. I have been for many years now. Der working life didn't agree wid me. Now I live wid my bike In summer I go nord and in winter I go south to der Mediterranean. It's warmer down dere.'

'What do you do for food?' I asked, trying not to stare at a thick scar on his left cheek.

'Dat's easy! Summer is a rich time for me. In the Scandinavian countries, dey simply give you money for feeding der bottles and cans into der automatic recycling machines in supermarkets. It's only a small amount for each one but people just trow dem out of der car window.'

Derek seemed happy and completely disinterested in me. He wasn't exploring and didn't burn with curiosity about the world. He wasn't desperate for company. He was just living in the way he'd decided was easiest and most pleasant for him. His simple motivations contrasted with my tangled ones. However, I couldn't help wondering if he was running from something. And, if so, what? Who did that to his thumbs? Did he not have family or friends?

Am I running from something? I asked myself. *Perhaps, but what? I have friends and a loving family. I have a home and a job if I want them. But I don't, not really. Is that it? Am I running from mundanity? From mediocrity? From the responsibilities of adulthood?*

As I rode on I pushed these thoughts to the back of my mind and, inspired by Derek, began plucking cans and bottles from the roadside. I was amazed and appalled at how many I could collect on a short stretch of road. The majority were alcoholic or energy drinks. I imagined drivers rushing from A to B and, in a frenzy fuelled by Red Bull and dated Europop, furiously flinging cans out the window.

For a fortnight I gathered what I spotted and in each town deposited the fruits of my labour in the supermarket.

People stared at me and my bike covered in bulging bags of cans but I was happy to have a little income. In the first two days I made 200 krona (£18) that fed me for the next four days. Cooked on a small petrol-burning stove, my meals were large, simple and cheap. I was averaging eighty miles each day and my appetite seemed bottomless. Breakfast was four or five sandwiches stuffed with chocolate spread and sliced banana. Second breakfast was the same meal two hours later. Lunch was dense bread with cheese and several cups of sweet black tea. Teatime called for more tea and plenty of biscuits, but supper was the main event: mounds of rice, sauce and maybe some fried vegetables as a treat. Occasionally I spoiled myself by adding the cheapest meat I could lay my hands on, usually tinned tuna.

In a supermarket one day, I found a stack of tins bearing a drawing of a tuna-esque fish and incomprehensible Swedish text. It was nearing expiry and discounted to an absurdly cheap price, so I bought three tins, one for each night until the next town. That evening, as I forked the first tin's contents onto my rice, I was surprised by its paste-like texture and the lumps of an opaque gelatinous substance. Ignoring the gag-inducing taste, I stoically struggled through it for three nights before reaching the next supermarket. Walking absent-mindedly down an aisle, I spotted the very same 'tuna' in the pet food section. The discovery ended my period of living on almost-expired cat food.

In Norway, the land grew more dramatic as the road swept me alongside a fjord edged by sheer cliffs. I emerged from the enormity of the Boreal forest onto treeless tundra. Clinging to the windswept ground was a patchwork of tough gorse with yellow wildflowers that filled the air with a faint coconut smell.

I had been on the road for five weeks without a rest and felt a deep fatigue. I could fall asleep within seconds of closing my eyes and slept nine hours every night. I knew the continuous exertion wasn't sustainable, but I wanted to reach Nordkapp before taking my first day off. I braced myself for a final push, and continued across the snowless summer plains for the last leg to the cape. Along the road were occasional houses with parked snowmobiles patiently awaiting winter. The light traffic consisted solely of caravans and tour coaches all funnelled onto the one road north. As evening tried to fall, the speeding coaches ceased for the day and I decided to cycle through the night as a fitting climax to my time in the Arctic summer.

The sun skirted the hills at 11.30 p.m. and I continued along a coastal road under the still-blue sky while it caressed the northern horizon. The thin clouds started bleeding vivid pinks and purples and the magnificent blaze was reflected on the water. The tranquillity was briefly shattered when I was dive-bombed by a flock of Arctic terns, whose cliffside nests I had disturbed in passing. Protective mothers swooped at me, knife-like, with wings folded back and beaks thrust forward. Several crashed into my body and one stabbed into the back of my head. In a panic, I thumped one bird out of the sky and the rest retreated to their young.

I arrived at 'the tunnel' in the small hours. Infamous among cycle tourists, *Nordkapptunnelen* is four miles long and drops 212 metres below sea level before climbing to emerge on the island of Magerøya, which Nordkapp crowns. I plunged into the dimly lit mouth in the cliff face and sped downwards, forcing myself not to use the brakes. Reaching a toe-curling 50 mph, I clenched my buttocks and bellowed a song at the top of my voice. The long echo thundered all around me.

At the bottom I passed an ice puddle and began the steep climb to the other end. After almost an hour I emerged into the daylight, body steaming like a racehorse, and flopped onto the grass to chew some stale bread. There was still thirty miles to Nordkapp, but I felt energised. As the road threaded a route through and over hills, mist fell and visibility dropped to just a few yards. I watched as delicate water droplets collected in the hairs on my hands.

After 170 miles and eighteen hours of continuous riding, I crested the last hill with legs throbbing and head pounding. The end of Europe: a 307-metre-high cliff thrusting into the Berents Sea at latitude 71°10'21", Nordkapp lies only a thousand miles from the North Pole. The view from the cliff top was of a daunting blue-grey nothingness. Sea birds swooped in and out of the fog, unseen waves struck the rocks below with muted crashes, and the invigorating smell of the sea surged up to meet me.

As the sun started to burn through, the mist thinned. It was not yet 6 a.m. and I had the viewpoint to myself. Leaning on the railing, having achieved my first goal, I started to cry. I wasn't sad. For the first time in my life I was crying with relief: a swell of gratitude and pride amplified by the accumulated exhaustion of riding a heavy bike three thousand miles in a few short weeks.

On reflection, I wasn't sure if I had ever truly believed I would make it that far. Before starting, Nordkapp was little more than an abstract concept to me, just a distant place at the end of several roads. Day by day I got closer to the target but thought little about it, busying myself with cycling, eating and gazing at the forest.

The milestone had crept up on me. I realised that if I made it this far, simply by getting up each morning and riding a little further, then I could *possibly* complete the whole journey. The thought was both exciting and intimidating. For the first time, I knew I was in it for the long haul: that I could and *would* go through with the whole journey. I was finally dedicated to the challenge with all my being, not just my words. This wasn't bravado in front of friends. It wasn't drunken boasting in a pub. This was me, alone, committing to something more completely than I ever had before. *I won't be going home for four more years.*

My life will never really be the same. My eyes continued streaming.

With the hiss of air brakes behind me, the day's first coachload of tourists arrived. A chattering group of German pensioners disembarked. I wiped my eyes on a sleeve and continued staring seaward. A woman came and leaned against the railing next to me.

'Are you OK?' she asked. I turned. She was staring at me through rheumy blue eyes with folds of pallid, baggy skin hanging above them. They were shining, watering slightly in the chilly breeze. My tears started running again and my jaw shuddered for a second. I felt vulnerable. I shouldn't have made eye contact. She laid a light hand on my shoulder as I buried my face in my fingerless gloves. 'Do you speak English? Vot's wrong?' she asked.

'It's nothing,' I shrugged. 'I'm just tired and being foolish.'

'*Nicht* foolish. It's OK. Vere haf you come from on der bicycle.'

'From England.'

'Englandt? Zooper! And vere do you going now?' I thought about it for a second. 'I'm going to Singapore.' My voice was resolute. 'Really? On der bicycle.' She sounded incredulous.

I said goodbye and wheeled Old Geoff down the slope. Singapore was half a world away. I would have to go through sand and snow to get there.

FOUR

AUTUMN

For my part, I travel not to go anywhere, but to go.
I travel for travel's sake. The great affair is to move.
- Robert Louis Stevenson

The thousand miles through Finland was fast. Autumn gathered pace behind me, sweeping south like a tide igniting trees into a seasonal blaze. The golden summer of my northward journey receded and I chased its tail, upping the daily mileage and taking no rest days. My first birthday on the road, a Friday thirteenth, saw my first puncture and the small treat of some freshly baked bread rather than the packaged supermarket variety.

The few Finns I met were relaxed, welcoming people. Slightly lost one morning in Lapland, I followed a forest track off the road to ask for directions. At its end was a small pottery studio where I was welcomed in by Hellevi and Juhani. Married for more than forty years, they had built the most peaceful life imaginable in their studio and wooden house with a garden sloping down to a small, sparkling lake. Their home in the forest clearing was originally used as a cabin for loggers in the nineteenth century, and the sticky smell of pine sap hung in the air.

We ate a brunch of homemade yoghurt with berries that they had foraged. Hellevi perched on a stool in her floral apron and clasped a coffee mug. There were smudges of dried clay on her forearms. She told me that every day of the year they swim in the lake and fire up their homemade sauna. 'When the lake freezes over in winter,' she said, 'we have a little electric churn to keep a small area open for our daily dip.

'The winter is so beautiful. On clear nights I like to wrap up in blankets and take a thin mattress onto the ice. I lie down in the centre of the lake to look at the stars. There is no light pollution here, even in the Australian outback it will not be better...and the Australians, they don't get the Northern Lights!'

Hellevi asked me where I was going. I told her I was on a four-year journey and her brow furrowed. 'But what about your mother? She will miss you very much, I think.'

'She will,' I replied, 'but I'm following my dream, which is also important. She understands that.' Even as I said it, I could hear it was simply the answer I *thought* should follow. I hadn't truly considered the question.

'I am worried for you on your dangerous journey,' she continued, 'but I am more worried for her. These four years will be extremely hard for her. She will always be wondering where are you and if you are safe. I am a mother too and I feel pain, literally physical pain, if I am separated from my children for too long. It is like a body part is being slowly torn away. You must contact her as often as possible. Use my computer now and write her an email, even if it is only a short one.'

Having sent an email, I thanked Hellevi and Juhani and left their tranquil home with a heavy heart. Apart from seeing my parents' tears at my departure, I really hadn't thought about the effect my absence might have on them. I started to accept that my plan was indeed a selfish one. I had something I wanted to do for unclear reasons and was pursuing it without the slightest consideration for anyone else. I tried to soften my guilt with the fact that my parents had been happily married for thirty years. They had each other for support if they fretted about my safety. Hellevi and Juhani seemed to have an equally unbreakable bond. They had found each other and created happiness in isolation with no settlements for miles around them. Feeling a mixture of envy and admiration, I pedalled back to the road knowing I would be unlikely to find love on my adventure. I had chosen a solitary existence and would likely forego the possibility of a relationship for the next few years.

From Helsinki I took a ferry to Tallinn in Estonia. The medieval heart of the city was a handsome introduction to Eastern Europe, but I was soon jolting south on crumbling, Soviet-built roads. The villages and small towns of Estonia, Latvia and Lithuania were uncanny stereotypes of the USSR in the eighties: portly babushkas in shawls and curtain-like skirts sold mushrooms on the pavement; the husks of characterless concrete buildings decayed on the outskirts with laundry hanging from windows on improvised lines; the rubbery smell of boiling cabbage wafted from cracked kitchen windows; antique tractors with open engines wheezed along pot-holed streets; middle-aged men with dense, greying moustaches loitered in maroon Adidas tracksuits; lean, elderly men creaked along on bicycles as old as themselves; and teenage boys with close haircuts and faux gold chains leered in small packs on street corners, drinking unlabelled bottles of beer.

I continued cycling fast, meeting few people and covering as much as 120 miles in a day. A week of unceasing rain and flooding swept me across Poland. In the mornings, I woke in my sodden tent and pulled on cold, soggy clothes, and the heavy wellington boots I somehow had thought were appropriate for a bicycle tour. The weather broke the morning after I entered Slovakia. Dawn cast its brilliance over the wet landscape and a million dewdrops glittered on the grass in the field I camped in.

The two days it took to traverse Eastern Slovakia were dreamlike. Morning mist receded down the valleys, theatrically unveiling quaint villages stretched along narrow cart lanes. Wild apple trees lined the roadside, boughs groaning with ripe fruit packing a pleasant citric tang. On Saturday morning I watched villagers flocking to church with grave expressions and sombre black outfits. An hour later, in similar villages a little further on, I saw similarly attired people spilling out of their old stone churches, talking and laughing in little groups, often with a chair-bound matriarch at the centre, dressed in mourning for a long-lost husband.

Slovakia's southern border marked the start of the Great Hungarian Plain. The road carried me through vineyards, blooming sunflower fields reaching to the horizon, and a few hundred flat miles of parched farmland. I regularly saw lone, early-teenage girls in scant, lurid costumes soliciting on the roadside. They had dark, eastern complexions. Prostitution is one of few professions easily accessible to Romani living in Hungary.

Once through the intimidating Soviet-style Romanian border post, I joined a pot-holed road heading southeast towards southern Transylvania. Climbing through the Banat Mountains, a southern arm of the Carpathian range, I followed tracks with the scattered remnants of centuries-old cobblestones that would soon be buried under a metre of snow.

Tracing a stream out of the mountains, I soon arrived at the Danube and followed it downriver for a few days. The lush, green plain the river inhabits rolls eastward, separating Romania from Bulgaria, before spilling into the Black Sea after its 1,777-mile journey from the source in Germany's Black Forest. Straying just a few miles north of this fertile valley brought me to tinder-dry fields being burned off, filling the sky with acrid smoke and lending a hazy, purplish appearance to the landscape. The smell reminded me of heaping armfuls of dried weeds onto the bonfire as a child. Leaning on a gardening fork, my father would watch the billows of dense smoke and warn me not to go too close. In these hills, I saw more horse-drawn carts than cars. This was the land of the Romani people. Thought to have migrated westward from India over a millennium ago, the travelling Roma are marginalised across modern Europe, but those settled in Romania live a simple agricultural existence. Their villages were reminiscent of the developing world: decorative and pitifully poor. Skeletal horses with lively red tassels bobbing back and forth on their foreheads pulled carts driven by wrinkled women in patchwork clothing.

One morning I woke in my tent to the jangling bells of a flock of sheep. Crawling outside, I was accosted by two surly Romani shepherds. They asked if I carried a gun and, when I said no, began fiddling with my kit. One produced a phone and made several calls, each time repeating the word *turista* with a toothy grin. I quickly began to pack up, on a whim slipping my camping knife inside my pocket rather than my bag. When I tried to leave, the two men grabbed me and I was frog-marched along a dusty track. I allowed myself to be led while the acidic taste of panic pooled in my mouth. *This would be an easy place to disappear*, I thought. *They could easily take my belongings and bury my body in any part of these hills.*

We reached a group of dark, stony-faced men loading crates of plums onto a truck. They didn't wave or shake my hand and I was soon at the centre of a circle facing a small, hairy man who appeared to be in charge. The others fell silent, watching him as he stooped to pick a plum from a crate at his feet. He produced a small pocketknife and wiped the blade on his once-white vest. His eyes firmly fixed on mine, he plunged the knife into the plum and removed the stone in one swift flick. He then crammed the fruit into his face and chomped, staring at me in a triumphant manner that was clearly a challenge. Juice trickled down his grinning, chewing chin and all eyes turned to me. I had been called out.

The scene was threatening, and farcical. Perhaps this was the Romanian equivalent of pistols at dawn. It seemed I had little choice but to also eat a plum, and to do so in a cooler manner than him. Despite looking like a comic scene from a spaghetti western, there was a real air of menace and I was afraid. My fingers quivered as I picked up a slightly bigger plum and pulled a larger knife from my pocket. Flicking the blade open with a theatrical flourish, I scooped out the stone exactly as he had done. I triumphantly stuffed the large fruit into my small mouth. There was a solitary gasp from the crowd. Unfortunately, my victorious grin was so wide that I couldn't chew properly. A glob of plum crossed my windpipe and instantly doubled me over into a violent choke. The tension dissolved to laughter as I turned purple and coughed the half-chewed plum onto the dust. Someone came forward, guffawing, and started slapping my back. A few minutes later, after we had all wiped away our tears and shaken hands, I was sent on my way with a large bag of plums.

On my last day in Romania I was waved off the road at high noon by a giddy group of men. The day was hot and I gladly accepted a cold beer. We sat awhile, engaged in staccato conversation, and before I knew it I had drunk three beers. Having had almost no alcohol since leaving England, three beers felt like ten. That afternoon, listening to Ennio Morricone's sweeping film scores on my MP3 player, I wobbled drunkenly through small, arid villages imagining them to be frontier towns in the Wild West. I honked the clown klaxon on my handlebars, high-fived roadside children, and doffed my sweat-soaked sunhat to pretty girls and toothless hags alike. The hangover kicked in late afternoon. I abandoned Morricone for Enya's sombre strains, stopping at the frequent roadside wells to douse my aching head.

A narrow bridge of Soviet ironwork bore me over the Danube and deposited me in Bulgaria. I rolled across the country towards Turkey feeling the magnetic pull of Asia more strongly with each passing day. While resting under a tree on the final climb to the Turkish border, I heard the slow approach of French language punctuated with out-of-breath gasps. A tandem bicycle rounded the corner carrying a handsome couple in colourful cycling clothes. The man was standing out of his saddle, treading through each pedal stroke with his full weight while the woman sat neatly behind him, her feet spinning in time with his. On spotting me, they waved and chorused *bonjour!*

Nicholas and Joanna were both twenty and had taken a year out from their studies in Grenoble to pedal a loop of the Mediterranean. Everything about them attracted me: they were both tall, tanned, beautiful, unashamedly cultured and spoke endearingly incorrect English with caricature accents. We spoke for a short while but we were all keen to reach the border, so we saved conversation for later and continued on the rutted back road to Turkey.

Late in the afternoon we made the pass and cleared immigration. 'Welcome to Turkey,' said a beaming official. 'Thank you!' we chanted in reply as a rush of excitement swept over all of us. We sped downhill on freshly paved roads shouting *Turkiye* as we went. Motorists honked greetings and we waved back from the safety of a wide hard shoulder. Dust clouds rose from the brown hills as herders brought their flocks back to the villages for the night. These dust clouds dispersed in the breeze and the earthy taste of Turkey settled on my sweat-moistened lips.

After six thousand miles of European Union roads, my passport finally had a stamp and I was in an exotic land. At sunset I heard the first of many muezzins singing the call to prayer from their rocket-shaped minarets that stand proudly over even the humblest of mudbrick villages. It didn't matter to me that it was clearly an electric recording. It was the start of a chain reaction as the imams in surrounding villages heard it and rushed to their tape decks to press play. The result was a cacophony of Arabic warbling but, for me, on that evening, it was the symbol of my adventure beginning in earnest. Gone was the relative predictability of Europe. New sights, sounds and smells would be my daily bread and butter. Languages would bear no resemblance to any I knew, and I would live a little closer to the edge of my comfort zone.

We camped on a hilltop under an astonishingly bright full moon and cooked a spiced vegetable stew on a small fire. The moonlit landscape lunged away from us: rolling interlaced hills with shallow valleys squeezed between them. Small clusters of distant lights marked villages among the hills. *Our* hills, I possessively thought, *our valleys*. We felt like kings and the hill was our throne. It was a magical night.

We talked around the fire until late; the all-knowing and irreverent talk of youth. My companions seemed so content and certain of themselves. They'd set out from Marseilles two months earlier and made a leisurely journey across Italy's thigh and through the Balkans. They aimed to cross Turkey and head south to Egypt via Syria, Jordan and Israel. All four of their parents planned to visit them in Cairo before they continued along the coast through Libya and Tunisia.

Unbeknown to them, events would cut Nicholas and Joanna's journey short and they would fly back to France to start a family. It was late 2010 and the region was poised on a precipice. Protest and revolution lay around the corner in most Near and Middle Eastern nations. However, sitting by the fire that night, we weren't to know. Joanne, with more English than Nicholas, could make more sense of my pidgin French and so did most of the talking. Nicholas stared happily into the quietly crackling flames, his head resting on her crossed legs. Illuminated by the flickering firelight, her animated face floated above her dark fleece while she spoke about adventure, social justice, art and *la futur*. Unlike most people I'd met, they genuinely believed me when I said I would cycle across both Asia and Africa. They asked me which countries I was most excited about and what ancient monuments I most looked forward to visiting. I asked about the exotic deserts and coastlines ahead of them and if they had picked up any Arabic living in multicultural

Marseilles. We shared a sense of boundless excitement, and my wanderlust for the journey ahead was reignited after the exhausting rush through Europe.

FIVE

TRANSITION

The heavens themselves run continually round, the sun riseth and sets,
the moon increaseth, stars and planets keep their constant motions,
the air is still tossed by the winds, the waters ebb and flow…
to teach us that we should ever be in motion.
- Richard Burton

30 September 2010

'Hi! I see you're travelling by bike,' I said, perhaps a little too enthusiastically. 'Where're you headed?'

The man looked up from the little camping stove on which he was boiling eggs. The combination of his light brown skin and dense, dark stubble made me guess he was from a Latin country. Italy, or Spain, perhaps. A copy of *Meditations* by Marcus Aurelius was splayed open on the table beside him. Narrowing his eyes slightly, he scrutinised me for a couple of seconds.

'Well hello!' he said suddenly, his eyes now opening and twinkling. The soft Midlands accent and jaunty tone took me by surprise. 'I'm on a round-the-world trip. Heading east. Take a seat.' I sat down. 'How about you?'

'I'm also going east by bike,' I said. 'I started from England about three months ago. Came here via Nordkapp. When did you get to Istanbul?'

We were sitting in the basement courtyard of a backpackers' hostel in the centre of the *Sultanahmet*, the heart of Old Constantinople. Next to us was the hostel's infamous thirty-bed dormitory, where I'd spent the last few nights trying to ignore the soft moans and heavy breathing of people having sex on a squeaky bunkbed.

'Nordkapp? Top of Norway, right? That's quite a detour,' he said. 'I got here about five weeks ago and have been kicking back a bit after my ride across Europe. I like to take things pretty slow.' He extended the final word, hovering on the *ooo* sound with a smiling face, while spooning an egg out of the water and ladling it into a crook in the table's flaking latticework.

'I'm Charlie, by the way.'

'Leigh,' he added. We shook hands.

After several beers that evening, we found ourselves sitting on a rock by the waterside. I looked across at the night lights on the Asian side of Istanbul, and their reflection in the unusually still waters of the Bosporus. We'd climbed a sagging fence and scrambled down to the water to escape the noise and lurid social scene of the backpacker area. It was quiet but for the eternal hum of the city and a dull baseline thudding from a nearby bar. The soothing smell of brine was tinged with fish just lightly enough to not be unpleasant.

I had taken to Leigh quickly and felt a kinship with him. We were both just months into bicycle journeys that we expected to last years, and yet we felt little need to talk about cycling. I had sometimes met other cyclists, often Germans, on the roads of Western Europe and Scandinavia. They asked me practical, no-nonsense questions which I found uninteresting and difficult to answer:

'What's your average daily distance?' they would ask.

'I don't know really,' I would admit. 'I stop when the light fades. Or when I find a nice camping spot.'

'*Ja*? Und what's your daily budget?'

'I don't have one. I try to spend as little as possible.'

'Und what sort of cadence do you maintain when pedalling?'

'What is cadence?'

'It's the number of spins of the crank each minute, of course. What's your daily calorie intake?'

Leigh and I were both glad for easy, meaningless

conversation with someone living out the same unusual lifestyle. We talked about music, our terrible personal hygiene on the road, and how hard it was to meet women as a smelly cycle tourist. I sensed that Leigh was like me: not a cyclist as such, but someone who saw the merits of travelling that way – slowly, cheaply and with a wonderfully tangible transition from one place to the next.

'So, listen,' said Leigh, 'you're headed to Iran and so am I. I've already cycled as far as Ankara but came back here to see a Turkish girl. I'm bussing back there soon to continue riding. If the timing works, we should ride Iran together.'

'Great! Let's try to meet up in Eastern Turkey.' I liked the idea of riding with Leigh. It would make for a change, and a little familiar humour would be comforting.

With visas to obtain, I stayed a week in Istanbul. It was the first time on the journey that I found myself surrounded by other travellers, backpackers mostly, all excitedly swapping stories and comparing notes on places they had visited. There was a pulsing night scene on Akbiyik Street, with wall-to-wall bars offering discounted drinks. On my first night, three months starved of contact with young women, I drank too much and, hand in hand with a backpacker, sneaked behind a bush against the outer wall of the vast, four-century old Blue Mosque. This hot-headed act of public lust could easily have landed me in jail and I felt shame within seconds of emerging. I would soon be entering one of the world's most conservative countries and would need to control my appetites better.

I needed visas for Iran, Pakistan and India to get me through to Nepal, where my family hoped to join me for Christmas. The Iranian visa was granted with surprising ease and needed only a few days to be processed. This bode well for the other two. The Indian consulate staff were almost excessively welcoming and polite, greeting me by name (*Mr Walker, sir*) on my second and third visits. As

I left with the visa stamped into my passport, I looked back to see the dutiful, Indian doorman making several precise, minute adjustments to the angle and positioning of the plain doormat in the musty corridor outside the fifth-floor office. He noticed me watching and stood upright again with a sheepish grin. He then wobbled his head, twitched his moustache and bowed slightly.

Pakistan, however, posed a problem. I met a Turkish man called Moses and a Latvian man called Jesus who also needed visas. Together we embarked on a four-hour expedition in search of the unadvertised consulate. With difficulty, we found what turned out to be the former location where a vague new address was given to us. Finally, at the plaque-less, flagless new location in an obscure residential suburb, we were curtly informed 'no visas' by a man bulging out of a brown suit. I resigned myself to trying again in other consulates on the route ahead and returned to the Iranian consulate to collect my visa.

In the peaceful, air-conditioned waiting room, I spotted a man I clearly recognised as a cycle tourist. Similar to me, there was an air of the unwashed about him. He was older, with dark bags under his eyes and a ginger beard that crept unchecked down his neck. His baggy, button-up shirt was disproportionately sun-bleached on the back and shoulders, his right trouser leg was turned up a few times to keep it from catching in a bicycle chain, and there were clear, tanned circles on the otherwise pale backs of his hands. He evidently wore cycling mitts with a hole featured in the design. An uncomfortable-looking bracelet made from a length bicycle chain ran around his right wrist. I sat scrutinising these telltale signs and feeling like Sherlock Holmes until he leaned back in his chair to reveal a bicycle helmet on the seat beside him. I wandered over and sat down.

'You're a cyclist, right?' He nodded. 'Where are you headed?'

'Home to New Zealand,' he said with a soft twang.

'Through Iran, I take it?' I asked with a glance across the waiting room.

'Yup. And you?'

'Singapore, via Iran.'

'I'm leaving town tomorrow.'

'Me too.'

'Want to ride together?' he asked.

'Sure.'

'That's settled then,' he said.

The woman behind the little visa window called out 'Mr Hooper' and he got up to collect his passport.

'I'll meet you outside town around midday on the main highway heading east,' he said, moving towards the door.

'OK. See you tomorrow. I'm Charlie. What do I call you, Mr Hooper?'

'Ash.' And he walked out.

We hadn't exchanged email addresses and I didn't have a phone, so it seemed optimistic that we'd ever meet again.

The next day, having crossed the Bosporus into Asia, I pedalled east until I felt certain I had cleared Istanbul and was in the first satellite city. I propped Old Geoff against a tree and sat down to eat biscuits. Minutes later, the familiar shape of a cycle tourist appeared in the distance and I hooted my klaxon to get his attention. We shook hands, agreed to save conversation for when we had reached the peace of the countryside, and rode on with him in the lead.

During three weeks and a thousand miles exclusively in each other's company, Ash and I gradually developed a close friendship and exchanged life stories. He had moved to London in 2000 and worked in the City as a computer technician. After seven years of an increasingly decent salary, and growing distaste of 'the system' he had become a part of, he quit his job and moved to a squat in Hackney for eight months, from where he founded and ran various eco-friendly projects. During this time, he shared the abandoned house with several similarly minded refugees from the city, and one addict. He recalled keeping everything that could be pawned on him at all times in case it was relieved of his possession and converted into drugs.

Ash then lived and worked on a permaculture farm in the Dordogne for a couple of years under the mantle of a charismatic womaniser who took his pick of the female workers. Now in his mid-thirties and starting to feel the pull of home, Ash was returning to New Zealand with plans to start a sustainable farm of his own. He had a fierce sense of morality and actively worked at wrenching me from my middle-England assuredness towards his more sceptical way of thinking. Ash was often sparing with words, and stories had to be coaxed out of him.

'So, what did you do for money when you lived in the squat?' I probed one morning over breakfast.

'I was mostly taking computers out of skips and fixing them up to sell online,' he said, with a glob of egg white lodged in his moustache. 'But you don't need much money to live in London once you take rent out of the equation. I actually became a freegan for my last few months there.'

'And a freegan is…?'

'A freegan doesn't pay for food. You know, like 'vegan', but free. We used to wait out the back of supermarkets and then rummage through their rubbish for recently expired food that they simply threw out. It was all fine to eat, but they'd report you to police if they caught you. There were lots of freegans lurking around, so you had to learn what time each supermarket would dump their dated stock to beat the others to the draw.'

In my mind, I saw Ash running through the streets of Hackney on all fours with a pack of other freegans. They hurled themselves into a big plastic wheelie bin, baring fangs at each other while digging for anything edible. The pack then jumped out and ran on, each with a slimy, greenish joint of meat hanging from their mouths.

When we pitched camp each evening, Ash would disappear while I put rice on to boil and started dicing onions. He would return with a handful of ingredients with which to make a unique brew of cloudy, greenish tea. Pine needles, nettles and rosehips were among the most drinkable, but some were so bitter or foul that I pretended to sip for a while before pouring my cupful away when he wasn't looking.

Always on the lookout for food that would otherwise go to waste, Ash gathered suspicious mushrooms in the fields and picked up sugar beets that had fallen off the back of trailers. Craggy men in sheepskin caps stared disapprovingly from the roadside as he put them into his pannier. I ate the mushrooms nervously and the fried slices of sugar beet politely, wondering what either might do to my stomach. Cycling with the resultant cramps left me exhausted and vomiting for a day.

Together we climbed into the mountains and followed the road ever eastward across northern Turkey. In headwinds, we took turns to cycle behind the leader, sitting in his slipstream. This went awry one day when, travelling downhill at 30 mph, I swung out from behind Ash to find one oncoming lorry overtaking another and speeding straight at me. I managed to bodily throw myself off the road and down a steep, stony bank just in time to avoid both Ash and the lorry. None of the several vehicles that must have seen the accident stopped, and I lay shaking and bleeding in ripped clothes on the roadside for a long time until Ash managed to calm me.

Frustrated by a spell of incessant drizzle, we decided to take a rest day. In the Kurdish city of Erzincan we bought ample food and rode on, looking in vain for a hidden camping spot. Night fell, the penetrating rain continued, and we finally chanced upon a freestanding hill ringed by high fencing. Having hoisted our kit over the fence, we dragged our bicycles laboriously up the steep, slippery slope. On the summit, weather-worn stone slabs were strewn about. An unfinished tourist information board informed us that we were standing on the ruins of Altintepe, a ninth-century BC Urartian castle. We pitched tents and settled in among the stumps of once-grand columns for an indulgent day of reading, sleeping and eating. The pitter-patter of raindrops on my tent in the morning felt comforting and reassuring. People were less likely to be out and stumble upon our trespass.

The morning we left the castle was clear, and we were treated to a view that biblical kings would have enjoyed almost three thousand years earlier. The shining, heavily waterlogged valley floor spread before us. Dappled by clouds of low-lying fog, the land stretched towards the distant valley walls, behind which lurked snowy mountain peaks. The ancient smell of petrichor rose from the sodden ground and reminded me of childhood, churning up autumn mud with a stick in my parents' garden. The minarets of village mosques pinpricked the mist below us and chorused the *adhan*, their call to prayer. The early reaches of the Euphrates cut through the valley on its eternal journey to the Persian Gulf.

Leigh caught us up a few days from the Iranian border, on his twenty-ninth birthday. He hugged me like an old friend and we celebrated with a large supper cooked on a fire of cow dung that Ash had gathered. The dynamic was different with three of us. Irrepressible Leigh bought an element of silliness and light-heartedness that had been lacking before. He took almost nothing seriously and found amusement in small things that I never noticed.

Increasingly vertiginous mountains surrounded us once more and, from a lofty pass, we caught our first glimpse of Mount Ararat, the supposed resting place of Noah's Ark. At 5,137 metres, the freestanding dormant volcano hovers over the surrounding landscape, aping Kilimanjaro or Fuji with its year-round snowcap.

Eastern Turkey was a wild place, far removed from the cosmopolitan streets of Istanbul. The sense of backward frontier land grew in the last few towns we pedalled through. This culminated in Dogubeyazit ('Dog Biscuits' in the traveller's vernacular), where swarthy children in tattered clothes pelted us with pebbles and even fist-sized rocks. Leigh was whacked several times with a long, leafy tree branch, not knowing whether to giggle or scream as the tiny boy ran at him repeatedly.

On our final night in Turkey we camped at the foot of Mount Ararat under a swollen gibbous moon. We sat outside until late, enjoying a last beer, and talking about girls before entering the Islamic Republic of Iran, where alcohol is illegal and pre-marital sex is punishable by flogging, hanging or stoning.

SIX

MISCONCEPTION

*Travel is fatal to prejudice, bigotry and narrow-mindedness…
broad, wholesome, charitable views of men and things
cannot be acquired by vegetating in one little
corner of the earth all one's lifetime.*
- Mark Twain

25 October 2010

'There shall be no drinking or womanising beyond this point. *None!*' the severe figure in the portrait seemed to say. 'And, in the name of Allah, put on some long trousers and a shirt with sleeves. Cover your skin. Where do you think you are entering? This is not some western beach resort, not some iniquitous infidel party where we feel free to show what God gave us to hide. We don't do that here. No, we don't feel *free*.

'And your memory – scan it. Everything you've said, everything you've done, *and* everything you've thought. Yes, that's right, don't forget the thoughts. Search your memory for impurity, for things you feel that I would disapprove of, that *He* would disapprove of. Now, feel ashamed. Welcome to Iran.'

I gazed into the eyes, wilting before the intensity of the Ayatollah's glare. His face hung forebodingly above the immigration hall at the Turkish–Iranian border. I was accustomed to seeing images on the evening news of purse-lipped men wearing beards and turbans. These men apparently wanted me dead, the headlines said at home. They didn't know me, but they wanted to kill me, and to kill almost everyone I knew, because of how we choose to live our lives. To me, with those firmly ingrained preconceptions, the stern man in the portrait symbolised hatred and evil.

Ayatollah Khomeini's white beard contrasted with his coal-black eyes that lurked in deeply sunk sockets. His frowning eyebrows rose steeply outward, creating an expression equal parts angry and quizzical. Capping his high forehead, a thick black turban denoted him as a Shia cleric, with alleged lineage from the prophet Mohammed himself. No hint of a smile buckled his tight lips, no stroke of warmth or happiness. There was simply disapproval and devout austerity.

While hurriedly zipping trouser legs onto my shorts, and pulling a shirt over my vest, I realised that I knew little about Iran beyond snatches of negativity half-heard on the nightly news at home. Words like *extremism*, *fanaticism*, and *fatwa* played across my memory. I knew there had been a revolution some thirty years before, and that a man despised by (and disapproving of) 'the West' had forcefully taken power 'in the name of Allah'. The country had plunged into deep Islamic conservatism. A theocracy based on the fundaments of the Qur'an, yet opposed to most of the predominantly Sunni Islamic world. Iran had become a pariah state, even among the basket cases of the Middle East, a nation allegedly developing nuclear weapons in hidden desert laboratories. A country I'd been conditioned to fear, and the first country that my parents fretted about me entering.

Ash, Leigh and I had nervously arrived at the immigration post in our ragged three-man peloton, the breadth of Turkey behind us. We all suspected some sort of difficulty at the border and were unsurprised when the official frowned theatrically as we approached his desk. We were quickly and unsmilingly ushered through to a side room where our fingerprints were recorded using inkpads. Before we knew it however, we were directed through another door and found ourselves outside, freely mounting up and cycling into Iran. *Why wasn't that difficult? Where was the suspicion, the interrogation, the bare, swinging lightbulb?*

After climbing steep hills into a sapping headwind throughout the following day, we stopped in a primitive-looking village to buy food before camping. The narrow lanes, flanked by crumbling mudbrick houses, were busy with children playing games. Musky smelling goats with dirty fleeces lay on the ground, and neatly coiffured men unselfconsciously preened in their motorbike wing mirrors. Ushered to a basic shop by a steadily growing entourage of villagers, we bought some vegetables and were about to leave when a young, sockless man arrived on an ancient motorbike.

'This night…you…to my house…are sleeping?' He asked with endearing shyness, reading the words from a mobile phone. 'I…Siamak,' he added by way of introduction, prodding his narrow chest with a stiff finger. Leigh, who seemed much more accustomed to being invited into homes, instantly reached forward to shake Siamak's hand and said, 'yes, thank you.' Ash and I exchanged a glance and a shrug. During the last four months, I hadn't been invited to sleep in anyone's home. I had been cycling so fast, and had become so accustomed to skulking into hidden places to pitch my tent, that this simple gesture of welcome took me completely by surprise. I felt suspicious, and then ashamed for feeling so. Siamak kickstarted his coughing motorbike, and we followed him through the village to a tidy, walled courtyard.

Our host welcomed us into his family's two-room home where we sat on an intricately patterned rug woven, we were told, by his grandmother. Tea and nuts were produced on scratched steel trays and I sat feeling awkward, unable to express my gratitude beyond repeatedly saying *mamnoon*, the only Persian word I'd learned so far. A queue of village men arrived to enthusiastically shake our hands. Siamak introduced each visitor by name. They would correct our pronunciation a couple of times before lounging on cushions and contentedly watching the procession towards the novel foreigners. Wearing headscarves and shapeless black cloaks called *chadors*, the women huddled out of sight behind a kitchen counter. Nobody could speak any English, but that didn't seem to matter. The men were happy to say Persian words, hear us repeat them, and then smile.

A plastic tablecloth, with holes worn at the folds, was spread on the floor and two women scurried in to lay plates of rice, chicken, vegetables and *sangak* bread before us. Ash flicked through a guidebook before informing us that *sangak* means 'little pebble' in Persian, and that the unleavened bread is cooked on a bed of small stones which dimple it in the process. Bread is the core of any Iranian meal, pieces being torn off and used to pick up, and bulk out, the more costly and flavoursome parts of the spread. The rice was served in a steaming cake with a fried, golden crust which released the sweet, perfume of saffron when broken open.

The best meal I had eaten in weeks was accompanied by an odd sense of guilt. Our hosts were treating us like honoured guests and heaped our plates with third, and even fourth, helpings. They were simple goat farmers, not starving, but living in relative poverty with few possessions. What could I possibly give them in return for their kindness? I sensed that offering payment for their hospitality would offend them. But I was uncomfortable with being given something so freely by someone who evidently had so much less than I did. It just seemed unfair. I couldn't help but view the encounter from a material perspective, which was perhaps the difference between them and me, and precisely why they were happy to be so generous.

After dinner, little bowls of seeds, roasted wheat and fruit were produced while we sat talking with the still-growing gathering of men. The teapot seemed bottomless. Similar to Turkish custom, Iranian tea is served in small glasses. However, the sugar lumps were not stirred-in. Instead they are pinched between the front teeth and the tea is sipped through them. Unsurprisingly, many of the villagers had hideously decayed and caramel-coloured front teeth.

Omid, a fifteen-year-old with broken but strangely imperative English, arrived and began acting as interpreter. Through laboured conversation, I soon started unpacking my misconceptions about Iranians. These men were simple, friendly farmers, cut off from the world by censorship, state-controlled media, selective education and an autocratic regime. Our hosts had endless questions about life in Europe and we soon dispelled some of the startling ideas about our cultures that they had been fed by Iranian media.

'No, it is not normal for a woman to walk in the street with her breasts exposed…'

'In our country the men will cook and clean too…honestly. No, really, it is the truth…!'

'No, petrol is not fifteen cents per litre all over the world. We pay two dollars per litre…'

Later in the evening, the numbers dwindled and some men began to fall asleep, chins resting on chests. The patriarch, Hassan, put down his tea, hushed those still awake, and turned to me with a grave expression. 'Are you friends with America?'

Noticing the serious faces, watching expectantly, I remembered the *Olum Amerikaya!* (death to America) graffiti I had seen scratched onto a wall the day before. A couple of men were nudged awake and caught up in whispers.

'I have some friends who are from America,' I began, cautiously. 'But, I am not friends with their government. I do not like many of the things the American government says and does.' I held my breath while Omid translated my reply. There was a short silence.

'OK. It is good,' decided Hassan, nodding. I exhaled. 'I understand. It is like Iran. We are your friends. But, maybe our government is not always your friend?'

'Exactly!'

'Good. Now listen to this,' he said with a smile, and fired some quick Persian at Omid. Moments later, an Iranian song entitled *Kill the Americans!* chirped from Omid's phone while he swung his arms happily above his head. Regardless of the song, I thought, Iran was already shedding its threatening veneer.

In the morning, Siamak led us back to the main road and waved us off. His blue eyes watered as he gave us each a hug. We had met the man only twelve hours earlier, but he had given us our first taste of Iran's humbling hospitality. His was the first of countless acts of kindness I was to experience in Iran. Grinning motorists pulled over to force nuts, fruit and drinks on us. Vendors jovially coaxed us into political discussions and bluntly refused payment. Businessmen invited us into their offices for tea and, with a timid national pride, to discover our thoughts on their country. We were forced to turn down most offers to stay the night as otherwise we would have progressed only a few miles each day.

I suspected that there was another reason for the overwhelming hospitality. In the eyes of Iranians, we were representatives of the outside world from which they were so isolated. Ambassadors of the West. Through us they could get a sense of our alien world, where bikinis, atheists, and criticism of the government are all commonplace. Like a West German crossing the Berlin Wall and talking of supermarkets with stacked shelves, we were a portal to the seductively forbidden other side.

As we continued, our new-found sense of security among the Iranian people made us increasingly relaxed about where we camped. A couple of nights later we pitched in an orchard after dark. Dinner was interrupted by a burst of gunfire behind a wall twenty yards away. A volley of shouts followed before an aged motorbike gunned to life and roared away. We finished eating in silence. I struggled to sleep. Clichéd scenes rolled across my mind's eye: crowds of men shooting rifles skyward while the statue of a toppled leader is torn down, a roughly stitched new flag hoisted over a baying mob, armed men in balaclavas with a haggard white man kneeling before them in dirty overalls, with a bag over his head. I told myself these scenes belonged to other countries, but was clearly yet to shake every uncertainty about Iran.

The road meandered east through steep mountain valleys of withered brush with the lingering fragrance of lavender. Signposts to a ski resort adorned the entrance to the provincial capital of Tabriz. Perched at an altitude of 1,400 metres and surrounded by a wall of lofty mountains, Tabriz would soon be blanketed with a thick layer of snow for the winter months. We dumped our bikes in a hostel and wandered into the labyrinthine alleys of the dark, aromatic market.

The bazaar is the heart of Iranian society, where people gossip over transactions, news spreads, and revolutions are born. Being the middle of the day, the bazaar wasn't particularly crowded and most *bazaaris* (merchants) were lunching on their shop floors. Young men in tight jeans and faux-leather jackets sat in quiet obeisance before greybeards reclining on stacks of beautiful rugs, postulating expansively about whatever sprang to mind. Small, chubby women, rendered shapeless by their *chadors*, waddled along with awkwardly clasped shopping bags. If they went out in public with their hair uncovered they could be arrested by the local *Gasht-e Ershad* (the Islamic 'morality' police, present in every Iranian town).

Feeling hungry ourselves, Leigh, Ash and I followed a tempting smell down a stone spiral staircase. We descended into a basement full of wizened men sucking on *hookah* pipes and wearing an assortment of old suits, fraying at their ancient hems. They eyed us nonchalantly and spoke sparingly to each other. The waiter (white shirt, black waistcoat, smudged half apron and resplendent moustache) fetched three servings of the only dish available: *dizi*. We were each presented with a roughly hewn stone pestle and a steaming terracotta pot of stewed and spiced vegetables. Taking our cue from a man eating nearby, we used the pestles to mash the vegetables into a lumpy paste before lifting pinches of it to our mouths with torn scraps of *sangak*. The bread tasted like the smell of a good bakery first thing in the morning, and perfectly complimented the oily, peppery vegetable mash. Leigh and I had soon finished ours, then shared most of Ash's meal as he had no appetite.

Ash had been weak for a couple of days and deteriorated rapidly after reaching Tabriz. By evening he was laid out on his bunk, yellow-faced and lifeless. He dozed for two days and nights, showing no signs of improvement but stubbornly refusing a doctor. We had a thousand miles of Iranian roads ahead and it began to seem unlikely that we would ride those miles as a threesome. Leigh and I waited a third day, hoping Ash might rally but, hating the time press of our short visas, we finally left him in the care of the friendly hotel manager. Ash said he understood, but we felt guilty regardless. I'd known him less than a month, and if we'd met in London I doubt that we would have become mates. However, a friendship had been forged over twelve hundred miles of nightly rice dinners and bitter cups of improvised tea. The intensity of a feral road existence effortlessly bridges the social gaps that otherwise keep us strangers.

Once out of Tabriz, we picked up the pace, breakfasting under the stars and riding throughout the day. We followed the eastward contours of the Alborz mountain range. Several long, unlit road tunnels plunged us into the sheer mountainside where we sprinted through, dizzy with exhaust fumes, trying desperately to reach daylight before the growing roar of a truck behind us could rush dangerously past. For these fearful tunnels, we somehow developed an unusual calming mechanism: blurting out the few lyrics we knew of Chris de Burgh's *Lady in Red* at the top of our voices. Tearing through the darkness, we would scream our fear into submission.

Before reaching Tehran, the weather turned for a couple of days. The temperature hovered around 5°C and we forged on in silence, hands gloved against the chill.

Desperate for a warming cup of tea one morning, we stopped at a tomato farm when two workers waved us into their storage hut. Assad was a diminutive, bald man with awful teeth and a weathered face. Jarved was handsome and younger with combed, bouffant hair and a brilliant smile. Neither had a word of English.

We all squatted around a gas burner on a threadbare rug, and rubbed our hands to warm up in the room, which smelled strongly of marijuana. Stacked crates of tomatoes lined the walls and a single bulb threw out a stark light that cast dancing shadows as it swung in a draught. A faded poster depicted a sardine-packed crowd of white-robed pilgrims circulating the *Ka'bah* at Mecca. Assad boiled a pot with a welding torch, and we gladly drank the glasses of tea he handed round.

'Charlie,' said Leigh out of the side of his mouth, maintaining a smile for our hosts. 'I think we're in a crack den. Look at the floor.' I followed his glance. Beside a rolled-up prayer rug, I spotted a tablespoon with burn marks on the underside. Several empty pill sheets were scattered about the packed mud floor. A Qur'an lay nearby, wrapped in a small green cloth.

'You might be right,' I replied. 'I'm not sure though. Shouldn't there be a tourniquet or something? I don't think I've ever been in a crack den before. Have you?'

'Can't say I have. I always imagined them to be less hospitable places. Fewer holy books.'

Just then Assad reached into his pocket and pulled out something small. He cocked his head at us with a grin and carefully began to unravel it. It was a scrunched length of clingwrap containing a small block of a black, resinous substance.

'*Teriyok!*' said Assad triumphantly.

We had no idea what *teriyok* was. It looked too dark to be hash. Jarved pantomimed that it came from Afghanistan and was illegal. Young, nervous and naive, I thought it might be opium. Leigh didn't seem to know any better, and when Assad offered it to us we gave each other a knowing look. We both felt the same mixture of excitement to do something insensible, and obligation to our hosts to try a small sample.

Slivers were cut from the block while a length of wire was heated on the gas burner. Assad rolled up a scrap of newspaper with thick-skinned fingers, and began to melt the resin with the white-hot wire. Before I had time to reflect, he shoved the paper straw between my lips and I was inhaling the smoke that was produced. I froze for a few moments, waiting for some drastic rush of euphoria, or terror. However, other than a slight fuzziness, and a pleasantly warm feeling of calm, there seemed no drastic effect. Jarved lit a hash pipe. I sat back while his smoke slowly filled the small room and Leigh took his turn with the straw. We smoked a fair amount of *teriyok* before having our hands shaken and being sent on our way with a bottle of strong, homemade cherry wine hidden at the bottom of my pannier.

That afternoon, we each picked a favourite playlist on our MP3 players (Stereophonics for Leigh and Bowie for me) and gave in to a floaty sense of joy. Riding before a tailwind, and not feeling the cold, we passed through towns singing along to our music. Camped in a field that night, we drank the illicit cherry wine, enjoying the giddy excitement of doing something illegal. It reminded me of drinking alcohol at school or my first pull on a joint. We wondered just what it was Assad had given us, that left us so feeling so light and immune to the cold. We were later to discover from a man in Tehran that *teriyok* is simply morphine, but, nevertheless, still an opiate from the same Afghan poppy fields that produce over eighty per cent of the world's heroin.

SEVEN

PARIAH STATE

*Those who insist on having hostilities with us, kill and destroy
the option of friendship with us in the future, which is
unfortunate because it is clear the future belongs to Iran
and that enmities will be fruitless.*

- Mahmoud Ahmadinejad (president of Iran 2005-13)

4 November 2010

The sun reappeared the day we approached Tehran. In the satellite town of Karaj, we passed a large demonstration of women in black *chadors*, many sporting full burqas. They were marching down the street waving banners and Iranian flags. I questioned a shopkeeper who was looking on with indifference.

'They celebrate anniversary,' he explained flatly, 'anniversary of win America embassy.' In November 1979, the events in Tehran had gripped the world. Buoyed up by the mood of anti-imperialism lingering from the revolution earlier that year, a group of fanatical students, with Ayatollah Khomeini's backing, forced entry to the US embassy and held sixty-six American hostages for 444 days. Mohammed Reza, the recently deposed Shah of Iran, had fled to America, and the Iranians demanded he be returned to stand trial for crimes committed during his increasingly autocratic reign. The Americans refused to give up Mohammed Reza and instantly imposed economic sanctions, setting the tone for Iran's relations with the West for years to come. Leigh and I gave the demonstration a wide berth and pushed on for Tehran.

As the various routes heading into the capital converged, we were fully immersed in the madness that inhabits Iranian roads. Frequent road signs read *KEEP LEFT* but bore an arrow pointing right. There were baffling roundabouts where traffic circulated in both directions at the same time. In one district, a city-planning slip had resulted in traffic flow being switched to the wrong side of the road. All this occurred in a continuously rising cloud of dust, with shopkeepers watering their stretches of pavement to keep the choking dirt down. As we neared the centre, the hindmost of three men on a motorbike (rarely was there just one) pulled me into the traditional triple kiss of greeting as they slowly overtook. Unsurprisingly the four of us tumbled to the tarmac in an awkward embrace. I couldn't be angry, and they each gave me a hug once we'd stood up, untangled ourselves, and clapped the dust smudges off our clothes.

Once we had checked into a hostel dormitory we split up. Leigh set off for the Turkmen embassy and I wandered the streets aimlessly, getting a feel for the city. Contrary to my expectations after spending time in the relatively conservative villages, Tehran was modern, cosmopolitan even. The streets abounded with women in figure-hugging thigh-length jackets, large designer sunglasses, and headscarves pushed back far beyond their hairline. This risqué defiance of the law struck me as the Iranian equivalent of a Victorian lady flashing her ankles. Denim clad young men in baseball caps told me of their dreams to study in Europe or America. Rows of cafés were fronted with outdoor tables where people drank coffee and slurped on milkshakes, chatting in the sunshine.

In a neatly maintained park, I met a jumpy man named Reza, with greying hair and fidgety hands. After some small talk on a bench he leaned forward, softly clutched my elbow, and told me his uncle had been a leading figure in the 1979 revolution. He was proud of his family's role in overthrowing the last Shah. However, both he and his twenty-something son were now quietly but firmly anti-government.

'The ideas the people revolted for have been corrupted

or forgotten,' he confided, his eyes darting nervously around, scanning for discreet listeners.

'What were those ideas?'

'They were not all religious,' he said, quickly. 'There were many different ideas. My uncle was with the National Democratic Front. Then there were the Marxists, the *bazaaris*, the liberal students, the zealous Islamic students…there were even Marxist Islamists if you can believe it!' His left hand grasped the thumb of his right and pulled in sudden, twitchy movements. 'And there were lots of unpolitical people who just wanted the Shah out. His men were torturing political opponents and people were scared to talk on the streets.' He discreetly surveyed the park once again. 'But after the revolution, Khomeini and his uneducated 'soldiers of God' – really just village boys given guns – squashed all the other groups.' Reza softly slapped a fist into an open palm.

'Do you think there'll be another revolution soon?' I whispered.

Reza exhaled slowly with a sense of mournfulness. His shoulders slumped. 'No. Not soon. Too many died last time. Too much was sacrificed. We are not ready for that again.'

His hopelessness saddened me. I knew little about the revolution except that it grew out of a sense of dissatisfaction. Reza felt a painful futility. Every educated Iranian I spoke with was dissatisfied. But, after three decades of repression and international isolation, many seemed to have lost hope.

In Tehran, I was finally forced to admit defeat with the Pakistani visa process. Having failed to make any headway with various consular officials in Turkey, Iran and London, I had to accept that, short of returning to London to apply there, I would not get a visa and would have to fly from Iran to India. I begrudgingly booked a flight to Delhi from Mashhad, the country's most northeastern city. Bound for

Turkmenistan, Leigh was also headed for Mashhad.

The fact that I would be flying weighed heavily on me. I had set off from home with the grand notion of getting to the far corners of the globe by bicycle alone. I had the romanticised vision of leaving an unbroken trail of tyre tracks behind me, from home to home, spanning continents in between. I began to question once more the objectives of my journey. I hadn't set off with a world record in my sights. I *had* aimed to cycle the whole route, yes, but why? I was beholden to no one. Did it really make a difference? Would the spinning of my feet alone make me a wiser, richer or better person? No, there had to be more to it than that. Curiosity had to be the root of my motivation. To see, to do, and to learn.

It was a shame not to visit Pakistan, another country I knew little about. Headlines told of danger, tribalism and fundamentalism. And yet, Iran had pleasantly surprised me. Would Pakistan have similarly defied expectations? Perhaps that was precisely the reason to visit somewhere with bad press.

I consoled myself with the fact that the situation was out of my hands. I had no visa, and had to take the flight. I could no longer say I completed my odyssey purely by bicycle. I would have to search harder for things to gain from my journey. I resolved to question more, and learn more, feeding my late-blooming curiosity. That would at least make me a more knowledgeable person, if not a wiser, richer or better one.

Leigh and I left Tehran in rush hour. We were soon hopelessly lost in the tangle of roads that interweave the city of twelve million. We asked people for directions but only drivers seemed to know the mysterious road system, and they were hard to stop. We finally questioned a man who had been filming us from his car for about five minutes before pulling over to say hello. He led us for half an hour, at bicycle pace in the middle of the busy highways, with his hazard lights blinking. When we reached the outskirts and the road to Mashhad, he pulled over again.

'I am happy I can help you. Now, of course, you will please sleep in my home tonight.'

'Thank you. That's very kind of you. Where do you live?'

'Central Tehran.' It had taken us almost two hours to escape the centre, so we politely declined.

We descended into the Kavir desert. Not a stereotypical desert of picturesque, rolling dunes, but one of loose, fine dust that gets everywhere: clothes, tents, hair, beards, eyes, nostrils, food and cameras. The sky was an immaculate cerulean blue, excepting for the horizon's perpetual, purplish dust haze. We didn't see a single cloud during our two weeks in the Kavir.

Our destination, Mashhad, was the holiest city in Iran, and the third holiest city in Shi'ite Islam. Every year, 25 million visitors flock to the city to pay homage to the shrine of Imam Reza (the eighth Imam in the Shia tradition) who was martyred in AD818. Less than fifteen per cent of the world's Muslims are Shia and, with over ninety per cent of Iran's 80 million inhabitants adhering to Shi'ism, the country has the world's largest concentration of the minority sect.

Due to our now swarthy, bearded appearance, we were often mistaken for Iranians. The fact that we were travelling to Mashhad in a slow and self-propelled fashion led some people to assume we were Muslim pilgrims ourselves. We were quick to correct this misunderstanding but we both felt that our crossing of Iran along the ancient Silk Road had become a sort pilgrimage anyway. Due to state censorship of internet and media, when travelling in Iran one feels so cut off from international news that there is an otherworldly sense. I began to entertain the idea that the outside world was standing still, waiting for my return before lurching back into action.

In the desert, I felt happier and healthier than I had in a long time. Leigh and I were getting on well and moving at a steady pace of about sixty miles a day. We took turns to cook meals, allowing the other a lie in or time to read and write. There was no alcohol, and we ate simple, ample meals. Months of living outdoors had left me feeling strong and vigorous. Although the nighttime temperatures were near freezing, the November days were still balmy. With a richly bronze face, and legs that could pump away for hours without complaining, I was in the best shape of my life.

Desert camping proved the most enjoyable yet: idyllic pitches surrounded by flat nothingness to the south, and the snow-capped Alborz to the north, just visible through the haze. Around the time motorists started pulling over, facing Mecca, and laying prayer mats on the dust for *Maghrib* (sunset prayers), we would follow dirt tracks off the road in search of a spot. We sometimes made our home among mud ruins. Their slow state of decay was as beautiful as it was desolate. There are abandoned buildings all over Iran. As mud bricks can't be reused, they are simply left to the elements. It was often tough to tell whether they were fifty or five hundred years old.

We also passed several crumbling *caravanserai* (Silk Road coaching inns with crenellated rampart walls for protection against bandits and large courtyards for accommodating camels). At the turn of the seventeenth century, Shah Abbas I ordered the construction of 999 *caravanserai* all across the Persian empire to boost the trading network and his tax revenue. Most of the abandoned mudbrick forts we saw were part of his project and had stood for over four hundred years. There was a melancholy to these buildings. They had once been the bustling heart of Persia's thriving international trade routes, but they now stood abandoned in a country that had, in turn, been abandoned by international trade.

EIGHT

BELIEF

*Isn't it enough to see that a garden is beautiful without having to
believe that there are fairies at the bottom of it too?*
- Douglas Adams, *The Hitchhiker's Guide to the Galaxy*

11 November 2010

In the quaint town of Shahrud, we sat in a park stuffing our dust-coated faces with cheap cream cakes. Two beautiful girls approached warily, and offered us tea in timid, halting English. Leigh and I were taken aback. It was very rare for Iranian women to talk to us. A few minutes later, they reappeared bearing a tray of tea, chocolates, dates, persimmons and pomegranates. We invited them to sit with us, but they skittered away with half-stifled giggles. Not long after, they returned to offer more tea.

'You are very dirty,' announced the taller and prettier of the two.

'Yes. I am sorry. We have been camping in the desert,' Leigh said.

'Wild desert men,' she declared. 'You like bath with us?'

Leigh caught my eye and smirked beneath his cream-encrusted moustache. Visions of harems and sultry bathhouses flitted through my mind, of dark girls in thin, clinging white robes, standing waist deep in steaming water, brandishing sponges and discreet smiles. We had evidently been in the desert in more than one sense.

'We home, there,' she continued, pointing to a building on the edge of the park. 'You use shower. No problem. Wait here, now. We brother coming.'

They slunk away and, thirty minutes later, Ali appeared to escort us home, as propriety demanded. Monireh and Moona were waiting for us, and they were much more talkative in their home. Meeting strange men in parks can attract trouble from the *Gasht-e Ershad*. In fact, since the revolution, being seen in public with a member of the opposite sex who is not a relative or spouse is technically a criminal offence.

Our clothes were thrown in the washing machine in their modern flat, and we were thrown in the bathroom to scrape off the caked desert dirt under a hot shower. Ali's wife, Neda, cooked spaghetti bolognaise and we all sat on their white and gold rug (a wedding present) to eat. Monireh (the English speaker) was a lifeguard, Moona an art student and Neda a nurse. It was a refreshing change to be in a household where the women ate with us. Monireh boldly took off her headscarf, allowing a yard of thick, glossy hair to fall down her back. She had a rebellious streak, and joked about the overzealous imams in Iran, describing them as *pashmaloo* – literally 'woolly' – because of their big beards.

The family asked us questions about Britain, its freedoms, and our lives there. The girls were particularly excited by the idea of cycling across countries. It is frowned upon for girls to ride bicycles in Iran, and few ever learn how.

As the light began to fade, it was decided that we should go with them to Semnan (a town we passed two days earlier) that night to attend a theatre festival the next day. Toothbrush in pocket, I climbed in the Peugeot 206 with the five others and, two hours later, we arrived at the house of their brother-in-law. Ismail's wife was away, but their teenage sons, Pooya and Pouria, were in.

The men embraced us with triple kisses and we were ushered through to the living room for a feast. Bowls of *ash-e sagh* (creamy spinach, leek and pea soup), plates of *tah chin* (the same saffron-suffused pilau rice we'd had with Siamak), lamb shish kebabs, colourful *sabzi polo* (steamed rice mixed in with chopped herbs, pomegranate and torn pieces of fried fish from the Caspian Sea) and several varieties of flat bread, all washed down with *doogh* (a slightly salty yoghurt infused with mint). Bowls of fruits, nuts and seeds were circulated after the plates were cleared.

The end of Iranian meals was always a pleasure. After sitting uncomfortably cross-legged for over an hour around a tablecloth laid on the floor, everyone spread outwards to the walls, propped their head against a cushion, and lolled almost horizontally, luxuriously submitting to drowsiness and heaving bellies.

Iranians excel at this particular type of social lounging around – sated, and happily whiling away the hours after eating. It's perfectly acceptable to let the conversation wash over you and drift into a light doze. In fact, usually everyone will eventually sleep. Conversation ceases when the least interested of the last two people finally gives in and lets their chin slump onto their chest.

We lounged like this until late at night. However, as the strange objects of attention, it felt rude for Leigh or myself to drift off. Endless questions were asked of us via Monireh's translation. Every time she spoke to me, I seized the opportunity to gaze longingly into her large, dark, oval eyes. Her long trail of hair was plaited and ran alluringly over her shoulder, hanging off the prominent contour of her breast.

In the morning we breakfasted on yoghurt, cheese, honey, quince chutney, butter and bread, still warm from the bakery. In the theatre, I was lucky enough to sit next to Monireh. She leaned over to whisper occasional translations to me. The brief brushing of her nose against my ear sent thrilling tingles down my spine. The play was set at a religious shrine and involved a murderer escaping from prison to find his friend had married his moribund sister. It was comically melodramatic with no shortage of clowning, face-slapping, and kneeling women wailing wretchedly. The long and enthusiastic standing ovation was a genuine surprise to me.

We returned to Ismail's house and the thickly carpeted floor so conducive to chatting, snacking and playing games. Due to Iran's conservatism, friendships are less common than in Europe, particularly between boys and girls. Resultantly, family bonds are much stronger, and people draw on their extensive web of cousins for company. The familial atmosphere that afternoon gave me a twinge of real homesickness for the first time since leaving home.

We drove back to Shahroud in the evening and met the small, raisin-faced family matriarch. Her wise, deep-set eyes grinned, and she insisted on feeding us again before bed. She had been married at fourteen to a husband seven years her senior, and had borne six children. Ali was the only boy among them, and her husband had died five years earlier. Monireh told me that her mother was a force to be reckoned with, and that various members of the *Gasht-e Ershad* had received tongue lashings for hassling her daughters about their headscarves slipping back.

In the morning, Monireh drove us to the shrine of Sheikh Abol Hassan Kherqani, a thirteenth-century poet and holy man, who allegedly could command lions and be in two places at once. The peace and contentment that this small building brought to Monireh was touching. She seemed completely refreshed after kneeling before the tomb and laying her head on the cool marble for a while.

I pondered my absence of faith. I had been raised in a moderate Church of England family. My parents said prayers with me when they put me to bed as a child, and I would often say them on my own, unprompted. Not rational, considered prayer, but the learned-by-rote prayers that had been recited to me from an early age.

Until I was sent to boarding school, on Sundays I was dressed in corduroy and marched up the hill with my siblings to our village's Holy Trinity church. The handsome little building had stood for well over six centuries and smelled like dust and old paper inside. Hymns were self-consciously mumbled to a slow tempo set by an organist who, to us children, looked almost as old as the church. Using soft modernisms and tepidly conversational language, the billowy-frocked vicar would desperately try to engage the diminished congregation, many of whom likely attended through a sense of duty instilled during similar childhoods to mine.

The services brought me no peace or enlightenment. They bored me, forming in me a distaste of my religion. I would look forward to the end (*go now with God's peace* was the cue), when the adults would stand gossiping among the pews with hot drinks, and I would race around, competing with my brother and sisters as to who could collect the tallest stack of hymn books in their arms.

At my prep school, from the age of eight I attended thrice-weekly chapel services with hymns, a squeaky reading from a near-pubescent senior, and the headmaster's sermon with wobbly morals crowbarred into obscure bible stories. However, it was different to the village services. School chapel was attended by a hundred and fifty other mischievous boys. There was always some game afoot, carefully obscured from the eyeline of the staff sitting at the back, scanning for troublemakers and plucking suspects out of the room for a dressing down.

In my second-to-last year, when my voice was breaking, I was ordered not to sing by the music master. Apparently, my bold, toneless chanting was ruining services and I was commanded to mouth the words instead. I did so until hearing one sermon about God's acceptance of all who worship and believe. Why did He not accept my voice? For the final year I stood through hymns with my mouth resolutely shut.

In classes we were taught bible stories as fact, not fiction. We were tested on Moses' twelve plagues, the names of the disciples, and the exact antiquated spelling of the Lord's Prayer. There was no mention of Islam, Hinduism, Judaism or Buddhism. And definitely no mention that some people chose to live without a god in their lives. The order of the six days of creation was drilled into us early, and with as much importance as the times tables. We were taught how a man named Adam and his wife (curiously, made from one of his ribs) were shown paradise but had it snatched away by an 'all-merciful' schoolmaster. As far as I could follow, this bully wanted them to experience pain and hardship, simply because they wore clothes and asked questions. Apparently, because of this couple and their loud-mouthed pet snake, we were all sinners, forever to be punished by our creator for the imperfections he created us with. Only after four years of this were we suddenly told about a contradictory 'theory' of evolution put forward by a monkey-faced man with a Father Christmas beard.

My secondary school was more liberal. There was a church available, but I distanced myself from religion. Not because I didn't believe in God. (I had never been told that I was allowed to *not* believe in God.) I didn't go to church anymore because I didn't have to. It bored me, and was all about rules. Why on earth would I go back?

Later than I would have liked, I began to read about other faiths, most of which professed to have the 'one true God', and some of which had untold thousands, seemingly one for every household item. They couldn't all be right. Maybe none of them were. Apparently, the ancient Greeks had this scandalous family of Gods who did as they pleased. They were forever having sex with each other, animals, or pretty much anything that they could. Yet it was these same Greeks who drew up the first blueprint for what we consider to be a fair society. Millions of people believed in and feared those incestuous, anarchic deities for hundreds of years. Nowadays we call those stories myths. I began to equate that with how millions of people have believed in the Christian gospel for hundreds of years. Perhaps those stories would also one day be considered myth.

I gradually realised that nothing bad was happening to me, despite the complete absence of religion in my life. I was leading a charmed, godless existence. At the age of eighteen I had a short conversation with myself and decided there definitely wasn't a god, at least not a god that I could ever be sure about, or that watched us and meddled jealously in our lives. Maybe some sort of 'power' sparked Monkey Father Christmas's evolutionary process hundreds of millions of years ago, or even lit the taper for the Big Bang billions of years before that. But the rest surely came down to chance and chaos. I liked the idea of chaos. It felt excitingly amoral.

Once I had consciously placed myself outside of religion, it started to become one of my greatest interests. The interwoven history of human religion is perhaps the longest and most intricate story of our species, leading from historical obscurity thousands of years ago through to today, where most people believe in a divinity of some sort. At university, I studied the influences of the ancient Mediterranean religions in the formation of Christianity. I saw how much of the Torah, the Bible and the Qur'an was a successively reimagined rewrite of stories passed down over millennia through verbal tradition. I discovered that societies often converted to a new faith either forcibly, through military conquest, or pragmatically through tax breaks and superior rights for converts.

Given the freedom to do so by the liberal society I grew up in, I had taken my faith into consideration and consciously turned away from belief in things I had been taught when too young to question. Having been through that process, it was easy to develop an edge of arrogance, and a dismissive view of those who hadn't yet 'liberated' themselves. However, the calm that visiting Kherqani's tomb brought to Monireh reminded me that, although it bought me peace, my journey away from spirituality was personal and worked for me in my particular situation. Not everyone is fortunate enough to live in communities that don't persecute those who think differently. Living in a theocracy, Monireh would have religion in her life whether she liked it or not. Even if she secretly questioned or resented aspects of that religion, she had found her peace with it.

A few days later, Leigh and I rode into the choking embrace of Mashhad's heavy smog blanket. The city was humming with pilgrims from all over the Islamic world. Marking the location of his assassination, Imam Reza's shrine is the third-largest mosque in the world, and can accommodate 700,000 people. I visited the few peripheral buildings permitted to non-Muslims. Foreigners are given an obligatory guide-cum-escort and mine was called Ali. Numerous traditional outfits, from Afghanistan to Indonesia, drifted past while Ali and I sat on a bench discussing religion. I claimed to be a Christian, as neither agnosticism nor atheism are understood in Iran, and tend to cause offence.

'Although they are *al khitab* – people of the book – I find Christians to be foolish,' said Ali. 'They believe in miracles and magic.' He was forthright in his opinions and no doubt accustomed to discussing religion with foreigners. 'It's crazy, you know, the idea that a man – *not* a god, but *a man*, who was born and died *as a man* – that this man did magic tricks and changed water into wine. It is bad to drink wine, anyway.'

'Yes, maybe you are right. I do like wine though,' I replied, unsure what else to say. 'You mentioned the twelfth Imam earlier...'

'Mohammed al-Mahdi. Yes, he is the final Imam. The Hidden One.'

'You said he died centuries ago?'

'Not died. Disappeared. He *disappeared* over one thousand years ago.'

'So where is he now?'

'We don't know, but he is still alive. He has made himself invisible, and will come back to save the faithful people at the end of the world.'

'I see. I think I was told about him at school when I was a child.'

Leigh and I had formed such an easy and uncomplicated friendship. We had enough in common to amuse each other, but enough differences to interest one another. He was several years older than me, and had told me he was riding to escape a cycle of depression. But I saw so much of myself in him, and I think he did, too.

He set out north, towards the mountains of Central Asia, and I took a taxi to the airport. We said goodbye awkwardly and hugged. I was sad to leave him.

I was an oddity in the departure lounge: wearing wellies and carrying the shopping basket from the front of my bike as hand baggage. We took off late in the afternoon. As the sun dropped towards the horizon, I gazed out of the window, briefly allowing myself to agonise and speculate over the potential adventures lying along the hundreds of miles below.

During the previous five months, I had cycled eight thousand miles across the face of the world. Touching, smelling, seeing, and feeling the landscapes, meeting countless people from all walks of life. I was now hurtling high over the earth in a metal fuselage. The sense of dislocation gnawed at me, but I reminded myself that the journey was not about cycling around the world. It was about seeing and learning.

NINE

CHAOS

I wanted to coast along, swallowing beetles in the wind,
alive to all the earth's pulses.
- Tom Freemantle, *Johnny Ginger's Last Ride*

23 November 2010

I sat in the arrivals hall of New Delhi airport for several hours, disoriented after thirty-six hours of flights and transit. The airport was newly refurbished, still bearing posters and slogans from the recent, corruption-mired Commonwealth games.

I was awaiting the arrival of my friend, James, on a flight from London. By first light I had grown cold from the air-conditioning, so I assembled my bike, wheeled it outside, and wandered around some building works. There was an unwashed *chai wallah* selling sweet, milky masala tea under a tattered golf umbrella. I bought a cup. He smiled and stared at me with fascination while I squatted on my haunches against a half-built wall, my hands clasped around the rapidly disintegrating paper cup. Rags of closely printed Hindi newspapers caught on the lengths of rusted steel cable that protruded from the uneven rubble. A dried human turd lay across a broken brick a few yards away.

The raw, ramshackle nature of the scene stood in stark contrast to the relative development of Iran. The bashful distance of the other men drinking *chai*, skinny construction workers, was also surprising after the friendly overtures of Iranians. The row of men squatted opposite me were having a long discussion in Hindi about my fully laden bicycle. I stood the bike up and indicated that they could try to ride it. All wobbled their heads in alarm, blankly refusing a go on my two-wheeled deathtrap. I pedalled back to the arrivals hall and joined the growing crowd awaiting the overnight flight from London. When the passengers started swarming out I easily spotted my old school friend James. He was a head taller than the crowd.

'Jesus! You look bloody ridiculous! Look at the state of that beard. And you're so damn skinny,' said his familiar voice.

'Welcome to my world,' I beamed.

'It's good to see you, mate,' he added, locking me into a firm bear hug.

'I hope you're fit, James. London life's not softened you up too much?'

We assembled James's bike and cycled to the wide, leafy boulevards of Delhi's diplomatic quarter. Through a contact, we'd been invited to stay at the British High Commission. I felt embarrassed by my rundown appearance as the gate swung majestically open revealing the facade of a grand, whitewashed colonial mansion. An immaculately attired butler informed us that Gordon Brown had left twenty minutes earlier, and then installed us in the pool house. On the trellised verandah, we breakfasted on bacon and eggs, slices of toast cut into triangles, and fine china cups of Earl Grey tea. We gossiped excitedly about friends at home and our plans for the month we had together. Monkeys scampered across manicured lawns and crashed through beds of riotously coloured flowers. Although only ten miles away, it felt worlds apart from the milky cup of spicy chai I'd slurped on the building site two hours earlier.

That evening there was a diplomatic dinner in honour of the visiting British Secretary of State for Defence. We kept ourselves scarce in the pool house, and the liveried staff brought us shepherd's pie with buttery boiled vegetables. We were also left with two bottles of wine, each bearing a sticker reading *For diplomatic purposes only*. Before each swig, we toasted one another with 'to peace!' or 'for the good of the people!'

The next day, eager to explore, we got on our bikes in the cool morning and headed for the city. We wandered around the seventeenth century Jamid Mosque and wove our way through the Chandni Chowk bazar. Old Delhi was a shock to my system. A sensory overload with garishly flaunted wealth alongside startling poverty. Beggars crawled along in the dust and pathetically clutched the ankles of passersby. Hawkers shouted and pedestrians spat. The clichés were true. There was such an arresting vibrancy of bright colours; Iran had been a palette of conservative browns, whites, and occasional flashes of Islamic green. In India, if there is a surface and a few rupees spare for paint, cheerful patterns and Hindi script will soon adorn it. Even the cows were painted with swirling patterns and Hindi mantras as they roamed the tight alleyways, grazing on wilted produce in piles of rubbish.

The route out of Delhi comprised several crawling lanes of traffic filtering onto a two-lane highway towards Agra. We dodged and wove our way onto this 'Grand Trunk Road' – the subcontinent's historic trade artery that has run almost 2,000 miles for over 2,000 years, from Chittagong in Bangladesh all the way to Kabul in Afghanistan.

The unwritten rules of the Indian road seemed to be as follows:

1. Drive on the left. But not if you'd rather not.
2. Never look to either side, only look forward. This rule also applies to those entering a roundabout at speed. Once a motorist has overtaken another vehicle, it ceases to exist, and he – it is rarely she – may swerve as dramatically as he wishes. (I learned this with a buckled wheel and a grazed elbow in Delhi, when a moped sped past me on the outside, braked sharply and cut across a second later.)

3. Never give way. Driving is for the bold, and needlessly risking death is the ultimate display of subcontinental masculinity. (A Spanish motorcyclist I met witnessed a fatal head-on collision on a single-lane road. He foresaw the accident several seconds earlier as he had come to know the stubborn nature of Indian drivers.)
4. Traffic lights and official rules of the road are laughable constraints, merely for the weak. (I saw a traffic policeman hit by a car that rolled slowly towards him as he helplessly whistled and waved his white-gloved hands.)

Unsurprisingly, the annual death toll on Indian roads is now over 200,000.

Every sort of vehicle surged in the seething crush on the road to Agra. Three-manned motorbikes and rusty, single-speed bicycles threaded through seemingly impassible gaps that opened for an instant when a driver was too busy honking to quite hug the bumper ahead. Scrawny men in dirty *dhotis* skillfully guided handcarts sporting battered car wheels with bald tyres. Top-heavy rickshaws needled into invisible spaces between cars. Buses and minibuses used their superior size in a vain attempt to cow the other, lower drivers into submission. The entire chaotic assembly lurched and jolted forward in a frenzy of self-interest, and with an absolute absence of courtesy. We all existed in a cloud of eternally rising dust, exhaust fumes, and unparalleled clamour of horns and shouts and grinding gears. James and I loved it. We nudged our way forward in fits and starts, yelling joyous abuse and greetings along with the most vociferous of our peers on the highway.

Among the argy-bargy, an ancient bull elephant with colourful markings painted on his leathery skin plodded stoically. A sleeping *mahout* lolled precariously on his neck. The creature seemed removed from its chaotic surroundings, and I could picture him in the wild with the same slow, determined gait and no impatient rickshaws hemming his flanks.

After two days, we entered another standstill scrum and prodded our way through a cluster of touristic hostels near the Taj Mahal. Having checked in to a windowless, ground floor room for a nightly pittance, we wandered around the buzzing alleyways. Many foreigners we saw looked harassed, down-trodden and disgruntled. They flinched defensively when people approached or passed too near them. They stepped cautiously over mess on the alleyway floors with thinly veiled disgust, and they studiously avoided eye contact with strangers for fear of someone trying to sell them something. Having escaped the anarchic road, James and I were, by contrast, relishing the space and peace, the opportunity to interact with people who wouldn't potentially flatten us.

We visited the Taj Mahal as sunset approached on the following day. Once inside the grounds, we were swept along on a tide of excited, chattering people, eager to see their country's most emblematic building.

With the jostling crowds shattering any potential serenity, I enjoyed watching the struggle for the dead-centre photograph spot more than the building itself. People thronged around the southern end of a long, narrow pond that reflects the onion dome of the four-centuries-old mausoleum. Everyone was after a photo of themselves appearing to pinch the distant dome's decorative spire, so it appears to be dangling from their fingers.

The noisy, colourfully dressed hordes swilling around the Taj Mahal slightly dimmed its majesty. However, as the sun sank, the clean marble facade began to glow an ever-shifting array of soft, sunset shades. The dome bulged with a rich orange, and elegant shadows were cast from the intricate masonry. A hush descended and the throng ground to a brief halt. At that moment, I understood why the building enjoys the reputation it does. Its ability to awe several thousand excited Indians into silent reverie, however brief, is admirable and perhaps unique.

I awoke with a hangover – my first in two months – and we shakily made our way out of Agra on a small country road. As we pedalled, we pieced together blurry snatches of memory from the previous night. While leaving the Taj Mahal, we'd met Jessie, an American with long brown hair who was also staying in our hostel. She joined us in a rooftop restaurant for beers and a cheap *thali* (a mound of rice and a stack of *roti* flatbread served with lentils, curds, vegetables, chutneys and pickles). Jessie worked for a circus in Macau, and was travelling with a warring gay couple that she seemed glad to have escaped. We later found ourselves in a bar where Jessie complained of the heat, and how itchy it made her head.

'So, shave it,' I suggested.

'Yes, definitely! I'm sure your skull has a nice shape,' added James.

Ten minutes later we were in a barber shop, and a man with electric clippers hesitantly mowed an irrevocable strip down the centre of her head. By the time we moved to another bar, she was left with nothing but a slim ponytail in the style of a shaolin monk. After midnight, we stumbled back to the hostel and James slumped into bed. I stayed up a while, smoking unpleasant cigarettes with Jessie, and spectacularly failing to woo her.

'I can't believe you were into her,' said James, as we rode east in the morning.

'James, you're fresh from the lights of London with it's nightlife and easy pleasures. You have a girlfriend too. I'm far from fresh after five months sleeping alone in a tent, showering rarely, and scaring women on sight.'

'Well you evidently scared this one off,' he said.

'Yes. It's become my most accomplished and least valued skill.'

It was Sunday and people lined the road, washing clothes, playing, and watching the world pass by. The road was an avenue of rich verdure dotted with small villages. Long-suffering camels from the deserts of nearby Rajasthan strode along, hauling carts and exuding dignity. Tethered water buffalo grazed in front of simple brick huts. The air was cool and lightly scented by fresh manure. Our heads soon cleared, and we began to relish every second. This narrow, rural road was blissfully quiet, and we soon turned onto even smaller tracks, little more than footpaths threading through the fields.

'Excuse me! Excuse me, sir!' I said. The five-foot-five man on the footpath stopped walking, turned around and looked at me, taken aback. 'Do you speak English?'

'*Angreezi*?' added James.

The man pensively tilted his white-turbaned head left and right a few times, looked from one of us to the other, and clasped his elbow with his hand behind his back. He seemed to be deciding whether we were a threat to be avoided, or a nuisance to be ignored.

I couldn't blame him. I was wearing a dirty t-shirt with the collar cut out and sleeves ripped off. My shorts were tattered and I had sprouted a bushy copper beard in the five months since leaving home. Six foot four, blue-eyed James involuntarily towered over the startled man, and wore a luminous green vest revealing pallid white arms, freshly plucked from British winter.

The man looked up and down the path. It was a deserted, two-yard wide corridor through the fields. Head-high bulrushes fenced it on either side. The sun blanched the milky white sky. There was no easy escape from the alarming foreigners on their strange bicycles.

'Yes. I spee-king *Angreezi*,' he said at last. 'How helping you?' We had found very few villagers with English in the state of Uttar Pradesh.

'Ah! You do? Brilliant! We are looking for the way to Dibiyapur,' I continued. He wobbled his head once more and looked askance. This strange Indian tick is an utterly ambiguous gesture that can mean *yes*, *no*, *what?*, *I don't know*, and much more besides. Many Indians do it contentedly to themselves while going about their business. The face remains forward and the nose stays put, while the chin and top of the head waggle alternately side to side.

'Do you know the village named Dibiyapur, sir?' I tried again.

'Knowing this village.' It rolled off his tongue with no gaps between words.

'Do you know which direction it is in?' I probed. He wobbled his head again. The action would have looked jaunty if it wasn't for the bewilderment plastered across his face.

'Is it this way?' I pointed forward in the direction we were facing. He wobbled his head mysteriously. 'OK. Is it that way?' I stretched my arm in the opposite direction. The head wobbled once more.

James cut in. 'Yes? It is this way? Dibiyapur?' Two eyes bulged in the still wobbling head. 'Yes?'

'Yes? This way?' repeated the man uncertainly, his eyes fixed on James and his hands nervously grasping folds of his *dhoti*.

'So, it is this way? This direction?' I pressed.

'This direction?' repeated the man. His head seemed due to come loose at the hinge.

'OK. So, we go this direction. Yes?'

'Yes?'

'To Dibiyapur?'

'Dibiyapur?'

'It's useless. He doesn't understand,' James mumbled from the side of his mouth.

'Understanding,' he said. His hearing was evidently

better than his English.

'Dibiyapur is how far? How many kilometres?' I tried.

'Vun.'

'One kilometre?'

'No. Vun furlong. Goodbye,' and he walked quickly away down the lane, glancing frequently over his shoulder.

'Great, let's go!' said James with thinly veiled sarcasm.

'James, what's a fucking furlong?'

'I was hoping you'd know the answer to that.'

All the land was fields, and all the fields were busy with people, so we pitched camp late that afternoon by a cucumber patch. A small crowd of leering boys watched us from a distance. This was a pleasant respite from the vast crowds that gathered around us anywhere we stopped in rural India. Home to two hundred million people, Uttar Pradesh is India's most populous region. It is also the second poorest (after neighbouring Bihar) and has the lowest literacy levels. English language was scarce. The state's agricultural economy is fed by millions of villagers manually working the flat land of the Ganges flood plain. It forms the majority of 'The Cow Belt', the ancient Hindustani heartland.

When we stopped in towns, scores of men and boys would silently close in, ringing us with a wall of indifferent gormlessness. They had never seen anything like us before: long white limbs, sunburned shoulders, scruffy beards, James' ice blue eyes, and our expensive-looking bicycles burdened with mysterious baggage. However, few onlookers appeared particularly friendly. No one spoke, asked questions, or offered guidance. They simply stood, a mass of stick-thin men with hands slung loosely behind their backs. These crowds often swelled to a hundred within a minute, and continued to grow.

For most of the way to Lucknow, we cut across country on bumpy cart tracks lined with bulrushes. To either side, dry rice paddies awaited the spring monsoon while women harvested crops with hand sickles, neatly tying and stacking the sheaves. A man at an endearingly rustic barbershop (a chair in front of a tree with small shelf and mirror nailed to it) wobbled his lathered face enthusiastically as we passed. Roadside vendors sold samosas and chopped vegetables served on plates of pressed leaves for a couple of rupees each (less than three pence). For the first time on my journey, I started dosing tap water with iodine before drinking.

One night we asked villagers for permission to camp among a clump of trees where thousands of potatoes were laid out to dry. A crowd gathered, and we slowly coaxed them out of their bashful silence and into a game of catch with a tennis ball. A boy soon fetched a gnarled cricket bat and we played with sticks for stumps, prancing over the potatoes blanketing the outfield.

Our rural route eventually joined a small road that carried us across the Ganges, four hundred yards wide at that stage. James fell behind me on the bridge and later caught up ashen-faced. He had spotted a cluster of about fifty corpses: a mass of swollen bellies, splayed hair and angular limbs jutting out of the sluggish, muddy water. Some families cannot afford proper cremation ceremonies, and their loved ones are quietly slipped into the Holy River.

After a few more days in the villages, we neared Lucknow. Due to roadworks, the city centre was a grainy blur of drifting dust. Once an important colonial centre under the British Raj, Lucknow today sees relatively few foreign visitors. At the start of the Indian Mutiny in 1857 (known, more fittingly, to Indians as the First Great War of Independence), colonialists from the surrounding areas quickly retreated to the Residency, the political and administrative headquarters at the heart of the city. The Indian revolutionaries surrounded the Residency and a siege began that would last almost six months.

James and I took a stroll through the grounds and the ruins of the once-stately building. The remaining brick walls were pockmarked with mortar damage and occasionally adorned with modern, anti-British graffiti. The gardens were in a charming state of overgrowth. As a symbol of both British exploitation and early nationalist resistance, the Residency is neither maintained nor destroyed, but left to the elements. Young Indian couples go there to walk hand in hand, and to laze on the lawns away from prying eyes.

That evening I phoned my grandmother to wish her a happy eighty-seventh birthday. She told me that her great-uncle Arthur – a grand, sepia, tweed-clad individual – had been a young officer in the Residency during the siege. His wooden chest had been used along with other furniture to barricade the main entrance, and he had been posted in a second-floor window as a sniper. Arthur received a head wound during the siege, but bandaged himself up and maintained his rifle vigil for six months until the relief party arrived. He was mentioned in dispatches for his bravery.

However, it seemed to me that the age of heroism was over. That I might end up barricaded in a besieged building for half a year seemed impossible. Of course, I didn't want that. But on some hubristic level, deep at the back of my mind, I craved a dramatic event, or a tragedy, in which to prove my mettle as a brave man. I wanted to see if I could be a hero. My great-great-great-uncle Arthur might not have been searching for the chance to show his bravery, but one landed in his lap and likely shaped the rest of his life.

James and I turned north towards Nepal on another rutted road with one lane in each direction and comedy-inducing railway crossings. The barriers would drop in anticipation of a coming train. Pedestrians and cyclists would continue to duck under them and scurry across the tracks until perilously late. The train would then clank languorously past for ten minutes. In this time, a single-file queue of beeping cars would form, until one particularly impatient driver would skip to the front in the wrong lane. More would follow his lead until both lanes were tightly gridlocked, inching pointlessly forward. The train would pass, the barriers would lift, and the drivers would discover that the same impressive idiocy had occurred on the other side of the tracks. All the cars would then lurch forward a few yards, only to reach a bumper-to-bumper standstill in the middle of the tracks. It would then take a horn-happy half hour to extricate themselves from the gridlock. We witnessed this phenomenon several times. It is hard to better exemplify how Indian drivers are not so much reckless as witless.

TEN

CALM

*Years from now you will be more disappointed by the things you
didn't do than by the ones you did do. So throw off the bow lines.
Sail away from the safe harbour. Catch the trade winds in your sails.
Explore. Dream. Discover.*
- Mark Twain

5 December 2010

We had seen Nepal from some distance as the border
marked the end of the plains of Uttar Pradesh, flat
as a chessboard, and the start of the Himalayan foothills. A
daunting green barrier of gradient and verdure rose before
us, stacked layer upon layer until lost in the haze.

Once we'd entered Nepal the world transformed. Gone
were the stony-eyed crowds and sullen indifference. People
waved and cheered us past. Villagers shouted 'welcome!', a
sentiment we had rarely heard during the previous
fortnight. The road tilted and we plunged into forested
foothills. Monkeys chattered in the trees and occasionally
loped across the tarmac, boisterous troops with large,
watchful elders standing sentry. That night we camped,
unseen, in a clearing by a crocodile-infested river. We lay
by our campfire until late, spotting shooting stars, chatting,
and feeling completely at ease. No one knew we were
there. No one came and stared, and the peace was
overwhelming. It was finally what James had envisaged
when he agreed to join me.

James had travelled in India years earlier and
remembered it fondly. He was at a crossroad in his life,
bored of odd-jobbing and bar work, but unable to find a
decent job in recession-struck Britain. Cycling through
India had sounded a nice prospect to clear his head and
gain some perspective. But the crowds and the staring and

the indifference were not what he remembered from his backpacking days, and he had not enjoyed himself as much as I'd hoped. In Nepal, however, things were looking up.

In the morning, the sweat and toil of hills came as a welcome change. We headed east, hurdling over rising valley spurs as they splayed down towards the plains. The climbs afforded sweeping views and made our progress feel tangible. The lush valleys had floors of lime green rice paddies which became terraced as the valleys narrowed and rose. We rolled through small thatched villages where beautiful girls giggled coquettishly behind clasped hands. Few cars plied the road, and we proceeded side by side, playing word games to pass the time.

At lunchtimes, we stopped into village restaurants in basic, wooden huts. The only meal available was *dhal bhat*, the nation's staple of rice with lentil soup. Costing only fifty pence, it was usually served with pickled vegetables and freshly foraged mushrooms. The beaming, stooped old women running the restaurants would sidle over to the sloping tables time after time to refill our plates. *Dhal bhat* is always an all-you-can-eat affair – a hungry cyclist's dream. A steaming mug of sweet, spicy milky masala tea (sometimes with a floating cinnamon stick or anise star) would round off the feast perfectly. We would then pedal a sluggish few hundred yards, find a grand, sweeping rudraksha tree, and flop down in the shade for an indulgent slumber.

In the bustling junction town of Butwal, we turned north and spent a day climbing up a narrow ravine with sheer green walls shooting skyward. At the top, we began a thrilling descent, making great, echoing shouts of joy while slaloming down the tight switchbacks.

We worked our way up and over several passes where the views added to our breathlessness. Atop one, James and I caught each other's eyes while standing silently, gazing across the far-reaching panorama. Our faces buckled, and we broke into peals of laughter. The simple joy of exertion and beauty. The silver thread of a distant river shimmered, and the mountains glowed all the shades of golden-green as the late-afternoon sun ripened. That evening we settled into a one-pound room in a village guesthouse and cooked a dinner of buffalo, onions, tomatoes, chilli and rice. After eating, we drank coffee by candlelight. The muffled clang and tinkle of gongs, bells and cymbals sounded from the village's Buddhist monastery. James said in earnest that the day had been among the happiest of his life and would set a high benchmark for all days to come. I felt relieved.

Two climbs later, we arrived in Pokhara. Set on a lake surrounded by mountains and presided over by the Annapurna range (several craggy peaks soaring to over 8,000 metres), Pokhara is a hub for hikers, mountaineers, and just about every visitor to Nepal. We spent a couple of days unwinding, swimming, rowing on the lake, and feasting on *momo* (traditional Tibetan steamed buffalo dumplings).

The final three days of riding to Kathmandu were challenging. It was almost entirely uphill, and fast buses swung around blind corners over daunting precipices. Many had 'drive slow, live long' painted on their rear, and we saw the twisted, rusting carcasses of several that had tumbled to the valley floor, doubtlessly killing dozens. I managed to latch onto the side of a slow-moving lorry for a particularly steep stretch. While I clung awkwardly to both my handlebar and the side of the lorry, a man popped his head out of the passenger window and waved. I wobbled my head, Indian style, in acknowledgement, and he disappeared. He appeared again with a bottle of water and a sympathetic expression. I tilted my head back, and relished the cool water he poured into my mouth. Seconds later he leaned out again, shaking a cigarette and a lighter. I wobbled my head once more, and he placed the cigarette in my mouth. He lit it, and I smoked the entire cigarette from his fingers while the lorry wheezed its way up the hill.

The ride culminated in an agonizingly steep twenty-five-mile climb, before the joyous descent into central Kathmandu. In the tourist district of Thamel, we found a basic room for two pounds a night, washed, and wandered around, looking at the tightly stacked stalls of souvenirs and the ambling travellers. Many wore the baggy, brightly coloured fashions more often associated with backpackers in the sixties or seventies.

James and I, for some reason, refrained from the numerous restaurants serving western food and found instead a basement dive serving *momo* and *dhal bhat*. Once fed, we picked up a foul bottle of *chhang* (locally brewed barley liquor) and wandered out into the night. The rest of the evening, our last together, was a blur of hugs and heartfelt words. I hoped James found what he came for.

James flew home and my parents, brother, and sisters arrived to spend the Christmas week with me. When I met them at the airport, I shocked them with my bushy ginger beard. We spent a couple of days on safari in Chitwan National Park (Asian rhinos, leopards, and pythons, but sadly no tiger sightings), hiked in the Annapurna foothills around Pokhara, and visited the various heritage sights in Kathmandu.

On their last day, we took a scenic flight along the Himalayan ridge to Everest. The towering granite spires looked an impregnable fortress guarding the endless Tibetan beyond. Then, all too quickly, I was waving my family off at the airport with a wrenching pang that felt like leaving home all over again.

Feeling lonely, I sought solace in a secondhand bookshop in Thamel. While scanning the shelves, I noticed an attractive girl also browsing. She pulled out *Daniel Martin* by John Fowles and began reading the back. I saw my chance.

'It's one of my favourites,' I said, truthfully, but instantly regretting it. I felt creepy with such an unsolicited conversation starter. She looked at me and said nothing.

'The book, I mean. He's a brilliant author and the book is a sort of, well, a deconstruction of Englishness and what it is to be a lone man increasingly outside of the social establishment.'

'You're English?' She said, with a North American twang.

'I am. And you? American?'

'No.'

'Oh God! Sorry, I'm always doing that. Very embarrassing. Canadian, right?' I babbled.

'No. I'm actually from here. I'm Nepali.' Her skin was fairer than mine, and I was confused.

'But...'

'Oh, your confused because I'm white, right?'

'A little, yes. Sorry!'

'Don't be. My mum's Nepali and my dad is half-Danish, half-Ukrainian but he grew up here. I've lived all my life here until I went to study first in Norway and now in Idaho.'

I gulped. 'Do you feel like a coffee?' It was a wild swing. Bushy bearded and deeply tanned, I looked vaguely Neolithic.

'Sure,' she said, simply. 'I know a place near here.'

Over coffee and chocolate cake, Ayesha and I got to know one another. I asked about her unusual heritage. She shrugged off the question, elusively saying her grandfather was 'quite an interesting man'. There was a book about him if I wanted to learn more. We spoke for hours, walking around the city's cramped alleys, and eventually chanced upon the *Losar* (Buddhist New Year) celebrations in a park. We sat with a family for a picnic lunch of *tsampa*, the Tibetan barley-based staple, and danced with the mostly elderly crowd. Ayesha asked questions about my journey and what I was planning now my family had left. I explained my aim to get into Tibet and the visa difficulties of doing so.

'So, you may be in Kathmandu for a while?' she asked.

'I suppose so. It's going to be hard to find a way across the border.'

'Come and stay with my family until you leave. My big brother is over from Australia, and my little brother and sister are on school holidays. We'd love to have you.'

I didn't have to think twice, and that evening I was welcomed into a family. Ayesha's parents, Alex and Kabita, installed me in the guest room for almost three weeks. They came to treat me like a lost son while I worked on various doomed schemes to get myself into Tibet, where the Chinese don't allow independent travel.

While staying with the Lissanevitches, I spotted a copy of *Tiger For Breakfast* on a bookshelf and began reading the most adventurous life story I'd ever heard. Ayesha's grandfather, Boris Lissanevitch, had been a twelve-year-old naval cadet in Odessa when the Russian Revolution began. As a White Russian, he fought on the side of the imperialists against the Bolsheviks and was shot in the thigh in battle. He lived under the Soviet regime for several years before escaping to Paris in 1924 with a forged contract to dance for Sergei Diaghilev's *Ballets Russes*, today considered the most influential ballet company of the twentieth century. On arrival in France, Boris quickly learned to dance, and was soon accepted by Diaghilev. The all-Russian troupe had lived in exile since the revolution, and toured Europe extensively. During his four years in the company, Boris married a fellow dancer, Kira, and met many Bohemian luminaries of the time, enjoying drinking sessions with Picasso and Matisse among others.

Diaghilev died in 1929, and the young couple became an independent dance act, largely performing in nightclubs across Europe. They were refused labour permits when they tried to move to London, but an Indian club owner offered them a six-month dancing contract in Bombay. They completed the contract and travelled east through Sri Lanka, Malaysia, and Java, before settling in 'Swinging Shanghai' for a year. They returned to India, via a three-month hunting trip in Laos, and settled in Calcutta to found Club 300, a private members club created to exceed London's Club 400 for exclusivity of clientele (being restricted to just three hundred members). The first club to open membership to both British and Indians, Club 300 became a favourite of maharajas, hunters, fighter pilots, and visiting royalty. The couple became estranged during the ten years he ran the club, and they eventually divorced.

Boris' next venture was a distillery which failed after four years when India partitioned. Most of his ingredients were sourced from Pakistan and became unavailable. In 1951 he met and befriended Nepal's King Tribhuvan in Club 300. The king was in exile, having recently tried and failed to overthrow the Rana dynasty (an increasingly tyrannical hereditary line of prime ministers who had reduced the monarchy to figurehead status over a century of rule). Allegedly with Boris's help (acting as a secret emissary), Tribhuvan finally overthrew the last Rana and restored power to the throne.

Boris was soon invited to stay at the royal palace in Kathmandu and took his opportunity to ask the king for a licence to run a state liquor monopoly. The licence fee was agreed, and Boris moved his new family (young Danish wife, Inger, and three sons) to Kathmandu. At this time, very few westerners were even permitted to visit Nepal.

When Tribhuvan died and Prince Mahendra ascended to the throne, his administration decided that Boris should have been paying a higher fee all along. When he failed to produce the inflated bill, he was imprisoned. He spent three months in a cell until the young king realised he had no idea how to accommodate or entertain the dozens of state leaders and dignitaries invited to his coronation. He went in person to Boris with a bottle of whisky and reportedly said: 'Well, you're free. No hard feelings I hope. And I have a favour to ask…'

After successfully handling the coronation, and the subsequent state visit of Queen Elizabeth and Prince Philip (including a tiger hunt and a line of 305 elephants kneeling in deference), he opened Nepal's first hotel, in a converted nobleman's palace. All the requisite furniture had to be brought over the foothills from India on horseback.

In 1955, Boris approached the king, now his friend, and asked him to begin granting visas to tourists. Mahendra was sceptical, but Boris persuaded him to grant a sample batch of fifteen visas to Americans on a round-the-world tour. The king visited the hotel to welcome the tourists, where Boris had cleverly laid on a display of local handicrafts. When Mahendra saw how eagerly the tourists bought the souvenirs, he instantly ordered that tourist visas be permitted henceforth.

For years the Royal Hotel (and Boris in person) hosted every international visitor to Nepal. He hosted memorable nightly parties in the hotel's bar (the Yak and Yeti) and welcomed those who couldn't afford the rates to stay as his personal guests regardless. It was said in the fifties that visitors knew only two things about Nepal on arrival: Mount Everest, and Boris. Boris died in 1985 and is buried in the British cemetery in Kathmandu.

A nomad most of his life, Boris never truly settled until his fifties. His inventiveness and ability to restart his life in new places so many times was inspiring. His rip-roaring adventures would live on as legend.

The time came to say goodbye to Alex, Kabita, and Ayesha. I had booked a flight to northwest China, from where I would cycle south and attempt an illicit entrance to Tibet. I reflected on Boris' story. I had recently parted with my family, potentially for several years, and was now feeling pained to be leaving another family that had so generously accepted me. The pain of parting is unavoidable for someone always on the move. Boris was an itchy-footed adventurer who saw and did unbelievable things. However, it struck me that he only truly found peace when he stopped moving and set up in Nepal with his family.

ELEVEN

COLD

It is the work that matters, not the applause that follows.
- Robert Falcon Scott

17 January 2011

The cold stuck me like an angry slap as I walked into the bright midday sunshine. Urumqi airport was a scrum of small, grim-faced people buried in thick winter clothing. Earlier, as the plane soared over the Tibetan plateau, I had squinted through the brilliant sunlight at the barren wasteland below, a purgatory of chaotic whiteness. Comfortably sat in the heated plane, the coldness and desolation outside was abstract. However, on approach to our destination, the captain came over the PA system and made a cheerful announcement in Chinese. He then repeated the message in English.

'Hello! Ladies and gentlemen. We are now beginning our descent to Urumqi International Airport. We hope you've enjoyed flying with Air China, and that we will see you again soon. The ground temperature in Urumqi is currently minus thirty-three degrees centigrade. Good day.'

I looked through the window again. It was midday with clear blue skies. *Minus thirty-three degrees! How can it be that cold when the sun's out? How cold will it be when there's snow and wind? What will it be like at night in my little summer tent? Will I freeze in my sleep?*

This kind of sudden transition, from temperate Nepal to frozen northern China, was new to me. For the past six months, I'd made happily slow progress across Europe, the Middle East, and South Asia. Now I felt a sense of terror. There had been no gentle ramp to these conditions. If the Chinese hadn't been so sensitive about Tibet, I could have simply entered, legally, from Nepal. But no such luck.

Foreigners struggle to get permits for the well-trodden tourist sites of Tibet, even on guided tours. I was planning to travel unaccompanied along the completely off-limits western road. I would have to traverse numerous military bases and police checkpoints. If caught, I would be arrested and likely fined, possibly even imprisoned. The Chinese government's patience with foreign travellers creeping around their politically sensitive regions withered after 2008.

Foreigners were allowed in with increasing ease from the early 1980s up until 2008. However, in the run up to the Beijing Olympics, violent rioting broke out in Lhasa. The Tibetan people were protesting the occupation of their country, an independent nation until the 1950 invasion (or 'liberation', in the Chinese Communist Party's vernacular). The salt in the wound was that Tibetans are forbidden from worshipping the exiled Dalai Lama, their spiritual leader and a living god in Gelug Tibetan Buddhism. They are not even allowed to possess his image, risking imprisonment if caught. The rioters in Lhasa reportedly killed eighteen Han Chinese. However, the government forces are believed to have killed over a hundred Tibetans in their attempts to quell the unrest. The riots ruffled the government's feathers and the Tibet Autonomous Region became more tightly controlled, with civic freedoms further restricted. Since then, over a hundred and fifty Tibetan monks have self-immolated in protest.

In Urumqi, I was discombobulated by the sudden cold, and irrationally decided not to hail a taxi to the train station. I hefted the box containing Old Geoff onto a shoulder and, panniers in my other hand, staggered under its weight. After only a couple hundred yards, one of my wellies slipped on ice and I crashed to the pavement. A stooped, toothless Chinese man pushing a handcart stopped, and lifted my things onto it. His bare hands, poking from synthetic, padded sleeves, were horribly raw and red. He looked at me until I made a pantomime of a train. With a gummy grin, he wheeled around and set off. I trailed stiffly behind with a slowly forming icicle of snot arrested in its escape from my left nostril.

The road signs were in Chinese, Arabic, English and Russian. Geographically, culturally, and traditionally, Xinjiang (China's largest province) has no business being part of China. The indigenous Muslim Uighur people have been fighting for independence ever since China's conquest of the region in the nineteenth century. Urumqi, the capital, had been the scene of Uighur protests eighteen months earlier in July 2009. Protest marches escalated into rioting and ethnic violence between the Uighurs and the Han Chinese, in which two hundred people died.

At the railway station, I gave the man with the handcart a negligible amount of money. It seemed to please him, and he merrily shook my hand with his rough claw before wandering off, pulling his cart behind him.

The station guards told me bicycles were not allowed on passenger trains, and that I must send it as cargo. The rail freight office was next door, and, after much confusion, I managed to send the box to Kashgar, from where I would cycle. By then, I had missed the passenger train, so I found a cheap *ludiàn* (hostel) for the night. The large, brutalist building was characterless, and heated to an unbearable temperature. I curled up on the bed that night and felt lonely. Nobody seemed to speak English and the prospect of spending the rest of winter outdoors in the ferocious cold compounded the sense of being alone. It was the first time I could remember feeling loneliness since leaving home seven months earlier.

The train journey lasted an uncomfortable thirty-two hours. My ticket was in the 'hard seat' category – an unpadded, upright plastic seat – crammed in with two thousand others on a two-storey train. The landscape scrolling past the window was a whir of brown and white nothingness. Seated on my left was a bespectacled student from Shanghai with enough English to lecture me haltingly on the great criminality of the Dalai Lama, and how non-Han Chinese regions are lucky to be administered by China.

'Daily Lama is very terrible man. He had all Tibet as slave peoples. They working all of time. No food. No school. No health. No TV. No karaoke. No fun. No free.'

'And Tibet has freedom now?'

'Now Tibet have school, hospital, club, supermarket... and free.'

'Free to worship the Dalai Lama?'

'Free *from* Daily Lama.'

We were disgorged in Kashgar after dark. The drive into town was not what I'd expected. Kashgar was a fabled Silk Road staging post that has captured the western imagination since Marco Polo visited seven hundred years ago. Visions of smoky bazaars, with mudbrick walls and blaring minarets, had wafted through my mind. However, what I saw was bright and lurid neon lights, ugly apartment blocks, and bold, red Chinese characters glowing over every shop front. Much of the Old Town had been bulldozed to make way for something that resembles any other modern Chinese city.

Despite supposedly travelling on the train a day before me, Old Geoff was yet to arrive. I passed a few days exploring Kashgar, searching for parts undiluted by modern Han homogeneity. The eighty-foot statue of Chairman Mao standing over the central square was disheartening. The 'Great Helmsman' had his right arm raised in a salute to the workers, but, in reality, his soaring presence and impassive face stood as a daily reminder to the Uighur people that the Chinese are their overlords. A cluster of Uighur men stood near the statue's base, engaged in a chaotic barter of used phones. They all wore tall fur hats coated with black velvet, and black, faux-leather jackets: a telling mix of cultural pride and reluctant acceptance of affordable Chinese goods. In a café one afternoon, a friendly Uighur man called Erik was horrified that I would be cycling south without a Uighur hat. Smiling broadly, he plucked it off his wide head and pushed it down low over my eyes: 'Now you have the warmth *and* the style of a Uighur man.'

The Sunday market was a refreshing taste of how Kashgar once was. The crumbling alleyways of the remaining Old Town were clogged with jovial Uighur men and women buying and selling everything from tattered business shoes to dried fruit. Steaming herds of livestock huddled for warmth while men energetically haggled over them. A couple of Bactrian camels stood unaffected by the cold, each with their two humps sagging sideward as their fat supplies from summer grazing slowly diminished. Smoke from food stalls billowed into the crisp air, scenting the scene deliciously. Butchers wearing timeworn, blood-smeared leather aprons maniacally hacked away at frozen mutton joints with rusted cleavers. The prized cut of the Central Asian fat-tailed sheep is the buttocks, which are pure, rich fat: an essential dietary requirement through the testing winter months.

Still waiting for Old Geoff to arrive in Kashgar, I began to fret. Fear of the upcoming journey through Tibetan winter swelled within me. The journey would not be safe or legal, and I wanted a partner in crime. I went to an internet café and emailed Leigh. After his ride through Central Asia, he was due to arrive in Kashgar soon, and I proposed we attempt the ride through western Tibet together. I wanted a companion to stave off loneliness and provide solidarity in the dangerous cold and remoteness ahead.

TWELVE

ALONE

Who knows what true loneliness is — not the conventional word but the naked terror? To the lonely themselves it wears a mask. The most miserable outcast hugs some memory or some illusion.
- Joseph Conrad, *Under Western Eyes*

23 January 2011

Old Geoff turned up in the hotel reception one morning, in his comically battered box. I quickly assembled and loaded the bike. It was heavy with winter gear and difficult to ride. I decided to wait two more days for a reply from Leigh. If he would arrive within the next week, it would be worth the wait. I also had a nasty, feverish flu. This was as good an excuse as any for delaying a little longer to allay my fears of riding across the Tibetan plateau, alone in the harsh winter. And then it arrived, an email from Leigh with the following paragraph:

I have a great fondness for the times we shared in Iran, the camaraderie, telling stories and cooking together. Someone to laugh with and to moan with, or just to share a coffee and a cigarette in the desert morning. The road can be lonely, but while travelling with you I also experienced a strange dislocation from the personal journey that I had been on previously.

It's clear we are looking for very different things, and have very different personalities, equal but different. A leaf drifting in the wind fell into a river with a strong current; the leaf no longer drifted but was carried downstream. It was no fault of either of ours, but at times I felt that I was no longer on my own ride, but a passenger on yours. I think it would be in both our interests to pursue the imminent future of our journeys alone.'

The last word stayed with me as I pedalled south from

Kashgar that afternoon. *Alone.* I'd not cycled alone for over three months. My entire journey in Asia had been with company.

Wrapped up absurdly against the relatively mild -15°C, I was soon sweating and stopping every few miles to cough up mucus while my headache throbbed ever harder. I should have stayed in Kashgar until I had shaken the flu, but the email from Leigh had struck hard. My decision to leave immediately was the ill-considered outcome of a strop. *If I'm such an unenjoyable travelling companion, then I'll show that I don't need anyone else.* A sulk is the wrong frame of mind with which to begin traversing the plateau in winter. I was woefully unprepared.

That evening, when I pulled off the road and pitched camp next to an ice lake, the sweat in my clothes quickly froze and began to chafe. The brittle plastic zip of my tent broke, and my stove failed to work. I couldn't cook any of the instant noodles I had planned as the mainstay of my diet for the next few weeks. Sitting glumly in my frigid tent, I snapped off chunks of frozen bread and gnawed painfully on frozen apples. The broken zip made it colder, and the tight confines of the one-man tent accentuated the sense of being alone.

I slept little, wracked by exaggerated shudders and explosive fits of coughing. By morning, the water had frozen solid in my two thermos flasks, cracking one irreparably. After sunrise, I pulled on my two spare pairs of socks before wrestling senseless feet into the rubber wellies that were my inadequate defence against the winter. Hungry, shivering, and miserable, I started cycling.

Thin sunlight filtered weakly onto a dreary, flat landscape that further depressed my mood. The only variations on the shades of steely winter grey were the anaemic brown of thin, leafless trees and the frosted grey-brown of turned fields awaiting spring. Everything was dead. Sensation soon retreated from my fingertips; my toes hadn't regained it after the night.

After a month out of the saddle, and with the weight of my food and gear, the pace was slow, and I grew colder still. I started mumbling to myself, dark thoughts and self-reprimands for undertaking such a foolish adventure.

Who are you trying to impress? I scolded. *What's the point in this? Why not just skip this part and lie low somewhere for the rest of the winter? A warm bed, hot food, people to talk to. You can tell everyone that you did it, that you crossed Tibet. 'How come you've got no photos?' they'll ask. 'My camera stopped working in the cold temperatures', I'll reply.* (Indeed, my video camera had failed to work that morning.) *But then what's the point? I might as well just go home.* The cold had crept into every corner of my body and, as my self-control waned, I started taunting myself. *You're pathetic! Toughen up and stop being such a coward. Coward, coward...COWARD!!*

In a sudden childish tantrum, I leapt off my bike, allowing it to crash to the road. I began furiously stamping feet and windmilling arms, desperate to force some blood to my extremities. In doing so I managed to cuff myself hard on the side of my head. Stunned, I paused, and was about to give an uncharacteristic shout of anger when the ridiculousness hit me. I broke into a chuckle. This induced a warm spread of adrenalin. The relief led me to laugh louder. It felt good, and I urged more to come. I began simultaneously crying, with the agony of thawing fingers, and laughing at the absurdity of myself. *You're a silly little boy who lost his temper and thumped his own head.*

I regained self-control when I saw the fright of an old man passing on a donkey-drawn cart. He was huddled against the weather in a patchwork of thin rags. His wife and three children were clustered behind him on the cart, similarly attired. My situation suddenly didn't seem so bad. *You've chosen to be here,* I told myself. *You've gone to a lot of effort to be here. So what if you're not quite sure why, or if it's not easy? Make the most of it.*

That morning was the first of countless drastic mood

swings I was to experience during my time in Tibet. Elated one day, and hopelessly despondent the next, it was the most emotionally inconsistent period of my life. I had never had to *try* to be happy before. I didn't even know it was something that could be learned.

The bleak road towards the plateau seldom saw motorised vehicles. Most traffic consisted of old Uighur greybeards sitting stoically on listing wooden carts. They flicked their donkeys harmlessly with thin sticks, more for the warmth of movement, I thought, than to motivate the donkeys. Rounded old women sometimes perched on the back of the carts, wrapped in sun-faded woollen shawls.

As I progressed south, the temperature dropped further. Keeping a small supply of unfrozen water in my one remaining flask became a daily struggle. Once frozen solid, it was extremely difficult to thaw, and I would have nothing to drink.

Villages became fewer and further between as I turned onto the G219 road, which runs 1,500 miles to Tibet's capital, Lhasa. The landscape morphed. I left the dull, wintry place of lifeless trees that had accentuated my misery. The Taklamakan stretched away on both sides of me, yellow, empty, and unyielding, while the jumbled white summits of the Pamir Mountains hovered faintly in the far distance over my right shoulder.

I have always found the cleanliness and spaciousness of deserts enticing. The peace and stillness are bewitching. I thought of the words Wilfred Thesiger used to describe the Empty Quarter in Arabia: 'It was very still with the silence which we have driven from our world.'

At the end of the desert the land tilted and the climb towards Tibet began. It grew colder still, and I was glad for Erik's fur hat.

As I neared the restricted area, I wore the hat low to mask my foreign face. I hid from the road when taking breaks, and turned my face away when vehicles passed. Two truckers had already stopped and told me to turn back, the occupants chanting 'Police, police!'

The road entered a valley and the climbing started in earnest. Tarmac was replaced by gravel buried in several inches of dust. The few people I saw now appeared Tibetan rather than Uighur: darker complexions with rosier, windburned cheeks. The gradient, the surface, the rising altitude, and my heavy load made the going painfully slow. Struggling to cover three miles in an hour was new to me.

I made the first mountain pass at 3,300 metres and was rewarded with a scenic revelation. Ahead of me spread a jumbled morass of mountains; brown in the foreground, towering and white in the distance: jagged throughout. I wondered how a road could find a path through that raging sea of geology. It was as beautiful as it was intimidating. *Maybe that's why I'm here,* I chided sarcastically, *to romantically marvel at the sublimity and power of nature. Like Wordsworth and Coleridge in the Lake District. Wandering lonely as a cloud...*

The descent was almost as slow as the climb, as I navigated winding switchbacks while dodging ruts and rocks strewn liberally across the track. Regular stops to clap and swing my arms maintained some feeling in my fingers, and thereby my use of the brakes. I never took off my bottom two pairs of gloves until camping each night, when I would notice that my fingers had an increasingly strange, orange tinge.

My nightly routine was simple: eat an unsatiating dinner of instant noodles cooked on my temperamental stove, close the poorly repaired tent zip as best as possible, try to think of times when I'd been warm and happy, and drift into dreamless, exhausted unconsciousness.

THIRTEEN

EMPTINESS

I am doing this for many reasons, some of which I don't fully understand. That there is an inner urge is undeniable.
- Sir Ranulph Fiennes

1 February 2011

It felt as though the alarm was beeping from within my skull, and it took several seconds before I remembered where I was. The wristwatch was tucked between the two hats on my head so I would hear the alarm through a dead slumber. The sun hadn't yet risen above the mountain tops, but it was light enough to see. I was in my tent, where I had pitched two hours earlier, utterly exhausted, twenty-five miles beyond the Kudi checkpoint. *I made it past!* A feeling of relief swelled within me, then quickly ebbed when I contemplated another day in the cold.

I stared with resignation at the glistening skin of frost that had formed above my head inside the tent. Vainly, I tried to avoid knocking it off while wrestling with the three drawstrings and two zips that locked me tightly inside two sleeping bags. Having retrieved a warm pair of gloves from my crotch, I hurriedly put them on.

There was a cold bottle of urine at the bottom of the sleeping bag where it briefly warmed my feet the previous night, and saved a trip outside before sleeping. I struggled into the bulky jacket that passed the night zipped around the foot of my sleeping bag. Despite all these measures there was still no sensation in my toes. I rubbed them together unfeelingly to prove this fact to myself, a daily exercise in frustration.

In the tent porch, my breakfast was laid out ready to be cooked. Perched on the unlit stove was a mess tin containing a block of brown ice – the broth from the previous night's instant noodles, a fork imprisoned in the murky freeze. An unopened packet of instant noodles sat beside it. After several minutes fiddling with the cooker, it spluttered into semi-efficiency. Above 4,000 metres it struggled with the thin air. I ate the small portion of unsatisfying noodles quickly and noisily. There was nobody within at least a twenty-mile radius, so manners seemed redundant. After slurping down the broth, I scooped the oily residue into my mouth with a finger and licked the fork clean. It was time to get up.

I was already fully dressed, except for replacing my two pairs of 'tent socks' with three pairs of moisture-stiffened 'day socks', which also passed the night in the sleeping bag to prevent them from freezing solid: the nighttime temperature sometimes dropped to -40°C.

With rapidly numbing fingers I packed up everything inside the tent, once again grumbling to myself. *It's so cold. These mornings are so crap. This is no holiday.* Next, I yanked on my stiff pair of wellies, opened the flysheet, and crawled outside. The frigid air felt like liquid as it gushed into my lungs. With what had become a daily epiphany, I looked around, and finally found a valid reason for being there. Purpose struck me anew with resounding force after just a few seconds surveying my surroundings. They were dwarfing, awe-inspiring, and trip-affirming. A clear, stingingly blue sky with a yellow eastern fringe yawned over the morass of rock and ice and snow. I felt miniature. *Perhaps this daily humbling is what I came for.*

Old Geoff lay steadfastly on his side, neglected in the winter night and with a light snow dusting on his rusted frame. Together we set off across the bewitching landscape towards a mountain pass.

Exertion and the sun began to warm me as the road climbed up tightly winding switchbacks. Every few hundred yards I stopped to regain my breath, the air getting thinner as I climbed. At the pass, I halted next to a sign announcing the altitude of 4,980 metres. My spirits soared again.

Ten minutes of floundering through knee-deep snow took me to a tiny peak marked with the red Chinese flag snapping in the wind. The intense mountain sun hadn't yet faded the fabric's colour, as it had on the Buddhist prayer flags tangled around the sign at the pass. From the vantage point I managed to pick out the monolithic peak of K2, the world's second tallest mountain at 8,611 metres, straddling the Pakistan border forty miles away.

Over the next week I rolled through eerily desolate valleys and crawled towards passes at speeds as slow as two miles per hour. The rubble-strewn, dusty track saw only one or two vehicles daily. When the often-furious winds were still, I almost felt guilty breaking the silence in such grand, peaceful spaces.

The only settlements were road-building stations and mining camps, mostly deserted for the winter and usually consisting of a single building next to a canvas tent or two. I made another four passes, two at over 5,500 metres, where there is just fifty per cent of the oxygen at sea level. When cycling at that altitude, my problem was not so much getting enough air, but remembering to exhale fully on each breath. I would suddenly realise I had been drawing deeply on the thin air until my chest was puffed out uncomfortably, forcing me to stop and regulate my breathing.

On rare occasions, I passed herds of goat and yak tended by old Tibetan men with wide, well-weathered faces. One herder beckoned to me and we squatted on our haunches beside each other in the sunshine. While established that we had no common language, I realised I was uttering words for the first time in four days. I wondered if maybe he hadn't spoken for longer. He offered me one of two cigarettes, hand-rolled in yellowing scraps of newspaper. We smoked in silence, watching his hardy goats tearing at scattered scraps of tough, dry grass.

As the unpaved road continued to bounce me around, I steadily accumulated an uncomfortable collection of saddle sores. My front pannier rack snapped in a fourth place, giving me a hellish two hours trying to bind it with numb fingers and strips of inner tube, which had lost their elasticity in the cold. Thankfully this stiffening of rubber also made my tyres tougher and I suffered no punctures.

I experimented with riding on a frozen river one morning. The jolting track had traced the river down a valley all morning, and it was too tempting when my saddle sores were so tender. The smooth surface was delightful for a short while, but I began slipping over every few minutes. I finally got stranded on the wrong side of the unfrozen trickle of water in the middle. I stubbornly rode on as the trickle grew wider and deeper, splitting into several more. Then, when I accepted I was stuck, I was unable to turn back as a fierce dust storm blew up. Grain-sized stones pelted my back, and the wind pushed me forward. With little choice, and nowhere to shelter, I let it drive me on. The afternoon became a four-hour hunt for a ford across to the road. Eventually the storm passed, and I waded across a series of streams carrying Old Geoff, while my leaky left boot filled with thick, icy water.

Passing a track leading to a clutch of three huts one morning, I noticed a smoke stack. I turned off to ask for water and was suddenly charged by eight dogs (two of them vast Tibetan mastiffs), barking and bearing pointed teeth. I had developed a terror of these beautiful animals a couple of nights earlier when three surrounded my tent. They snarled and barked and bayed and growled while I cowered inside, hoping they would leave. They eventually did, after two hours of the most blood-curdling noises I have ever heard.

I cycled fast through the pack of dogs, and darted straight inside the door of the hut where I knew they wouldn't follow. A Chinese couple, winter guardians of the road-building station, welcomed me in and produced a bowl of warm soup with large chunks of chewy goat. Mei and Huang lived in a small room with a bunk bed, an archaic iron stove, a small table and a few shin-high stools. They were from Henan province in eastern China, and they showed me photos of their two-year old daughter who lived with her grandparents. I asked myself how this friendly couple ended up so far from home in such an inhospitable place. I wondered if it was a punishment, or if they had volunteered to come and were relatively well paid. They must have been asking the same questions about me.

Another dust storm began to pull and suck at the sheet metal roofing, and Huang insisted I stay for the night. Relieved almost to tears, I gladly accepted and sat by the stove all afternoon.

We had no common language, but Mei fussed over me in a kind, motherly manner despite being only two years my senior. I gladly took the opportunity to wash my filthy face, feet, socks, and underwear for the first time in over a fortnight. The generator was fired up in the evening and we watched an emotionally manipulative Disney film about an abandoned pack of sled huskies surviving a winter in Antarctica. I was in tears for the last twenty minutes.

Supper was a towering dish of goat and vegetables, fried in a two-foot-wide wok and served with homemade noodles. I watched as Mei expertly rolled and stretched the multiplying strands of dough and smiled delightedly at my enjoyment of the spectacle. Huang led me to a bed in a room next door, lit the coal-burner, and loaded it with enough lumps to last the night. I slept warmly and well for the first time since Kashgar.

After a steaming breakfast of rice porridge with walnuts, I was waved off into another mounting dust storm with several flat breads and a dozen hardboiled eggs in my bags. I wanted to hug them both goodbye, but that sort of physical contact with a new acquaintance is impolite in China. I settled for handshakes while my eyes welled up once again.

The wind was in my face that day. Six hours slogging through a thick swirl of sand and snow on a corrugated dirt track took me only fifteen miles. The flap and snap of the tent in the wind kept me awake most of that night, and billows of dust were blown in through the mesh windows at each end. Everything was coated in the morning.

While climbing towards the next pass, my odometer reached the landmark ten thousand miles. The Khitai pass, at 5,200 metres, presented a new and very different scenery. I stood next to the wind-blasted sign and stared at the arid plains of Aksai Chin: an empty, dusty wasteland at the top of the world, speckled with bulbous brown hills. As at every hard-won mountain pass, my spirits momentarily soared. The landscape before me was both beautiful and haunting.

The desert plateau of Aksai Chin is only a hundred miles across. There are no permanent settlements and the few bodies of water are all saline. However, it has been the cause of much international tension. The Chinese and the Sikhs fought over this mountain-ringed void in 1841, and when the British defeated the Sikh Confederacy in 1849 to claim Aksai Chin as part of their newly acquired Kashmir, China never relinquished their claim.

The region was disputed for another century with the British, Chinese, Indians, and, briefly, the short-lived Uighur breakaway nation of East Turkestan all claiming it. The dusty track that I followed across it was built clandestinely by China in the early 1950s and wasn't discovered by the Indian government until 1958, when it appeared on a newly published Chinese roadmap. Aksai Chin, that otherworldly cauldron of dust and diplomatic breakdown high in the Himalaya, then became one of several disagreements (including India granting asylum to the Dalai Lama) that sparked the one-month Sino-Indian war in 1962. The plains are now administered by China, but they are still inhabited only by small groups of chiru (the, long-horned, black-faced Tibetan antelope) that galloped gracefully away in a cloud of dust whenever I came within half a mile.

Pitching camp halfway across the desert, I piled dust around the flysheet's base to seal out the wind. Sleeping in these high places brought about strange dreams, and it often took an effort upon waking to re-establish my grip on reality. I had to consciously disregard the elaborate fantasia that played through my stretched mind in the moments before opening my eyes. That night in Aksai Chin, I became convinced there was a man called Khotak standing guard outside my tent, and that there were two of me inside. I woke several times and had to switch on my torch. *Are you really sharing the tent with another you?* I asked myself in a tangle of sleep and confusion. *No! No, you're not. I mean,* I'm *not. I'm just losing my mind. Go back to sleep.*

The next day, at Aksai Chin's southern rim, another 5,200-metre pass sat on the unmarked official border of the Tibet Autonomous Region. I didn't celebrate my arrival as it is a nominal boundary and I had long been on the Tibetan plateau.

The road wound up another valley, and I came to a building. Only having a few packs of instant noodles left, I asked to buy food. The stooped old man indicated he had none to sell but stroked his wispy goatee pensively for a few moments before taking my arm and leading me indoors. He cooked a simple omelette for each of us, and we communicated haltingly for half an hour. He warned me of roving packs of wolves, and three-foot snowdrifts on the road just ahead.

'*Nǐ!*' You! The man pointed at me. '*Zhèr!*' Here! He waved a finger at the building around us and then, placing his hands together, he laid his head sideways on them in the international gesture of sleep. However, it was early, and the sky was a brilliant blue, so I thanked him for the offer and pedalled on.

The old man's warning rang in my ears as I snaked up switchbacks to the next pass: Satsum La at 5,360 metres, roughly the same altitude as Mount Everest base camp. The road rounded a mountain's shoulder and I saw snowfields in the near distance. The sky lowered and snow began to fall, swirling in the strengthening wind. Thick drifts soon lolled across the path, and the wind carried an increasing flurry of powder that blurred everything. The drifts deepened into impassable piles and I began long stints of pushing Old Geoff, often sinking up to my knees in search of passage forward. The wind flared up further, pushing the temperature down with a probing chill. It stung my face and made it hard to think. I was frightened, and soon lost in a complete whiteout, trying to use my compass to keep in the rough direction of the road.

Progress slowed to a few yards a minute, and I began to worry that I might be stranded on the mountain. My hands had long since lost sensation. I had to look down to check both thumbs were actually hooked around the handlebars each time I started pushing. My feet had become a pair of ice blocks. It felt as though I was just walking on stumps slotted into the tops of my boots and I feared I wouldn't be able to walk much longer. For the first time in my life, I feared death.

FOURTEEN

FEAR

The traveller buffeted and bruised by storm and mountain,
cherishes the most worthy foe of his steel.
- Frank Kingdon-Ward

13 February 2011

*H*elp! *I'm lost! What do I do? What can I do? This is serious.*
I'm too cold. I want to give up. Oh shit, shit, shit, SHIT! The
old man warned me, but I thought I knew better. Now I'm up to my
knees in snow, I've lost the bloody road, my compass has frozen up,
and I can barely move. This is it. I need to lie down. I'm going to give
up. I won't be found until summer. What am I thinking? Nobody
comes here. I won't be found for many summers. Just a lone, bleached
skeleton on a remote Tibetan mountainside.

No! roared another voice in my mind. *You can't give up.*
You fucking idiot! There must be a way out of this. Think, think,
think. THINK!

Perhaps I could dig down into the snow? Get in my sleeping bags
and bury myself, seal myself in. Yes! That's the answer. Warmth and
rest, relief. God I'm cold!

No, you fool! That would just be an icy grave?

OK, OK! Compromise…I'll keep going for thirty minutes.

But which way will you go?

It doesn't matter! I'll keep going for half an hour, and if I find no
better option by the end of that, I'll start digging.

During the minutes that followed, I began to seriously
think about what dying would feel like. The wind kept
whipping snow all around me and stabbing into any gaps
between clothing. I didn't think of friends or family or
times I'd been happy. As I struggled onwards, hopelessly
slowly, I thought of how stupid it would be to die out
here. How all the people who told me I was a fool would

be proved right. How I wasn't the heroic explorer I fancied myself. I whimpered aloud. I felt embarrassment, self-pity and, most of all, naked fear.

After twenty-five minutes of this pathetic stumbling, a trace of something flickered out of the whiteness ahead. Just a glimpsed trick of the light at first, a vague grey shape in a cold white world. But then another, longer vision, and finally I knew they were real. A clutch of small buildings.

I approached the first, abandoned Old Geoff to the elements, wrenched open the door, and staggered in. The small Tibetans turned to look at me, frozen with terror. They stared at the windburned, crack-lipped, ice-bearded madman who looked past them so lovingly at their stove.

I tried to speak but my mouth refused to make a sound. I shuffled past them, sat next to the stove and pulled off my three pairs of gloves with my armpits. The deadened, orange-grey fingers inside shocked me. After a short silence, the mother brought me a bowl of cool water to thaw my hands, and held a cup of yak butter tea to my lips. She smiled sympathetically while I sipped.

Feeling slowly returned to my fingers, accompanied by excruciating pain. It was half an hour before I managed to speak, but my hosts seemed content to let me sit in silence. I was deeply shaken, so tried to calm myself down by taking in the surroundings.

The home consisted of one small room centred around a couple of stoves that were fed dried yak dung from dawn until dusk. There was one large, south-facing window running the building's eight-metre length. A narrow bench ran right the way around the walls, which were decorated with bright, patterned paintwork. On one wall hung a large picture of the Potala Palace in Lhasa, where the Dalai Lama traditionally lived. The government forbids images of the Dalai Lama, but his former residence is now a tourist attraction and so deemed acceptable.

A smiling grandfather, with thickly matted hair under a

woollen cap, sat in the corner watching me. He was chanting Buddhist mantras and gently spinning a finely engraved prayer wheel. Two children of about three and four ran raucously around in the cramped space. They were wrapped up in several layers and had filthy faces. Curiosity outgrew their fear, and they began touching my face, hair, and beard, giggling with delight.

In the evening, I was handed a large joint of roast mutton and a sharp knife covered in scratches and dents. I watched the parents and grandfather for guidance. They pared off and ate strips of meat, occasionally handing tender tidbits to the children. When the meat was gone, they gnawed at the bone. Once picked clean, the bones were placed on the stove for a while, then deftly cracked so that the liquefied marrow could be sucked out.

Satiated, everyone took a place on the bench, stretched out, and pulled numerous covers over themselves. The storm still raged outside, and I was glad not to be buried in it. I slept deeply, and vaguely recall the father spreading his large overcoat on top of my sleeping bag as I drifted off. He and his family had probably saved my life.

Under a mercifully clear sky I continued, pushing Old Geoff through the deep snow that had piled up overnight. My fingertips still had only partial sensation and had developed blisters, a clear symptom of frostbite. These were extremely tender and needed draining on a daily basis. The road climbed yet again and after five hours I had made only as many miles. A truck chugged along, slipping and skidding, and getting stuck despite its extra high chassis clearance. I waved it down and got a lift for the next thirty miles until the snow was again navigable by bike. I paid for my passage with vigorous shovel work every few miles.

There were fewer passes now that I was moving away from the edge of the Tibetan plateau. The road unfurled through shallow valleys with long, gentle climbs. Nearing the village of Domar, the second checkpoint, I pitched camp early to rest for another night of sneaking past guards. Sleeping in my cramped and frozen tent just outside the village, I wondered if anyone in Domar spoke English. Being so close to people, and yet having to hide for fear of arrest, made me all the lonelier. I hadn't had a real conversation since leaving Kashgar three weeks earlier.

Dinner was a small and unappetising mush of thawed flatbread and instant noodles. I added a processed sausage given to me by the truck driver. I rarely had any protein, and this was a genuine treat. All too late, the wrapper informed me that its contents had expired several months earlier. The midnight stomach cramps climaxed with me vomiting inside the tent after a desperate fight with the numerous sleeping bag zips and drawstrings. Mercifully, the vomit froze in under a minute, so I chipped it off and scooped it out of the tent with relative ease. The odour was thankfully locked up in ice.

I gladly rose at 4 a.m. after the uncomfortable night of food poisoning. The checkpoint was less keenly guarded than at Kudi, and I passed the road barrier with ease. I then took a wrong turn in the village, managing to ride into the police station's courtyard, before continuing a couple of miles down the wrong side of a lake. Eventually, I had to turn back to the village and find the road, just as the sky was paling. Someone waved me over from a doorway but, terrified of arrest, I looked straight ahead and rode out of the village as fast as I could.

Later that day I sat in a low mud hut with a Tibetan couple, their young son, and two goat kids. The boy was an excellent mimic. He sat next to me mirroring my every movement much to the amusement of us all, not least him. Stacked against the side of the hut were several towers of dried yak dung that fed the smoky stove and kept us warm. I was poured cup after cup of tea and, as attempts at conversation led nowhere, we happily sat smiling at each other. The tea was made with earthy, spiced yak butter, slightly rancid, and was something I had come to enjoy over the weeks. It smelled claggy, like it would stick in the back of the throat. I suspect that the greasy fat it contained was so vital for my increasingly emaciated frame, that my taste buds were coerced. Tibetans start their day with several cups of this protein-rich drink and continue drinking cup after cup throughout the day.

Just beyond this break from the cold, I reached the southern shore of Palgon – a long, snaking lake, stretching 100 miles northwest into Kashmir. The shifting, expanding ice had thrown up huge slabs that jutting up at the shore and spilled onto the bumpy track. I raced past; each jolt in the road agonised my saddle sores and, for the first time, I considered turning myself in at the next police station and facing the consequences, rather than enduring more pain and cold. However, an hour past the lake I rounded a corner and abruptly hit a new, immaculately paved tarmac road. Overcome with joy, I dismounted and did a little dance, both to celebrate and to warm up. I felt sure this tarmac would whisk me all the way to Lhasa.

Wanting to record this landmark moment, I set my camera on timer, knelt down, and kissed the start of the tarmac after hundreds of painstakingly slow miles on dirt tracks. Unfortunately, the road had a skin of ice. My top lip stuck to it and tore as I lifted my head. Caught between the pain from my lip and embarrassment at my stupidity, I glided off along the gloriously smooth road with a reddening wodge of toilet paper clasped in my mouth.

I passed another checkpoint with ease before I reached the town of Ali, which I had planned to slip straight through. Lingering would likely lead to arrest and, despite some moments of despair, I wanted to continue cycling. I had come this far, and the worst was likely behind me. My progress was improving with the good road, and my camping routine was getting slicker, making the nights more bearable. I also still feared what punishment I might receive if arrested. However, when I approached the outskirts of Ali, I saw it was larger and more modern than expected. There would be shops, and food, and internet access. There would be a laundry: I smelled terrible. Perhaps I might even find a hotel that would quietly accept me without a Tibet travel permit. I decided to risk it.

Pulling my hat low over my face, I slipped into the centre. I searched for the particular two of the few Chinese characters I could recognise which meant guesthouse. I asked an old man pushing a cart laden with stiff goat carcasses, and he pointed at an adjacent building. The hotel seemed closed-up for winter, but a tiny woman scuttled over and said something in a kind voice before scurrying away. A minute later she returned with another smiling woman carrying a huge ring of keys. We went inside, and I was shown to a cavernous room with a huge double bed and purple mock-velvet wallpaper.

I wasn't asked for my passport but simply made to understand that the cost was forty yuan (£4) a night and that they would bring a thermos of hot water twice a day (the pipes were frozen). The room was unheated and a glass half-filled with solid ice sat on the bedside table. There was an electric blanket and the power worked.

I undressed for the first time in a month, and caught my reflection in the mirror. I was shocked. Each rib cast a clear shadow over the pale, stretched skin. My back ran down to the backs of my thighs in a straight line, with no hint of a buttock. Despite the cold, I stood naked for some time, examining the shattered fragments of my former reflection. The yellowish skin stood out in goose pimples, looking simultaneously slack and taught. The fingertips on my left hand still blistered daily, and the fingers on my right were cold and grey. The face was the most appalling. Brown and peeling skin, lips swollen, cracked and bleeding, and hollowed cheeks framed by dreadlocked hair. A pair of scales told me I'd lost a quarter of my bodyweight.

After washing with a bucket and cup, I dressed and carried my bundle of oily clothes to the nearest laundry. There was an internet café nearby where I was cheered by heart-warming messages. I sent no replies beyond a simple *I'm still alive* to my family. Typing was painful and frustrating. I stepped into a shop for dried fruits, dried meat, nuts, cakes, bread, fizzy drinks, chocolate bars, sweets, and plenty more noodles. Laden with these spoils, I returned to the hotel and got into bed for four days.

Weeks of accumulated exhaustion swept over me, and I slept almost around the clock. When awake, I ate ceaselessly and listened to podcasts on my MP3 player. I could charge it freely, no longer having to ration myself to thirty minutes' use a day.

I returned to the road with renewed motivation. South of Ali was a different world to the sparsely inhabited northwest of Tibet. Homes started to dot the roadside at more regular intervals, flocks of yak and goats roamed in uncountable numbers, and prayer flags proliferated. Each hilltop had a colourful, chaotic tangle of wind-shredded flags. Buddhists believe that the prayers written on the flags go to heaven each time they flap in the wind.

The tarmac made an incredible difference to my progress, and I regained my pleasure in riding. I stopped briefly into homes a few times each day to warm up and make cheerful, wordless conversation over cups of tea. My passing of Kailash was anticlimactic, as the venerable mountain hid her head in the clouds. Sacred to Böns, Buddhists, Jains and Hindus, Mount Kailash is a major pilgrimage site during the summer months. Also sacred is nearby lake Manasarovar, the highest freshwater lake in the world at 4,590 metres, which is said to cleanse bathers of their sins. Drinking the lake's water allegedly purifies the soul, but its cleansing contents were locked up in ice so I pedalled on by, impure as ever.

The road once again crawled up into the whiteness and I followed it through light snowfall, up and over the

Marium La pass at 5,180 metres. A string of cars floundered on the buried road, and I stopped several times to help push. Night was falling, but I rode on hoping to descend further before camping. The higher altitude nights were the coldest and most restless.

I spotted another military checkpoint ahead and, complacent after the previous five, I decided to wait a short while for complete dark and steal by instead of waiting for the small hours. All went well until I slipped on the ice and clattered noisily to the ground a few yards from the guard's hut. I lay still for several seconds and heard no sound. It seemed I had got away with it. Carefully, I stood and regained my balance with a half-step backwards. This landed my heel directly on the squeeze part of my klaxon. The resulting comedy honk, and then another, slower honk as I lifted my foot, brought out two guards who saw me hurrying around the edge of the barrier. They shouted. I stopped and raised my arms. They approached me, rifles slung over their shoulders.

The soldiers were respectful, kind even. As far as they were concerned, it wasn't their responsibility to sentence me. A short soldier, with octagonal glasses and some English, listened attentively as I concocted a backstory of innocence and ignorance. *Why, Tibet is part of China isn't it? And here is my China visa.*

My baggage was searched thoroughly, especially my camera and the photos on it. Thankfully I thought to slip my video camera into my pocket unnoticed. The detailed surveillance footage of checkpoints on it would have refuted my claims of ignorance about the permit system.

The soldiers gave me tea and said I must go to Lhasa to be dealt with properly. By this time it was midnight, and a five-car convoy I had helped on the mountain had arrived. They heard of the situation and offered to take me to the capital. After some barked phone calls to the police headquarters in Lhasa, it was arranged. I was to be taken in the convoy, escorted by a friendly young soldier who was due leave.

With Old Geoff thrust unceremoniously on a roof rack, I slumped disconsolately next to my guard in the back of the Land Cruiser. I fell asleep berating myself for being impatient and getting caught.

When I woke it was sunrise and we were well on our way. The mesmerising first hour of the day put me in a better frame of mind. Everything glowed golden and the snow sparkled brightly with traces of pink and orange. I had had a good run in a place few tourists ever reach. The western approach to Tibet is one of the highest, driest and most remote areas on Earth, and I'd penetrated it in winter. Any longer in the deep freeze might have left me with lasting damage. My fingertips had begun to peel, and still looked corpse-like.

Slipping in and out of sleep, I gazed out the window at the villages, yaks, and mountains, until I was suddenly looking at characterless apartment blocks towered over by the Potala Palace. Lhasa had the feel of an occupied city in wartime. People went about their business, but on every pavement corner was a glass box with six fully armed soldiers standing rigidly to attention. Almost half of the 250,000 inhabitants are Chinese and paid no heed, but the Tibetans lowered their eyes and voices as they passed the intimidating military boxes.

The light was failing when we pulled up to the police station, and the soldier went inside to fetch an English speaker. The driver and his companion, eager to get home, took my bike off the roof and leaned it against the car. I saw my chance and took it. Saying a quick thank you, I mounted Old Geoff and rushed off around a corner. With my pulse thumping in my ears, I hurtled along side streets and down alleys for ten minutes while considering my options. The police would be searching for me now.

I decided I would continue east, as planned, to Yunnan province. I would need supplies and should stay one night in Lhasa, leaving at first light. I began searching for somewhere to sleep. That I didn't consider finding somewhere hidden to pitch my tent, suggests to me now that the plan was rushed and insincere. In the fourth hostel I tried, I convinced the receptionist I had lost my passport and would be going to the police station in the morning to get my permits re-issued. I showered, set a pre-dawn alarm, and went straight to bed.

I must have slept through my alarm. I woke after sunrise to find an immaculately uniformed police officer standing to attention at the foot of the bed.

'Good morning, Mr Walker. I've heard about you. We've been looking for you.' His easy English took me by surprise.

'Good morning, sir. What have you heard?'

'That you're here without a permit.'

'Really? I'm sorry. I didn't know I needed one. I have a Chinese visa and I thought that Tibet is part of China. That's OK, isn't it?'

'It *is* part of the People's Republic. But you must have a permit to be here.' He paused and pensively stroked his chin. 'You are with a bicycle. Where have you come from?'

'I came from Kashgar.'

'Were you not cold? It is dangerous in the winter.'

'I was freezing. It was difficult.'

'You are brave. You are very foolish, but very brave.'

'I'm sorry. I didn't know the rules. I am just a tourist.'

He smiled knowingly. 'How did you get past the checkpoints?'

'What checkpoints? Oh, I sometimes like to ride during the night, so I can look at the stars, you see. Maybe I passed them without knowing it.'

'I don't believe you. But it doesn't matter.'

He smiled again, and I stifled a sigh of relief. He explained that I would have to leave Tibet by train immediately. The following day marked the anniversary of the 2008 riots, and the region would be closed to foreigners, with or without permits, for a month.

'I hope you've enjoyed your stay in Tibet.'

'Thank you. Yes, some of it.'

Lakeside camping spot, Sweden

Late summer sunset, Finland

Author at a pass near Mt Ararat with Ash and Leigh, Turkey

121

Camping by Mt Ararat, Turkey

Author with Siamak's family, Iran

Camping among ruins in Kavir Desert, Iran

Leigh smoking teriyok with Assad, Iran

Boy at the Taj Mahal, India

Sunday bazaar in Kashgar, Xinjiang Province, China

View from first pass on the road to Tibet, China

Road across Aksai Chin, between Xinjiang and Tibet, China

Nordkapp, Norway

Author in tent, Tibet

Camped beside frozen river, Tibet

Host family during a blizzard, Tibet

Windswept road, Tibet

125

Snowy road, Tibet

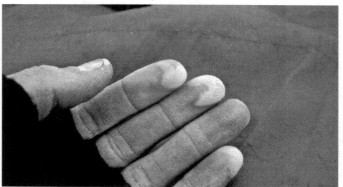

Frostbitten fingers, Tibet

Yaks and prayer flags, Tibet

The road to Lhasa, Tibet

Harvesting rice, Yunnan Province, China

Terraced rice paddies, Yunnan Province, China

Author after motorbike crash, Laos

Looking across the Mekong to Myanmar, Laos

Aumnuay, Thailand

Village children at Angkor Wat, Cambodia

Skulls at Choeng Ek, or "The Killing Fields", Cambodia

Camped among karsts, Guanxi Province, China

Author and "Little Geoff", Hunan Province, China

Michi, Hubei Province, China

Author on arrival at the Forbidden City in Beijing, China

FIFTEEN

RUNNING

Travelling is a fool's paradise. Our first journeys
discover to us the indifference of places.
- Ralph Waldo Emerson

22 March 2011

'I left home about three years ago and have been mostly nomadic since then.' Mariosh looked up from his glass of watery beer. A pair of intense green eyes fixed on mine. 'I left because I was suicidal. I didn't want to live anymore. So, I thought I'd try travelling to find a reason to live. People say that travel helps you find yourself.'

'And have you?' I regretted the question, but hadn't known what else to say. He sighed and sat in pensive silence for a few moments. A Jack Johnson track twanged from small, portable speakers behind the bar.

'I think so. Sometimes. I go through phases. Perhaps the happiest I've been since childhood was walking across Siberia. I liked the space and the peace. I worried I would think too much, but it wasn't a problem.'

'You crossed Siberia? On foot? Really?'

'Yes. I hitchhiked from my home in Poland to the Ural Mountains in Russia. At that point, I realised I enjoyed the hiking more than the hitching, so I just kept walking.

'When winter came it got tough, but the Siberian villagers were kind. They always rang ahead to their friends in the next village. I would often arrive in the evenings to welcome committees. I almost never slept outside.' He spoke through a smile, and I wondered why he'd stopped if he was so happy then. He seemed very down about life now.

'That's amazing! How far did you get?'

'All the way across to the Mongolian border. About

two thousand five hundred kilometres. From there I hitched again, through to China, and down to Yunnan province. I eventually ended up here in Dali. There's a little community of foreigners here. I felt at home very quickly. We started this bar together. There aren't many customers, but we survive. It's interesting being among such a diverse group.'

'So, you'll stay here?' I asked.

His wiry moustache twitched. 'No. I will leave soon. This is not the paradise I thought it was. My girlfriend left me last week. She is Chinese. The same night she left, one of my friends had an episode. He's not really stable, you understand. He took a piece of wood and hit me in the arm. When I tried to stop him, he hit me on the head and knocked me out. That's all I remember. Another friend found him kicking my body on the floor, and managed to calm him down. So, I will leave soon.'

Dali was four days' ride from where the train dropped me in Yunnan province. I met many drifters there. I came to refer to them as 'Lost Soul Travellers', and got the sense that most had something to run from. Many said they had set off in search of themselves. Each had a story of traipsing across the world to find their own Shangri-La, a hedonistic hideaway in which to slowly self-destruct on a cocktail of drink, drugs, and emotional instability. There were, of course, the dreadlocked rich kids too.

On the evening I met Mariosh, I ended up in loud bar called The Bad Monkey. An American man of roughly my age locked me into a conversation about 'the nature of things'. He spouted generalities about freedom and truth while rolling joints which he stored in a tobacco tin for later. On stage was a collective of foreign musicians called *The Quebec Redneck Bluegrass Project* who raced one another on their banjos and harmonicas. They struck up a song in German, about an irate rat with swollen testicles, and the American droned on.

'I can be myself here, you know, man? I can feel myself,' he said, fingering his waist-length dreadlocks with nicotine-yellowed fingers. I reminded myself never to grow dreadlocks.

'Home was stifling, you know, man? Too many *rules*. I never felt *truly* free. And, college was a waste of time, man. But now? Now I know who I am, and I'm completely free here.'

'Will you ever go back?'

'Woah! Bummer, man!' He looked angry with me for mentioning 'the real world'. 'I guess I will eventually. My dad wants me to join his company. They manage business developments in urban areas.'

As I sloped back to my hostel bunk that night, I wondered if he knew how fond the Chinese government was of rules, or their reputation of cracking down on freedom. The Lost Soul Travellers I'd met seemed genuine: lost in life, but genuine. This man uncannily fitted the stereotype of a wannabe hippy born of comfort, who talks too much about the world and does too little in it. His greatest vanity was his orchestrated effort to not appear vain. He carefully curated his image, eager to appear laid back, anti-establishment, and enlightened. Was that a reason to travel? Or a byproduct of travel? In some ways, he reminded me of my younger self, travelling in West Africa as a blissfully naive nineteen-year-old. *You had no idea what you were doing back then, did you Charlie?*

SIXTEEN

NAIVETY

Travelling – it leaves you speechless, then turns you into a storyteller.
- Ibn Battuta

During my first year of university, besotted with the self-image of a wise and dashing wanderer, I booked the first affordable flight I found to an African city I'd never heard of. Landing at 3 a.m. in Mali's capital, Bamako, I resentfully bribed an airport official to release my backpack and paid several times the going rate for a taxi to a rat-infested hotel. Having made my way east towards Timbuktu, merely because of its alluring name, I was disappointed to find a dusty, ugly Saharan slum. I'm not sure what I'd been expecting. An oasis of culture, perhaps. I was too impatient to hang around, wander the back alleys, and 'put my finger on the pulse' (as guidebook authors advised, in lieu of providing actual information).

On the way back west, I met a couple working for an NGO. They had just come from Guinea. 'Honestly, don't go there,' they warned me. 'It's not safe, particularly down in the southwest, near the borders with Sierra Leone and Liberia. The fighting only ended a few years ago. There are still militias in the forest, and tens of thousands of refugees who've been abandoned by the aid agencies and have turned desperate.'

A week of cramped bus journeys later, I arrived in Kissidougou in southwest Guinea, about one mile from the Liberian border and six miles from Sierra Leone. I went because I wanted to flirt with danger. I wanted to have stories with which to impress girls when I returned to university. But, when I got there, it seemed completely normal. No different to neighbouring Mali, which was deemed safe. It was hot, poor, and Francophone. People smiled and chatted with me on the waterlogged mud streets. A short woman approached and addressed me in an English with lilting cadences.

'Hello! Are you an Englishman?'

'Hello! I am.'

'Thank you, God! Nobody here can speak English with me. My French is too poor. My name is Ellen Watta. Do you have some availability to speak with me?'

'I do.'

'Sierra Leone is my country. I fled from the war and came here as a refugee. There are nine hundred of us living in the forest, and nobody cares for us. We are not allowed to integrate into Guinea. The government here wants us to leave. "Go home! The war is over. It is safe now," they tell us. But we know. We know that if we go back to our homes we will be caught and killed as suspected rebel collaborators. They are still hunting the RUF in the forests.

'We are in a limbo. Neither here nor there. And we have no food.' She looked me over carefully, and changed her tone. 'Can you help us?'

I was fascinated and, with little else to do in that forgotten corner of Guinea, I suggested we go to the camp to see the situation. I had recently had my first inclinations towards journalism and thought I had stumbled on a good story. I asked Ellen if I could interview her about her experiences of the war before we set off. She hadn't spoken about it for five years, but reluctantly agreed. We sat down with cokes in the deserted restaurant of Hotel Kissi, and I asked her when she first knew there was a war.

'There was screaming and shouting in my village one morning. It was a small village, one hundred people, called Kamalu, and was near the Moa river. People suddenly started running everywhere, saying that the rebels were coming and that they were killing people. In the confusion, I lost my family so ran along the road in the same direction everyone was running. After two hours, we reached the town Pendembu where there was also chaos.

'I was frightened and my head was hurting. I couldn't think properly and was fainting a lot, but the hospital was already abandoned. I found my family who thought I was already dead, and we continued to a small village to hide and wait.

'After three days, the rebels arrived and set fire to all the huts. They were assaulting anyone they caught. We hid behind some trees and looked out. The rebels had caught a man and were kicking him and laughing. Then they held his arm on a wood block and cut his hand off with a machete. He fell to the floor and they carried on laughing. The man got up, holding his bleeding wrist, and tried to run away, towards me. But they shot him in the back and he fell in the dust. I watched him die.'

Ellen was looking into space over my right shoulder while she spoke. Her coke remained untouched. There was no need to coax her with questions.

'When we tried to sneak out of the village, we were caught. My father was shot and my mother's throat was cut. My brother got away, but I was taken by an old man, a senior rebel. He took me as his wife. I was forced to live this way for two months until he was bored of me and chose another wife.

'The rebels gathered all the women from ten villages and collected up all the village devils.'

'What are devils?' I asked. She seemed surprised.

'The devils are a traditional mask and costume, one for each village. They are worn and danced in for sacred ceremonies. They have strong black magic power. A rebel held a machete to my throat, and forced me to set fire to the pile of devils. Then they put a gun to my head. I was told that I would be killed if I struggled. They raped me. Many of them. I was only thirteen…'

I was silent for a few moments while Ellen stared at the table in front of her. 'Maybe we should talk about something else,' I suggested. But it was no use. A sequence of flashbacks had triggered in her head, and she continued reliving the horrors of her adolescence.

'The other women, also captives, went against me. They said I shouldn't have burned the devils, I should have let them cut my throat instead. They made a plan to kill me. When they attacked, I fought them and managed to run into the bush. A rebel shouted and fired his gun, but God made him miss. I walked through the bush by myself, completely lost, for seventeen days. I was so hungry and I only ate leaves, any leaves – they all tasted the same and made my stomach hurt. The dirty water I was drinking off the ground was not helping this.' Ellen winced and placed a hand gently on her stomach.

'I was getting weaker, but God sent me a palm wine tapper who shouted to me from up a tree. He showed me the direction to Guinea and walked with me for three days. He left me at the border. I thought I was safe. I made my way to an area where the refugees were gathering, but the Guineans arrested me. Some of the women who saw me burn the devils arrived, and they told the troops I was a rebel. I was flogged in public and put in the jail.

'They gave me no food or water, but I had to survive. Each night I was forced to go away with a different soldier. I gave them my body, and they gave me some food. I was there for four months.' Tears had started from her wide eyes.

'How did you get out of the prison?'

'The UN came from N'Zérékoré to inspect the refugee conditions. They rescued me. They put me in a camp where I found my brother. For two years I was taught textile skills and learned a bit of French. I had two children. I didn't know who their fathers were. I only knew that they were two of my rapist tormentors. I began to work with the children who had been rescued from life as child soldiers. They had been brainwashed and drugged. Some were forced to murder their own parents. Many were very violent. They didn't care if they died.

'Then, a few years later in 1999, fighting began in

Guinea. It was connected to members of the RUF, the rebels who had crossed the border. The Guinean troops violently searched our breasts and legs for markings or inscriptions cut into the skin by RUF, mostly on children. They killed many of us. I was suspected but the International Rescue Committee saved me. They took me here to Kissidougou and put me in Boreah refugee camp. But the camp was shut down by the UN three years ago. And now we are starving in the forest.'

I searched for something to say.

'And your brother? Where is he?

'He died.'

'I'm so sorry.' My words had never felt so redundant.

'He returned to our village. The village elders told him to bring me to them because I burned the devils. They threatened to kill him if he didn't. But he said I was dead already. They didn't believe him. The witch doctor blinded him using spells, and the gong, and a knife. They made him mad and he killed himself.'

We sat in silence for some time. Ellen cried and sipped on her coke. I brought her a meal but she didn't touch it, just stared at it with glazed eyes.

Ellen and I left Kissidougou at dawn. I had hired a couple of Sierra Leonean boys with motorbikes – Amadou and James – to drive the forty miles of footpaths leading to Boreah refugee camp. I bought four large sacks of rice, and they used strips of rubber to strap two on the back of each bike. The journey was slow going through dense rainforest and mazes of head-high elephant grass. We finally came to a clearing in the forest. The motorbikes must have been audible and the refugees must have known we were coming. There was a crowd of men, woman and children charging towards us as we dismounted.

'Diplomat! Diplomat! Welcome, Mr Diplomat! We are saved!' they chanted.

Sadly, I was not the solution to their problems. Far

from being a diplomat, I was a patchy bearded teenage student in sandals, tattered t-shirt and floral shorts. Excluding a Swiss photographer a couple of years earlier, I was the first European to stumble across the camp since the UNHCR officially 'closed' it on 4 July 2004. They understandably thought I was the alleviation they had been ardently praying for.

About half of the nine hundred refugees came out to greet me. I was ushered into a dark, mud-floored building and introduced to the leaders of this lost little community. Embarrassed, I explained who I was, and that I had simply come to see the camp. I had never felt more of an inappropriate tourist, prying into their plight. I presented them with the rice sacks by way of limp apology. Their formal acceptance was so dignified that I felt yet more embarrassment.

Knowing I wasn't, but wanting to believe I was at least a journalist, they decided I should stay a couple of nights. I would be shown around the camp, meet the refugees, and interview some of them.

They said I must always be on high alert for the arrival of motorbikes. Guinean soldiers regularly visited, trying to intimidate the refugees back into Sierra Leone. They would beat the men, occasionally killing one, and sometimes rape the women. I was to hide if they came. No one knew what the soldiers might do if they found a *tubab*, a white man, meddling in the camp. As far as the government was concerned, the refugees had outstayed their welcome and were a nuisance. No one would employ them in Guinea, and they all believed they would be executed as collaborators if they crossed the border.

I was led around the camp by 'the chairman'. The buildings, mostly in ruins, were scattered through the forest. The inhabited ones were thatched with palm fronds, as soldiers had stolen the corrugated metal at gunpoint. The school was roofless – little more than a wall with a blackboard washed clean by tropical downpours.

There were many pregnant early-teenage girls. I was told they went into the bush and prostituted themselves to Guinean villagers. They were paid with pitifully small amounts of ground cassava.

A sorrowful fifteen-year-old boy read me a heart-rending poem he'd written entitled *Why I Cry*. It spoke as much about the death of his culture as it did about the death of his parents and siblings.

I was introduced to several maimed men, most with severed hands and forearms. One man showed me the remains of his penis. It had been ripped off by women in his village after he refused to perform female genital mutilation on his daughter.

Everyone smelled terrible. There was no soap in the camp and they were afraid of the nearby river. Several children had disappeared in it and they believed evil spirits inhabited the water. It was more likely crocodiles.

After a light dinner of rice (the first in the camp in five months) and stewed potato-leaf, which I could hardly stomach, I was shown to an empty thatched building. There was a heap of dry grass in one corner, and I gratefully slumped onto the makeshift mattress and went to sleep. Twice in the night, young girls entered and tried to sell themselves to me. They bared their shockingly withered bodies and begged until I managed to force them out and wedge the door shut.

In the morning, I was summoned to the unlit 'committee room'. Stark sunlight slanted in through a small window in the wattle and daub wall. One by one, a procession of refugees sat on an upturned wooden crate in front of me, and told me of their horrific experiences, or showed me their mutilated bodies. I sat hurriedly scribbling down everything I was told, feeling ever more angry and disgusted. The list was endless: rape, torture, starvation, humiliation, lips literally sewn shut, and being forced at gunpoint to rape relatives.

I was at breaking point when Ellen burst into the room.

'Quick, now! Come with me. We must hide you. They are coming!' There was a faint sound of engines in the distance.

'Who is coming?' I asked, my throat dry.

'The troops! The Guineans! Follow me!' Ellen ran out and I followed her to another hut. She opened a small, waist high cupboard. 'Get in.'

'I don't think I'll fit,' I replied.

'GET IN!' She shouted. I hurriedly squeezed myself into the cupboard with knees drawn up under my chin and feet splayed painfully outwards. Ellen shut the door and pulled a wooden bolt across.

The motorbikes drew up nearby and the engines were killed. I sat in the dark, terrified, for two hours. There were shouts and cries outside. Occasional gunfire sent chills down my spine. Harsh male voices came into the hut at one point. I held my breath as they rattled aggressively in a language I didn't understand, while a man and a woman seemed to be pleading with them. They left after a couple of minutes and I breathed again.

The commotion culminated with more gunshots. I heard the sound of several motorbikes grunting to life and driving away. I was crying when Ellen let me out. My legs had seized up and I couldn't stand for a minute. I felt pathetic. Ellen assured me that the shots had been fired into the air and that nobody had been raped this time.

After another night on the grass bed, I photographed as much documentation as the refugees could produce, and got on a motorbike back to Kissidougou. I resolved to help the refugees in any way I could.

After returning to Britain, I first consulted with civil servants and bank managers about the logistics of starting a charity to alleviate the suffering of the Boreah refugees. I wanted to help them win resettlement in the West. I contacted UNHCR to ask why the camp had been abandoned, and what the UN intended to do about the nine hundred souls eking out a sub-human existence in the forest. In reply, I received indifference and condescension. I was hot with indignation on behalf of the hapless refugees. I would pursue the injustice until it was resolved. I wouldn't rest until something was done.

But then term started. I returned to university with a beard and long, sun-bleached hair. A sleeve of metal African bangles jangled on my forearm. There was an Indian summer that year. I continued wearing my sandals, faded olive vest and tatty shorts well beyond the point of comfort.

People asked what I'd been doing all summer and why I'd been incommunicado. I gradually began to relish telling the stories of my adventures in West Africa: of desert oases in Mauritania, of reaching fabled Timbuktu, of chimpanzee trekking in the rainforest, but mostly of being locked in a cupboard in the jungle by Sierra Leonean refugees because government troops were hunting for me, firing their guns into the air.

In my bedroom, while Malian music drifted from tinny speakers, I drunkenly told drunken girls how unfair the world was, and how deeply this upset me.

'Those people in the forest having literally nothing,' I would say. 'They survive by eating leaves and selling their bodies. And here we are with all our technology and food and comfort. It's just so unfair.'

I would then change the track on my laptop, and refill our glasses with cheap Irish whisky. My bracelets, more numerous than theirs, would glint in the candlelight. Sometimes, the girls would melt before my big heart and tortured soul. I quickly lost sight of my purpose. My resolve to help the refugees eventually dwindled to a mild regret and little more. Back then, I travelled to appear a 'traveller'. Had that continued much longer, I probably would have grown dreadlocks.

SEVENTEEN

CONTENTMENT

I preferred being on my own. I could set my own rules, stay wherever I
wanted to and take risks without having to consider anybody else.
- Tom Freemantle, *Johnny Ginger's Last Ride*

16 March 2011

My last evening in Dali was spent with a Frenchman. We drank two-*yuan* (20p) bottles of beer, sitting on footstalls outside a corner shop. Loic had left France in his early twenties and spent the last seven years living first in Burkina Faso, and then in Dakar, Senegal. He spoke as much English as I spoke French, and we enjoyed our confusing mish-mash of language. I told Loic of my plan to cycle through West Africa on my way home at the end of my adventure.

'*Bien*! Email *moi* when you are close to Dakar. Be my guest, *oui*?'

We optimistically shook hands on the idea of our next meeting, and I wondered if I would make it that far. Would I really still be pedalling slowly across the globe in three years time?

I rode out of Dali, clearing modern streets and suburbs, then climbed into lush, green hills that unfolded in a jumbled stack. The weather was warm, and I relished riding in just shorts, sandals, and a vest.

The feeling of movement, the simple thrill of progress through exertion, and the enticement of unknown lands before me – these had been lacking for the last couple of months. But, in Yunnan, I once again felt the heady rush I used to feel on cycling out of every city. It's like the feeling at the end of a particularly exhilarating film, a book with an uplifting ending, or even while listening to a stirring piece of music. At these times, I feel the urge to get up, go outside, and run: to sprint. To run in no particular direction, but to go as fast and far as I can. The urge to flood my veins with energy and endorphins. There's an urge to charge headlong into projects that have lain too long neglected. I call this feeling 'the death of inertia', and it has been the birth of all my adventures.

The road snaked through various hill villages. People in conical straw hats worked the land and waved enthusiastically as I passed. Women carried buckets on yokes across their shoulders, reminding me of Victorian milkmaids. Despite headwinds that started light each morning and steadily grew throughout the day, the going was good, and my high spirits were unassailable.

Yunnan had so much to see. The province is in the very southwest of China, bordering Tibet, Myanmar, Laos, and Vietnam. Sitting on the crossroads between China, Southeast Asia, the subcontinent, and the Tibetan plateau, the area has always been fought over by various Burmese, Tibetan, Mongol, and Chinese empires. In later years local warlords controlled much of the region, until World War II. Yunnan then became a front line in the guerilla war between the Allies in Burma and the Japanese in occupied China. The border with the volatile Shan State, in northern Myanmar, is still porous, and opium is smuggled across from the poppy fields of the lawless Golden Triangle. Han Chinese have now settled Yunnan en masse, but a third of the population is still made up of twenty-five ethnic minorities. In a country that is ninety-three per cent Han, Yunnan is unparalleled for diversity.

I cycled south on a minor road, descending through fertile mountain valleys, where people lounged happily outside their homes in the cool of evening. On a misty day, I crossed the still-narrow Mekong for the first time. It was an eerie experience. The brown water slid silently under the bridge and disappeared a hundred yards downstream, where a dense wall of fog clamped down on it like a shroud. I imagined the long journey the waters had taken from their source, high on the Tibetan plateau. I pictured the long route ahead to the Mekong's mouth in southern Vietnam, some of which I would be following.

At some point, I crossed the Tropic of Cancer. The weather grew hotter and the humidity rose. The landscape was a mesmerising but exhausting knot of hills. On one long, steep climb, I grabbed the side of a slow-moving lorry. The driver instantly swerved towards a deep storm drain, forcing me to let go to avoid dropping in. Later that day, I clung to the back of another lorry for the final mile to the top. The driver pulled over at the pass, cheerily shook my hand, and invited me to eat with him in a woodshack restaurant. We sat and chattered cheerfully away at each other, mutually incomprehensible, while tucking into oily bowls of fried cabbage and spiced pork fat.

In one village, a group of teenage boys invited me to share their lunch. I ate and watched with interest as a small shard of mirror was passed around the crowd. The boys, all dressed in ostentatious and unusual fashions, patiently awaited their turn to preen into the mirror – tweaking heavily gelled hair, smoothing eyebrows with licked fingertips, and proudly stroking sparse, downy hairs on upper lips. I noticed at least three wearing eye make-up, and a couple of suspiciously rouged cheeks. I'd noted this phenomenon of young men grooming excessively elsewhere in China. They tried everything in their power to catch the attention of girls. It brought to mind wildlife documentaries capturing birds of paradise tirelessly trying to attract a mate with eccentric dances and odd rituals.

An unforeseen effect of China's one-child policy is the uneven numbers of boys and girls in the country today. There are significantly more males than females, as daughters are less desired than sons. Baby girls are often aborted before birth (and sometimes shortly afterwards).

There are now thirty million young men who will never find wives. This in a country where unmarried men are view with distrust.

Ironically, this gender imbalance, born from a bias for boys in a male-dominated society, has inadvertently empowered women. Young Chinese women no longer feel pressured to marry early, and they can choose from a disproportionately vast pool of men. The competition among Chinese men in the marriage market is fierce, hence the excessive vanity these village boys were exhibiting.

I rolled through banana plantations where huge leaves flopped over clusters of yellowing green fruit. However, most of the region was dedicated to the labour-intensive process of rice growing. Neatly terraced paddies prettily contoured the landscape, stacked high up the valley walls to a point where the highest levels were just a yard wide. No land is wasted.

It was early April, and the paddies were being prepared for planting. In the lower, wider rice terraces, weathered men with trousers rolled to the knee drove ploughs drawn by water buffalo. Once the seeds were sown, the paddies would be flooded by centuries-old irrigation systems, starting with diverted streams and ending with bamboo gutters distributing water to the furthest spots. Small fish would be released among the rice and allowed to grow and multiply. When the paddy is drained for harvest, the fish are simply collected off the soil and taken to market.

As I progressed further south, towards the border of Laos, I took an ancient cobblestone road which wound steadily up the wall of a gaping valley. On the opposite side were a number of immense concrete pylons, some reaching up one hundred yards from their base. A new expressway was being built, and those pylons would act as stilts, carrying the road towards its destination on a perfectly horizontal plane. Further along the valley, where the land rose up to meet the pylons, I could see the mouth of a tunnel which would burrow through the heart of the mountainside, bearing the road ever onwards without climbs or descents.

My old cobblestone road zig-zagged up and over the crest of the valley and into an area covered with neat tea plantations tended by quaint wooden farmsteads. The most tender tea leaves from this region are handpicked, sun dried, rolled, steamed, and pressed into bricks before being dry roasted, bruised, and aged for up to three years. During that time, the leaves slowly ferment, and the end result is the particularly dark and mature *pu'er* tea. The highest quality bricks sell for thousands of dollars per kilogram.

That evening's ride was joyous: cool air, clarity of thought, the sweet smell of wood smoke coiling from sleepy farmhouses, children giggling as I passed, splashing my face in a cold stream. I bought a cold three-*yuan* (30p) beer from the last village and drank it with supper, camped on the hilltop commanding the broadest view. As the sky faded from splashed sunset hues to a deep, star-speckled purple, I lay back in my baking tent, sweaty, dirty, and physically spent, a smile on my face. I fell asleep to the rasp of cicadas. Wearying at first, this sound had finally become a comforting lullaby to me.

At sunrise I enjoyed gentle birdsong, fresh air, and a golden panorama. I breakfasted on porridge and locally grown coffee (filtered though a scrap of t-shirt). I loved those mornings alone in Yunnan, sitting beside my tent. At last, I was content with my own company. I did not feel rushed or cold. I had finally made a positive step after my battle with loneliness in Tibet. Now I was experiencing simple, painless solitude, and drew much from it.

EIGHTEEN

PI MAI

It is sometimes an appropriate response to reality to go insane.
- Philip K. Dick

17 April 2011

Sabaidee pi mai! Sabaidee pi mai! cooed the minute Laotian granny as she tipped a glass of water down the back of my neck. While pouring, she reached over my shoulder and gently patted my chest in a reassuring manner. *Sabaidee pi mai!* Happy New Year!

I sat on a wooden stool and smiled as she walked around me until we where facing each other. Her stooped frame was only as tall as I was when seated. She grinned toothlessly, with a twinkle in her close, clouded eyes. The flower-perfumed water had just symbolically washed away the demons of the previous year, leaving me cleansed and ready to face the year ahead.

Sabaidee pi mai! Khup jai lai lai, I mispronounced by way of thanks, and placed my palms together in front of my face. The extended family of sun-darkened villagers nodded their approval. The beaming granny continued her round of the table, cleansing each person in turn, lavishing particular attention on the young children.

I watched with delight as the old woman, in her faded pink sarong, reached her seat and flopped down, physically exhausted, but looking invigorated. Her daughter stood and, dipping her glass in the petal-skinned water, began her round of the table.

The scene was so benevolent that I was almost tearfully happy. The water had refreshed me. My t-shirt had been plastered to my back with sweat. *Pi Mai* falls at the hottest time of year in Laos, just before the monsoon arrives. Riding dirt roads from the northern city of Luang Nam

Tha had left me sticky with sweat and coated in grime. The tang of dust hung long on my tongue. The tightly packed hills and dense tropical forest were unruffled by even the slightest breeze. I had been relieved when the extended family had beckoned me over to join their gathering under a roadside veranda.

Once the previous year's demons had all been washed away, the women went inside the wood-slatted house to fetch the meal. We ate from large communal plates of fried pork fat with spinach and bamboo shoots. Each person was given a length of thick, charred bamboo that had been split in two lengthways and tied back together with tough stems of grass. 'Sticky rice' is wrapped in a banana leaf and then sealed in these bamboo sections to be cooked.

Once the meal was over, everyone leaned back in their seats and an elderly man served the *lao-lao*, a rice liquor that can range from forty to eighty per cent proof. Little glasses were handed around and tipped down throats.

Some of the older men spoke French and asked me, with a suspicious air, if I was *falang*. The word is commonly used in Southeast Asia and usually means foreign – a bastardisation of the English due to Asian difficulties with pronunciation. However, this man had grown up in a colonised Laos and used it more specifically to mean French. He seemed to resent his former colonial masters and asked me again.

'*Vous sommes falang?*'

'*Non! Anglais, Angleterre!*'

'*Ah! Ankit! Tu détestes les Francais aussi!*'

'*Er...d'accord. Bien sur!*' I exclaimed with a tipsy flourish, and poured into my mouth the shudder-inducing liquor he had passed me.

I produced a world map from my panniers to point out *Ankit*. On seeing the map, the men soon lost interest in Europe and became absorbed in a five-minute search for their own country. One of them was shocked when I pointed out the relative enormity of neighbouring China.

Someone turned on garish Thai pop music and the drinks kept flowing. Through increasingly glazed eyes, I watched the adults quickly incapacitate themselves. Aged men and women were stumbling around and crawling on the floor, all in hysterics. I decided it was time to move on and find somewhere to camp.

It was getting dark when I got back on the bike and turned towards a village on the Mekong river called Xieng Kok. Evidently celebrations were going on in every village, and I'd attended the tamest of parties. The road was busy with swerving motorbikes, each carrying two or three singing drunks. People were setting off homemade fireworks on the roadside, dancing maniacally a couple of yards away as the rockets exploded.

There was madness in the air. It seemed the entire country was pissed. I didn't want to pitch my tent somewhere that would be found by a group of drunk young men with fireworks. I soon spotted a Buddhist monastery with a steeply towering tin roof. Thinking this, at least, would be a bastion of sobriety, I approached. A teenage monk was slouched, semi-conscious, across a bench by the entrance. His saffron robe had fallen from his shoulder, and was bunched around his waist. His shaven head was sweating profusely. I prodded him with my foot.

'*Sabaidee pi mai! Excusez-moi, mon frère. Je voudrais faire du camping ici ce soir, s'il vous plaît?*' The monk stirred and looked me over with confusion. He had deeply bloodshot eyes. I knew my French was poor, but I might as well have spoken Swahili. Some vague remnants of sense arranged themselves in his addled brain.

'*Sabaidee pi mai!*' he yelled belligerently before calling through the doorway. Several more equally drunk young monks emerged, saw me, and cheered. They shoved my bicycle up against the monastery wall, and ushered me to another party. I was fairly lightheaded myself, and before I knew what was happening I was thrust onto a bamboo palanquin and paraded around the party at shoulder height by a troop of topless monks. I managed to jump off just before they waded into a small lake, dropped their burden, and started splashing each other. I stumbled back to my bike and rode a few hundred yards before fumbling my tent up in a dry rice paddy. The music and shrieking lasted almost until sunrise.

In the hot, still morning, the road was all mine. Laos was sleeping off its hangover, and there was barely a stir in the simple settlements I passed. Towards noon, I wheeled into a village and spotted a small gathering under a tree. I approached to find a cockfight, circled by thirty bleary eyed men. *Lao-lao*-scented sweat seeped from their pores and some of them swayed slightly where they stood. They watched in concentrated silence. Several young boys perched in the tree overhead.

Two thinly feathered birds were squaring off in a makeshift ring about three yards wide. There was no blood yet. The bout had evidently just started.

I had never seen a cockfight before, and usually wouldn't have lingered for such an event. However, I was glad for the relief of the tree's shade and the chance to catch my breath.

The two chickens were performing a surprisingly elegant martial dance, almost choreographed. Circling one another, back and forth, they remained beak-to-beak, ready to protect their eyes from fast jabs with lightning quick parries. Each was weighing up the other, looking for weaknesses and testing balance.

Suddenly they both launched a yard into the air, slashing with claws in a frenzy of flapping and squawking. Then, just as suddenly, they landed and resumed their tense, circling staring match. It was an instant's action, but the crowd murmured appreciatively. A couple of men cheered. These attacks were repeated periodically throughout the fight. Sometimes one cock got the other in a sort of headlock with a wing, while the captive desperately struggled to free himself. The other made several low darts at the other's genitals and tried to flip him off his feet.

The 'sport' was more tactical, more like wrestling, than I had imagined. I was fascinated and instinctively revulsed in equal parts. There were no artificial spurs attached to their legs, only their blunt natural ones. This was a fair fight between two birds, a manufactured form of Darwinism for the dubious purposes of entertainment.

As the fight progressed, small cuts started to appear on the birds' thickly scarred heads, and blood began to smear across their bodies. The obscene heat of the day quickly dried and clotted the blood. Feathers lay in the dust, dancing into action with every nearby wingbeat. The crowd grew; newcomers strained their necks to see, and a few more boys shinned up into the branches. There were no women present, and nobody heeded the incongruous white man. The outbursts of cheering grew in volume but were still punctuated by strained silence whenever the fighters resumed their wary, circular scrutiny for the next angle of attack.

The engagement ended abruptly, and seemingly without reason, after twenty minutes. The two owners stepped in and scooped up their prize fighters. The birds knew it was over. They didn't look at each other while being sponged down, side by side, with great tenderness. Both cocks seemed self-controlled and proud. No money changed hands, and the crowd melted away into cool, dark, hut interiors. I had no idea which cock had won.

A day later, I reached Xieng Kok. I wasn't certain why I'd ridden there. It was a draining one hundred miles from Luang Nam Tha, which led me to a dead end on the banks of the Mekong. The lure of the river had been strong, and I wanted to taste the less-visited far north of Laos.

I stood at the end of the dusty road and looked down

at the fast-flowing water. A loudspeaker behind me was winding up its shouted morning propaganda message, no doubt of national unity through communism. I heard these long broadcasts almost every day in Laos. A sermon in a staccato female voice with an authoritative air would commence at sunrise and continue for an hour. I couldn't understand a word, but the tone felt clear: you should all be better. I imagined what the voice might be proselytising about: *you must work harder, for the people. You must work longer, for the people. We must become a great industrial nation, for the people. We are the people. Long live the people!*

I had known nothing about Laos before arriving and didn't expect to find myself in one of the world's five remaining self-proclaimed communist states. I was soon to learn that the modern history of the country was much more turbulent than I could ever have imagined. Laos was tacked onto the protectorate of French Indochina in the last years of the nineteenth century. However, it was never much more to the French than a buffer zone between their precious, resource-rich Vietnam and British-influenced Thailand. After fifty years of colonisation there were still only six hundred French living in Laos, a country roughly the size of Britain.

During World War II, the county's strategic position led to a string of occupations by Thailand, Japan, China, and France (both Free France and, later, the Vichy Republic). When the war ended, the French regained *de facto* control, but the Laotians had grown hungry for self-governance. Finally, in 1953, Laos declared itself an independent constitutional monarchy, and the French withdrew. America soon stepped into the power vacuum, hoping to influence the new government against the rising red tide of Pathet Lao – a communist guerilla movement gaining traction in the north. The guerillas were well protected by some of the densest jungle in the world and had the backing of the Soviet Union, the North Vietnamese Army, and the Vietcong (who were just embarking on their two-decade conflict with America).

Laos descended into civil war, and American B-52 bombers began their exhaustive campaign. From 1964 to 1973, the Americans dropped a bomb load on Laotian territory every eight minutes, on average. More ordnance was dropped during America's 'Secret War' with Pathet Lao than was used by all parties during World War II. To this day, Laos holds the upsetting title of 'most heavily bombed country on Earth' and seems likely to retain that record for a long time yet. Villagers still regularly find unexploded shells in the jungle.

After the fall of Saigon and the American withdrawal in 1975, the royalists in the capital, Vientiane, were overthrown. The new Pathet Lao government rebranded the nation as the Lao People's Democratic Republic. North Vietnamese troops were stationed throughout the country and the daily propaganda broadcasts began. Today the Vietnamese have gone home, but the broadcasts continue.

The Mekong continued sliding silently past Xieng Kok. I thought about the countless jungle stories told by books, films, and veterans of the twentieth-century wars. They told of suffocating humidity, claustrophobically dense vegetation, and the unique way that the jungle can simultaneously support those with the requisite knowledge and extinguish those who come unprepared. Conrad wrote of a madness slowly gripping white men travelling into Congo's 'heart of darkness', and Ford Coppola re-imagined that story on the Mekong in his film *Apocalypse Now*.

Perhaps unable to think straight after so much heat and cloying humidity, I decided I wanted a taste of that madness. I wanted to see that river and its surrounding jungle. *I'll build a raft! I can drift downriver by day, and camp on sandbanks by night. It'll take me effortlessly through some of the thickest jungle at a leisurely pace. It'll be a nice break from cycling.*

NINETEEN

JUNGLE

Going up that river was like travelling back to the earliest beginnings
of the world, when vegetation rioted on the Earth and the big trees
were kings. An empty stream, a great silence, an impenetrable forest.
The air was warm, thick, heavy, sluggish.
- Joseph Conrad, *Heart of Darkness*

18 April 2011

The village mechanic pointed at the folded-up inner tubes, then at a nearby car, rusting on the roadside with no wheels. He smiled toothily, nodded, and gave the thumbs up. He pointed at the tubes again, before prodding a finger in the direction of my bicycle. He shook his head with a frown. I pointed at the tubes and then towards the river. Nonplussed, he shrugged before repeating his mimed explanation that the tubes would not fit in my bicycle's tyres. I made the mime of paddling a raft, but he remained confused, scratching his bare stomach.

With crude sketching in the dust with a stick, I at last got him to understand my purpose: to build a raft from the tubes. He sold me the only three he had for £10 and, after I had paid, indicated that his foot pump was broken. I spent the next hour inflating the tubes with my miniature bike pump. He lay in a hammock, watching with bemusement.

Just as I was gathering up my tubes to take them down to the river, the mechanic drowsily rose and picked up the stick I'd used to draw my raft. He added jagged lines to my drawing, either side of the raft, and then gave a mime of perilous waves. Frustrated, I nodded my comprehension. He led me to a footpath leading south into the jungle, used his fingers to indicate the number forty, and gave another thumbs up. I sighed. The river had dangerous rapids. I

155

would have to follow the footpath for 40km (25 miles) until it became safe. I had little choice but to trust him.

Loathe to let the air out of the tubes, I strapped their bulging mass to the back of my bike, shook the mechanic's hand, and rode into the trees.

The world darkened awhile, and my eyes struggled to adjust. It was the densest jungle I'd ever seen. The heat and closeness of the atmosphere was oppressive. Vines hung into the gloom from tangled treetops that blotted out all sunlight. The narrow, rutted path was deserted, but I could see from tyre tracks that motorbikes occasionally crashed through.

The air was filled with the competing sounds of thriving life; the ceaseless cacophony of the jungle. Monkeys screeched. Exotic birds gave unfamiliar calls, occasionally flitting across my eyeline, a blur of shining, primal colour. Untold thousands of insect species paraded back and forth, flaunting their diversity on every leaf, branch, vine, or scrap of sandy earth. Clumped bamboo trees creaked and snapped. Vast dead leaves fell through the foliage, kerplunking their way to the ground. I could hear the faint rush of the nearby river, muffled by the jungle.

The going was slow. I often had to push, taking frequent rests, my breath rasping with exhaustion. When I stopped, inch-long ants raced up my legs and biting flies attacked. The path loosely followed the river, rolling up and down miniature valleys feeding the Mekong. Occasionally the trees opened for a few yards, allowing a glimpse of the river's enticing waters and virgin banks crowned by countless soaring trees.

After five hours, I emerged from the greenery into a village called Xieng Dao. A man cradling a mangy hen did a double take when he saw me approaching. He dropped his charge and deliberated for a moment before running off after his chicken. I continued through the village until a chubby, grinning man with a leathery chest waved me over. Laughing, he shook my hand and introduced himself as Kimo. Pouring us each a shot of *lao-lao*, he wished me Happy New Year. Evidently Xieng Dao was clinging to the festivity for as long as possible.

After several more drinks it was getting dark, and I gladly accepted Kimo's offer to sleep in his family's home. The house was typical of Laotian villages: a bamboo frame with rattan walls and a grass-thatched roof. It stood on eight-foot stilts over a communal seating-area-cum-kitchen. Upstairs was one simple bedroom with gaps between the floorboards large enough for the children to reach their hands through. The bathroom, in a separate hut, contained a long-drop toilet and a large concrete trough of water. I gratefully sluiced the sweat and grime off me with several cups of the cool water.

For the next hour, I smiled politely as the whole village came in twos and threes to incredulously inspect the wild-looking stranger who had cycled out of the trees. Many carried bottles of *lao-lao* and drank frequently.

There was a tiny *wat* (Buddhist temple) being built opposite the house. I watched as a couple of adolescent monks, perhaps 14-year-olds, approached a neat mound of sand, evidently to be used for building. They drew decorative, swirling lines in the sand with their fingers. Once the entire, waist-high mound was covered in patterns, they thrust a small dead branch in the top, and wandered off.

Dinner was eaten in near total darkness. I cautiously prodded a set of rough bamboo chopsticks into one of the bowls, and pulled out the first lump I could get a grip on. The family had urged me to eat first, and watched with interest as I began to chew. It was hard, crunchy and unpleasant, but I was determined not to spit it out. I crushed it all up noisily and, eyes watering, managed to swallow it. At this point, the family burst into laughter.

Kimo slapped me several times on the back, shouting '*La tête de poulet! La tête de poulet!*'

After eating, I sat in the doorway picking shards of beak and skull from my teeth. The sounds of the village, still celebrating, drifted across the warm night. The two monks returned to the sand mound with a burning torch, singing as they came. They lit the dead branch, then danced around it, chanting mantras and waving their torch as they went.

The women of my host family went next door to stay with cousins, while Kimo, his three sons, and I settled down on the roughly planked bedroom floor. I was just nearing sleep when shouting began. Heavy steps clunked up the stairs, and four elderly women burst into the room. Each was more pissed than the last. Chanting, guffawing and stamping their feet, they grabbed me, my host, and his eldest son. We were slapped on the arms, backs and legs. I didn't know whether to fend them off or not, but Kimo was submitting, so I followed his example. After two minutes of this, I was released after one of the grannies fell to her knees and loudly emptied her stomach. The others chuckled, and danced out into the night.

The room reeked of alcohol and stomach bile. I stood in the doorway to escape the smell. Equally amused and disturbed, I felt a little like I was in a mad house. Kimo walked over, smiled, and put a reassuring hand on my shoulder. Laotians seem to be always smiling or laughing. I returned to my space on the floor and fell asleep. The granny alternately snored and retched a couple of yards away.

In the morning, I walked Old Geoff down to the river, unloaded the tubes, and began building my simple raft with some discarded lengths of bamboo for a frame. As I was nearly ready to launch, Kimo ran down and, gripped my arm, pulling me away from the river. After much gesticulation, he finally used some familiar words.

'Police! Police! *Bang, bang, BANG!*' He clasped an imaginary rifle, and jolted it at me threateningly, while pulling the trigger.

Something clicked in my head. I was in the Golden Triangle, rife with opium smuggling. The Mekong marks the frontier between Laos and Myanmar. Border guards would assume I was a smuggler. The only option was to reload my bike and ride south, cutting across more hilly jungle to the point where the river no longer acts as the Myanmar border. Exasperated, I deflated the tubes, thanked my relieved host, and delved into the trees once more.

Although still a mud track, the path was wider now. It left the river to cut across land, and occasional cars rattled along it. Without tree cover, the sun's heat was aggressive. Large patches of vegetation were being slashed and burned for future cultivation. I panted past hillsides engulfed in flames. Falling ash clung to my sweat-soaked body, and I began to resemble a survivor from a house fire.

I stopped at one hut to ask for water. Two children, swaying in a hammock, pointed behind me to their approaching mother. Her face was split with a wide, gummy smile. She was carrying a live, brown rat she had trapped. It was the size of a small cat, and the family was evidently in for a big dinner.

The monsoon arrived that afternoon. The sky quickly bruised, and drained of light. The long-anticipated rains began, among the heaviest I had seen. The track's hard-packed dirt quickly turned to a slippery ooze. The mud jammed my brakes, and the wheels turned reluctantly. Wet through, I shivered under a tree for two hours until the first downpour eased just after nightfall. Squelching onwards, pushing with bare feet sinking ankle deep in brown sludge, I searched for a flat spot to pitch my tent.

I struggled up a long hill in a murky moonlit mist. The movement warmed me up, and I was oddly happy. I felt no rush. I had wanted this: to experience the jungle and its hardships. I wasn't uncomfortable, and I didn't *need* anything. The coming of the rains eased the heat. They also seemed to wash away the sense of madness that had characterised the last few days, in a way that a glass of water tipped down the back never could.

At the top of the hill, with dense bush all around, I simply pitched my tent on the track. I tumbled inside with mud-caked feet, content that I was having an adventure.

The journey back to the river took three days. A paved main road ran the last fifteen miles to Huay Xai, a border town situated on the river. Thailand was visible on the opposite bank. The river had swollen to 600 yards wide from only fifty yards at Xieng Kok. It was finally safe to build my raft. A mechanic re-inflated the tubes in seconds with an electric pump, and I pedalled a little way out of town to a quiet, sandy bank, collecting a few lengths of old bamboo as I went.

The design was simple: a triangle with a tube at each corner. The shortest side (about two yards), would have a small plank fixed in the middle, dipping into the water, to keep the raft straight. I cut an old bicycle tube into strips and used them to bind the structure together. The bicycle would sit on the front and I would paddle, or laze, at the back. It was about two hundred river miles to Luang Prabang, and I estimated that ten days would see me arriving in that tourist hub, triumphant on my ramshackle raft.

After a couple of hours work, I loaded the raft, dragged it to the water, and timidly hopped aboard. The bamboo frame creaked and the tubes almost submerged. It couldn't safely take the weight of both me and my kit. But the current already had me, and sucked me from the bank. I drifted helplessly for five hundred yards with my bags semi-submerged and my bicycle close to falling off. Had it gone, it would have been unrecoverable. Using my paddle (made from a stick and half a plastic bottle), I finally managed to regain the bank. I had a think. Me and my gear were simply too heavy and would never survive the journey. The raft was too low in the water and too sluggish to manoeuvre.

I could have cycled to Huay Xai and bought another tube or two. However, my appetite for the venture had waned after nearly losing Old Geoff to the river. There was a slow boat taking tourists to Luang Prabang that left Huay Xai every morning. I bowed to temptation and decided to take it. Feeling slightly deflated, I dismantled the raft and pedalled back to town. By the time I found a bed for the night, I was already laughing at my aborted attempt.

TWENTY

WHISKEE!

Show me the way to the next whisky bar.
Oh, don't ask why, oh, don't ask why.
- Bertold Brecht, *Alabama Song*

21 April 2011

The boat chugged downstream, and the fifty or so tourists onboard sat chatting, drinking, and watching the jungle slip by. Thirty yards long and three yards wide, the open-sided slow boat was furnished with seats cannibalised from old minibuses. Most of the passengers had just crossed the river from Thailand and seemed to have met each other before, at some point along the backpacker circuit of Southeast Asia – the so-called 'Banana Pancake Trail'.

I found myself suddenly surrounded by English-speakers eager to party. Most of the passengers were drinking *'Finest Blended Lion Whisky'*. They poured heavy handed servings of the liquor which was described on its label as *'Smooth & Mellon'*. In Laos, a bottle of whisky is cheaper than a bottle of mineral water.

Although I enjoyed meeting people on the boat, some snatches of conversation I overheard made me glad I was travelling by bicycle and alone.

'...and then, the night after her,' drawled a thick Australian brogue, 'I ended up shagging her best friend in the hostel showers! Complete coincidence. I didn't even know that they were travelling together! She was furious, but it was heaps funny...'

'...have you done Cambodia yet?' said an American. 'No? No way! You've gotta go! You know the temples? Angkor Wat and that? Right, just near them there's this awesome bar where they've got a dancing midget. Ha! I know, I know. I got hammered drunk! That was the best night of my trip so far...'

'...when you get to Hanoi, you've got to stay in this new backpacker's place. They have, like, three happy hours a night and some of the coolest bars in the city just around the corner. It's close to loads of cultural stuff if you're into all that...'

'...*oooh* my God! That sounds *toootally* amazing,' drawled a plummy English voice. 'I missed the full moon party when I was in Ko Phangan. I was *sooooo* gutted. But I might head back that way to meet up with this Israeli guy I was seeing for a bit last month. Do you know when the next full moon party is? Are they, like, every two weeks or something?'

I spotted several pristine sandbanks on the river. I pictured myself washing in the water next to my unwieldy raft, tent pitched behind me, and a small campfire smoking some fish. I felt a twinge of remorse. I could have persevered with the raft: I gave up too easily. With difficulty, I pushed those thoughts to the back of my mind and tried to get into the spirit of the boat.

It dawned on me that I was now in the Southeast Asia I had envisioned for years, when hearing tales of beaches, booze, and debauchery. I would still be cycling most days, slowly covering the 5,000 miles down to Singapore, then back up to China. I tried to view the few months ahead as a holiday of sorts, and embrace it. The weather would never be cold, and I would be able to stop into hostels occasionally for a shower, drinks, and easy conversation.

I soon came to accept the nickname of 'bicycle guy' on the boat. The other tourists were impressed that I was cycling, and for some reason this embarrassed me. I heard myself diminishing my trip, lying about its length. I'd spent years as a student, happily bragging about my unremarkable backpacking exploits, but now that I had achieved something to be proud of, I was bashful. I tried to deflect questions by joking about my ridiculous failure with the recent raft adventure.

As the afternoon drew shorter, I saw an empty seat next to a woman I'd met on the riverbank that morning. When I first saw her, Clare had been staring out at the water. From her blonde hair, athletic frame, tiny blue shorts, and threadbare pink vest, I guessed she was Scandinavian. I hastily fabricated some question about the boat journey, and wandered over.

'Do you know if this thing's ever going to leave? The ticket guy only says "soon, soon".' I blushed. It was a crap line.

'You're the guy with the bicycle, yeah?' Her accent was English, and she looked at me with startlingly blue eyes. We started chatting. Clare was a journalist in her early thirties who had taken a six-month sabbatical to travel through Australia, New Zealand, and Southeast Asia. Her dry humour and cynical wit was infectious. I liked her straight away.

When we spoke to each other over whiskies in the afternoon, I felt able to tell her more about my adventure. Her wry jokes and coaxing questions put me at ease. I spoke about leaving home, how long I planned to be away, and how I'd struggled with loneliness and doubt in Tibet. Unlike with the others on the boat, I didn't fear sounding arrogant or proud when talking to Clare. This swing between self-consciousness and confidence was to become a pattern over the following months. I would go through periods on the road, starved of conversation and companionship, and then, all of a sudden, find myself surrounded by people I could talk to but who I feared wouldn't understand what I was doing.

'I don't know what you are more – brave or stupid,' Clare said.

'It's a fine line, isn't it?' I replied, topping up our small paper cups. For the first time in months, I felt the giddy excitement of liking a girl.

On arrival in Luang Prabang, the passengers fanned out into the darkening evening, searching for the cheapest accommodation. I buddied up with Brodie – a boyishly handsome Canadian, recently graduated from high school, and with the easy accent of a British Colombian. We found a strange room in a rickety hostel with dark, hardwood panelling. Brodie genuinely seemed to think it might be haunted, so we didn't linger.

Luang Prabang is a world-famous cultural destination, and a UNESCO world heritage centre. However, it was dark and we were drunk. We decided on more drinks and picked up another bottle of whisky. This time the label read '*Lion King Whisky – True Manhood*'. We polished it off with unwise expedition over a bowl of spicy beef noodles from a riverside street stall.

Brodie's guidebook described a popular bar, and we stumbled towards it while another monsoon storm gathered loudly overhead. Utopia was packed with young, overexcited westerners and, on that night, I fitted right in. People played volleyball on a small, sandy court and extreme sports videos were projected onto a large screen.

Throngs of sexually charged tourists screamed, laughed, and one-upped each other's stories in a hotchpotch of accents. We stood at a table, talking to a couple of Americans about how overpriced the drinks were. Brodie suggested one of us dash out to buy more whisky and sneak it in. The rain was coming down in torrents, thrummelling loudly on the roof. Neither of us was keen to volunteer so we played rock, paper, scissors. I was soon sprinting through the downpour along dark alleyways, my bare feet splashing through ankle-deep rivers of rainwater. I was quickly lost, and started running towards any lights I could see, shouting, 'whisky, whisky, whisky!' Drunk enough for this to amuse me, I chuckled as I ran, continuing to shout 'whisky' into the night.

After a little while, my pace slowed and I began to wheeze. I chanted the word once more, and thought I heard something. I shouted again.

'Whisky, whisky, whisky!'

'*Whiskee, whiskee, whiskee,*' came a faint, accented echo.

'Whisky,' I shouted.

'*Whiskee,*' came the response, a second later. I kept calling and listening, working my way towards the voice. I soon found the tiny kiosk, roofed with tarpaulin. The chuckling vendor gave me an excited thumbs up. I bought another bottle of Lion King Whisky from him.

'*Whiskee, whiskee, whiskee,*' he called as I jogged away, bottle in hand.

Another fifteen minutes of confused running eventually landed me back at Utopia. Still talking to the Americans, Brodie was holding a couple of empty glasses he had found. We opened the bottle, but it would only drip frustratingly slowly due to a plastic stopper designed to prevent people from binge drinking. Brodie tried in vain to lever the stopper out. Drunk, a show off, and fed up with this delay, I picked up the bottle and smashed its neck off on a low brick wall behind me.

'Alright, that's enough! You gotta leave now, man. That's *not* OK! That's *not* cool!' It was one of the Americans we had been talking to.

'What's the problem, mate?' I slurred with indignation.

'What's the problem, *mate*? I'm the owner is what's the problem, *mate*. This is my bar. I was just about OK with you guys bringing in your own booze, but you can't go smashing bottles on my wall like that. You gotta leave.'

Suddenly sober and contrite, I apologised profusely. I insisted on clearing up the mess before I left. I was ashamed. It had taken only one evening for me to become the archetypal boozing, backpacking hooligan. After sweeping the floor of half the bar, I went to the manager to apologise again before leaving. He looked me over with a quiet smile.

'You know what? You're OK. You can stay. I appreciate you clearing up properly. We've all done stupid things. Now, why don't you pour us both a glass from that broken bottle.' Grinning, I tipped a couple of drams from the bottle's jagged neck, and the party continued.

When Utopia closed, a little after midnight, someone shouted 'bowling alley,' and the crowd cheered. It was the last place to serve alcohol. The storm had blown over and the night was deliciously cool. The entire bar spilled into the street and flagged down tuktuks. I allowed myself to be swept along on the tide of enthusiasm.

Brodie and I hopped in the back of a tuktuk with a few others and agreed a price with the driver. When we reached our destination, a couple of miles outside Luang Prabang, the driver decided that the price should be double. We tried to reason with him, but he pulled out a knife, and started swishing it around in our faces. Ridiculously, instead of paying the extra couple of pounds, negotiations continued, and the driver finally accepted a fifty per cent raise. I later heard that these incidents are common. The drivers are known to take amphetamines to get through the long night shifts.

The first person I saw inside was Clare, seated at a lane with several men. I tottered over to say hello. She jumped up and gave me a kiss on the cheek.

'I'm so glad you finally made it here. I've been missing you,' she said in a swooning voice. 'Come and sit down.'

She pulled me onto a chair next to her where she could whisper in my ear.

'Sorry about this. Please play along. You're my boyfriend tonight. This guy won't leave me alone.'

I slipped my arm awkwardly around Clare's shoulders, and looked around the group. There were three English boys on a gap year, whom I had met on the boat. Their fresh, innocent faces spelled no trouble. Opposite me was a sharp-featured man I hadn't seen before. He was staring at me without smiling. There was a recent cut on the bridge of his nose, and I wondered if he had been punched. He carried an intensity born of drunkenness and distrust.

'Hello, I'm Charlie. It's nice to meet you. What's your name?' I stretched out my hand.

'You are this woman boyfrien'?' He spoke with a leer, and an unusual French accent, Québécois, perhaps.

'Of course! Clare's my girl,' I beamed with unconvincing falseness. She smiled, and placed her hand on my thigh.

'*Moi*, I don't believe you. Then why did you come to here not together?'

'Clare likes bowling more than me. Don't you, love?' I said.

'That's right, Charlie's terrible at bowling,' added Clare.

'I still don't belief you. If you are together then you will kiss,' challenged the man. I leaned over and pecked Clare on the cheek.

'Is not enough. Kiss 'er on 'er mouth.' I looked at Clare who looked back at me. She shrugged, and we locked lips for a couple of seconds. The three English boys, who knew the jig, chuckled.

'OK! That's nice. It is love! What beautiful couple. I will get us drinks. Whisky?' He wandered off to the bar in a drunken zigzag. Clare thanked me. Her hand remained on my thigh.

Clare and I stayed at the bowling alley, talking and laughing, into the small hours. When all the other tourists had gone, the staff finally ejected us. Outside, there wasn't a tuktuk to be seen. Hand in hand, we began the walk back to the town. As red light began bleeding into the eastern sky, a farmer gave us a lift and we made it back to my hostel. Brodie was unconscious, his covers half thrown off. Giggling, we stripped off and cuddled up in my narrow bed.

TWENTY-ONE

LOTUS-EATING

Tourism was an escape from all that was messy and hard about life.
Travel was an embrace of it.
- Frank Bures

24 April 2011

In the late morning, Clare and I strolled through the city, seeing it for the first time by daylight. Founded in the seventh century, Luang Prabang was the capital of several empires before the communists took over in 1975. The city is wedged between a large tributary of the Mekong and the river itself. It is perhaps best known for its hundreds of golden-roofed *wats* scattered throughout the town.

Sitting in a café drinking dark, viscous Laotian coffee, we watched the monks pad along the sedate street with its nineteenth-century French colonial facades. The elegant, whitewashed buildings didn't have the sad sense of decay often found in past-their-prime colonial cities, but rather an aged sense of dignity. Street vendors were selling fruit juices and baguettes. I spotted several burned-out French hippy types who had never left. They had long, scruffy grey hair, bare feet, hemp clothing and vacant, mysterious expressions. Something about Laos evidently made it hard for some to leave.

Brodie took a bus south, Clare moved into the room, and we pushed the two beds together for my last night in Luang Prabang.

Early the next morning, I wrapped a towel round my waist, and began to pack my kit into carefully prescribed places in the four panniers. Clare lay on her front, stretching luxuriously, the sheet slipping below the small of her back. She rolled over and looked up at me. A beam of sunlight from the small window slanted across her chest, and she smiled enticingly.

'I have an idea,' she began.

'I have several ideas at the moment,' I said, re-arranging my towel.

'Some others from the boat are leaving today, too. I was going to go with them, but why don't we stay behind for a bit? Just the two of us. It would be nice, wouldn't it?'

It *would* be nice, and I nearly agreed on the spot. But some sense of momentum, of commitment to the journey, held my tongue. After a relatively decadent couple of days, where I had spent well beyond what I could afford, I felt torn.

You 'cheated' by taking that slow boat, I told myself. *You've already lingered here without really* doing *anything. And you've been drinking far too much. This isn't a world tour of hedonism. You need to get back on the road.*

But I like her, pleaded the other voice, *and why shouldn't I enjoy myself for a few more days? When's the last time I spent time,* really *spent time with a woman. Can't we compromise?*

I suggested Clare went ahead to Vang Vieng, and I would cycle the 150 miles as fast as I could, hopefully arriving the next day. Then we could spend some time together. I had initially planned to bypass Vang Vieng. I had been unnerved by the stories of excess and debauchery, but a few days couldn't do much harm. I appeased the budget-conscious taskmaster in me by reasoning that I would at least have someone to split the price of a room with.

The only road heading south was Route 13 – Laos's one national highway. It says much about the diminutive country that this quiet single carriageway is its arterial road. I followed it out of town and into a steep climb through another heavy downpour. Once I was already wet through, cycling in the warm tropical rain was thrilling. The aftermath was even more so. My clothes steamed dry, and swirling mist wisps danced as they rose from the tarmac, their moisture sucked back into the atmosphere.

Eight-inch geckos, basking on the warm, damp road, were startled by my approaching wheels, and sprang into action. They sprinted alongside me at full tilt, tails swishing and flailing front legs raised off the ground like the prow of an accelerating speedboat.

The climb continued for fifty miles, and I camped at the top on a burned-out field by a neat stack of charred kindling. It was chilly after dark, and I gladly retreated into my sleeping bag with a book after my simple rice dinner.

Heavy mist slumped, slug-like, in the valleys and slowly receded as I forced down a breakfast of plain rice porridge. There were one hundred miles to Vang Vieng. I hadn't cycled that far in a day since Hungary, but I knew the last sixty miles would be downhill.

I eased past tourist minivans on the descent and overtook dangerously on inside corners when they slowed to navigate the sharp curves. The previous day I had imagined tourists to be laughing vindictively as they sped past me on the long uphill slog. Now, the bored faces of cramped Europeans looked out jealously as I zigzagged my way to the valley floor, topless, unhelmeted, hair streaming behind me.

The road joined another tributary of the Mekong, the Nam Xong, which runs across a valley floor pierced by sheer limestone karsts. They looked like vast, jagged arrowheads dropped from the heavens, stuck deep into the fleshy earth. It was a bucolic Southeast Asian paradise, with water buffalo wallowing in the river and lime-green paddies spreading from the feet of the karsts. Villagers in conical straw hats worked the fields, and a briefly unblemished sky arced over all. A small group of children, on their way home from school, cycled alongside me, chanting questions they had learned by rote in English lessons: '*Hellohowareyou? Whatisyourname? Whereareyoufrom? Iameightyearsold*'.

I entered the infamous Vang Vieng and the quaint pastoral scenes disappeared. Slow-moving farmers were replaced by staggering tourists in swimming shorts and bikinis. Many had crude slogans or penises scrawled across their bared chests, backs, and buttocks. Only fifteen years earlier, the town had been a tranquil farming village. But some enterprising locals saw an opportunity, and it gained a reputation for unfettered excess, an unmissable pitstop on the Banana Pancake Trail.

I walked my bike along the main drag, looking for an internet café to check for an email from Clare. The street was lined with bars and 'happy cafés' openly advertising a variety of 'happy' milkshakes, teas, cocktails, and pizzas, containing any desired combination of marijuana, magic mushrooms, amphetamines, and opium. This explained the zombie-like appearance of many of the tourists milling around. The bars were either part-owned by the police or paying protection money so they looked the other way.

By chance, I spotted Clare, who'd just finished lunch with some other tourists and was about to go for a balloon ride over the karsts. She gave me her room key and directions to the hostel, saying she would meet me there a few hours later. The Cliff View Bungalows lay across the river on the other side of a swaying bamboo footbridge. The room was a standalone bungalow with clean white bed sheets, a walk-in mosquito net, and a hot shower. I couldn't remember the last time I'd stayed in such comfort.

I showered and handwashed my clothes before walking back to the centre to explore the town by evening. There were several '*Friends* bars' which showed episodes of the American sitcom twenty-four hours a day. A spaced-out clientele lounged on piles of cushions, mouths agape and pupils dilated. I also noticed an unusual number of people clanking along on crutches, with bandaged heads or arms in slings. Everybody was smiling. I had the feeling the town could be my undoing, and I wasn't at all sure I wanted to be there. As if to confirm my fears of unravelling, I caught sight of a familiar face weaving towards me with difficulty.

'Hey dude! How you doing, maaaan? It's good to see you, man.'

'Hi Brodie. I thought I might bump into you here. How're you?'

'I'm *fucked*, bro! In a good way…fuuuucked! They have some *crazy* opium here. It's legit man. Whatever you want, Vang Vieng has it. I was planning to stay, like, two nights, but it'll probably be more like, ummm, I dunno, two weeks? Have you been tubing yet?'

I'd heard about tubing from numerous friends over the years. It was what first put Vang Vieng on the map as a backpacker favourite. Tourists pay a few pounds to hire a car tyre tube and are driven up-river. They then float down a couple of miles of river past lots of rickety bamboo bars selling cheap drinks and drugs. I was curious and cautious in equal parts.

'It's the shit man! I've been down the river for the last few days. There are chicks everywhere. You'd have to be an idiot not to hook up. Oh, this is…' He looked at the petite girl in a neon-pink bikini, hanging airily off his left shoulder. 'This is um…'

'Ellie,' she offered in a laboured exhalation. 'Brodie, can we go to bed now?'

'Just one more 'shroom shake baby.' They tripped off, supporting each other and struggling to walk in the same direction. The charming young Canadian I met on the boat now belonged to Laos's land of the lotus-eaters.

In the morning, Clare and I decided we should at least go and look at what happens on the river. We caught a tuktuk with her group from the balloon ride, most of whom I'd briefly met on the boat: Loc, an older, easy-going Californian with a twinkly smile; Ansie, a somewhat confused Afrikaaner with a round, innocent face; Scott, a stocky, bearded Ohioan with a shaved head and a quickness to laugh; Wolf, a hirsute American my age, keen to be the alpha; and young Matt, with a quiet, friendly demeanour. They were a band of travellers drawn together by that fact they were solo. Due to Wolf's unusual name, the group had semi-sarcastically started to self-identify as 'The Wolfpack' – a group of lone wolves running together.

We dismounted from the tuktuk and filed down a narrow footpath. The music became audible halfway down, and we came out onto a sandy riverbank. I hadn't known what to expect, but an all-day rave is the simplest description. Clusters of people, starfished across yellow-painted tubes, were floating down from further upstream. Most cradled little plastic buckets, the type that children play with on the beach. These buckets are refilled in the riverside bars with heady cocktails of whisky, fruit juice, and a Thai energy drink called M-150 which is alleged to contain amphetamines. The whisky is free, but partygoers must pay for the soft drinks to mix with it.

We had arrived at the densest concentration of bars – five or six strung along a hundred-yard stretch of river, each competing with the others for the loudest music to attract customers. The thumping sounds of psytrance, techno, dubstep, and electro all merged, making normal conversation impossible.

Each bar jutted out over the river on bamboo stilts, on which the near-naked revellers gyrated to the beats. Teenage Laotian boys stood on the platform edges, throwing out ropes to those on tubes and hauling them in. I tried to imagine growing up in a conservative farming village and then being thrust into this drug-fuelled orgy of western decadence.

We half-drifted, half-swam across the river to the first bar, and clambered up a ladder to the 'party platform'. A couple of 'volunteers' standing atop the ladder offered us welcome shots of whisky.

'Go on mate! Have another!' goaded one of them, a young Englishman who'd been 'working' at the bar for a couple of months. I obliged. 'And another. Get it down you, mate!' Down went a third shot. 'One more, one more! They're free after all.'

Having heard about both the free whisky and the likelihood of losing possessions, I'd left the bungalow penniless, barefoot, and wearing only shorts and a vest. Most of the carousers were playing high-energy drinking games punctuated by cheers and whoops. The crowd was mixed, but the largest contingents were British and Australian teenagers on gap years. They had escaped parents and school for the first time in their lives and found a place where they could buy drugs with no fear of trouble from the law. There were also scores of angsty young Israeli men, recently released from their three-year conscription.

The volunteers whipped up the party and earned their keep by handing out body paint and encouraging races in downing beers. I noticed several people with 'last day' scrawled across them, as though the end of their week or two in Vang Vieng was as notable as graduation. 'Last day' was usually followed up with 'fancy a shag?'

I wasn't particularly drawn by the party atmosphere, but then I spotted something I *could* get enthusiastic about. Across the river were two bars with a trapeze slung high from a tree between them. People were queuing at the bottom of the tree, waiting their turn to scale the wooden blocks nailed to the trunk and launch themselves into the river. If people held on until the trapeze was at it's full extent, they would arc into the air and plummet 45 feet into the water. Cheers or groans rose from the crowd every time someone slapped painfully into the water. I swam across and joined the back of the line.

I took my leap of faith with arms bent. When I reached

the bottom of the arc my bodyweight pulled my arms straight and ripped my fingers from the trapeze, sending me helplessly spinning towards a loud, crowd-pleasing bellyflop. Winded, I doggy-paddled towards the bank and was shocked when my feet felt jagged rocks in the centre of the river. The monsoon was young, and the water level was dangerously low. Clare met me with a mock sympathetic grin. I had some more whisky and spent the rest of the afternoon on the various diving platforms, rope swings and ziplines on offer.

I made it through the day with little more than cuts and bruises and was relieved when Clare dragged me back to the bungalow. We were asleep by 9 p.m.

I had enjoyed the day but knew I wouldn't return. The land of the lotus-eaters had cast a fortunately weak spell on me. As I later learned, there are many that come and truly never leave. Just four days earlier, a boy of my age, who lived only thirty miles from my home village, died on the same trapeze. That year, twenty-seven tourists died in Vang Vieng's hospital, and several more made it as far as the hospital in the capital before succumbing, usually to overdose or injuries sustained on the river. But people kept coming, regardless, not in spite of Vang Vieng's lack of cultural wealth, but because of it. The tourists enjoyed spending time in a place with no obligation to visit temples or learn anything (apart from which flavour of milkshake best helps one come down after an opium binge).

TWENTY-TWO

SCOOTER

You see, I don't know how to ride a motorcycle, actually.
- Henry Winkler (*aka* 'The Fonz')

1 May 2011

'So sorry, sir. You no stay here. We full. Please, go now!' The hotel manager stood behind the reception desk, plastering over her curt words with a thin smile.

'Please. I've just arrived, but I *am* staying here...with my friend. She's already checked in. If you will please let me look at the registration ledger then I'll point her out and you can call her room.'

'You fren? Man or woman?' She eyed me again with suspicion. I couldn't blame her. I didn't look like her usual guests. Clare had chosen a relatively comfortable hotel in the capital, the sort with air-conditioning, a television, and a fridge. I arrived in Vientiane after dark, dripping wet from a thunderstorm, and spattered with mud. In place of a shirt I wore an orange high-vis vest, the kind that road workers favour, so as to be seen by drivers on the unlit road.

The ride from Vang Vieng was a hilly hundred miles, but I decided to tackle it in a single day. I didn't like the thought of sweating it out in my airless tent when I knew Clare would be in a big, comfortable bed, not far away. She had made a playlist to accompany me on the road, and the song playing as I reached the city's outskirts was Simon and Garfunkel's 'Mrs. Robinson'. High on adrenalin, and giddy with exhaustion, I rode through the streets searching for the hotel, laughing and slapping my thigh to the song. 'Mrs. Robinson' was the name I affectionately teased Clare with, in reference to our eight-year age gap.

'My friend is a woman, my girlfriend—' I stopped. My

choice of words had caught me by surprise. I hadn't had a girlfriend in years.

'Yes, my girlfriend,' I repeated. At that moment, Clare happened to come down the stairs.

'You made it! Look at you! We need to get you showered. What are you doing dripping all over this poor woman?' Seeing Clare made the eleven hours I had spent in the saddle worthwhile. The manager's demeanour switched, and she graciously welcomed me to her hotel before barking orders at one of her staff to help with my bags.

'Girlfriend, eh?' Clare said with a smirk, as we walked upstairs.

That night, Clare told me more about her life at home. Two years earlier she had broken up with a boyfriend of ten years and, aged twenty-nine, suddenly found herself single for the first time since she was a teenager. They had been in a relationship long enough to watch most of their friends marry. She had plotted their future lives together: when to have their first child, when to leave London, where to settle in the countryside.

Clare had struggled with clinical depression all her life, and her partner's sudden departure sent her into a tailspin that she had fought hard to pull out of. Once recovered, she took a sabbatical and flew to Australia. She had wanted time to assess her life. She hadn't had an easy ride by any means.

'You lead a charmed life, Charlie Walker,' she often told me, when I spoke of the hairier moments of my journey, and subsequent lucky escapes. 'Things always seem to work out for you.'

Clare used those words without bitterness. I should have simply agreed, because I did. It was true. I had been lucky all my life. But I didn't know how to gracefully acknowledge that in front of someone I cared about who had had less luck.

In the morning, we looked around the city. There was little to do but stroll down the wide boulevards and enjoy the space. A small, neatly laid-out city, Vientiane encapsulates the work ethic of all Laotian towns. People seemed to sleep all day. Shopkeepers, waiters, tuktuk drivers, and street vendors must all be roused from their hammocks before any service can be procured. I found a little bicycle shop where the owner, a caricature Frenchman, helped fix various problems. He chastised me for my lackadaisical approach to bicycle maintenance.

'*Sacre bleu! Mon ami, la condition de la chaîne…c'est terrible! zut alors!*' I rode away on what felt like a new bicycle.

The Wolfpack had decided to take a bus south to a town called Thakhèk and rent scooters for a four-day loop of the surrounding countryside. Clare suggested we tag along, and I needed little persuasion. I had time left on my visa, could easily leave Old Geoff in the hotel, and relished the prospect of travelling by scooter rather than the laborious bicycle miles I had become accustomed to. I also wasn't ready to say goodbye to Clare. Across the Mekong from Vientiane was Thailand, where I knew I would be continuing by myself.

We reached Thakhèk after sunset, yet another town on the banks of the Mekong. Once checked into a small guesthouse – where we had heard a man rented out scooters – we settled in with playing cards and whisky. The game became increasingly raucous and the staff gathered around the table, finding entertainment in the noisy, excitable *falang*.

In the morning, we rented three 125cc scooters from a lean man with a long hair sprouting from the mole on his chin. The helmets were a scratched ragtag collection and mine had no visor. I had a quick crash course in how to drive a motorbike. Clare said she wasn't a confident driver and would rather ride pillion. Loc and Ansie would take it in turns to drive their scooter, and Scott looked very at home on his, a frequent biker in America.

We fuelled up and rode out of town to begin the 300-mile loop. The route soon turned onto a dirt track, weaving among yet more limestone karsts and taking us to a secluded creek. The undisturbed, emerald-green water mirrored the lush karsts. We swam in the warm water and lay on the rocks, letting the sun dry us. An easy-going English couple, Jeff and Bev, arrived on another rented scooter, and continued with us. We mounted up and followed a winding track through jungle festooned with low-drooping lianas.

The track felt like a sanitised version of the route I had struggled with in the north. It wasn't claustrophobic, the surface wasn't washed away, and there weren't so many bugs. We rode in formation with the others, taking photos and holding shouted conversations as we went. I was having fun. Not the 'type 2' sort of fun, like most of my cycling (fun in hindsight, but tough at the time), but real, uncomplicated, straightforward fun.

That night, we stayed in a nameless village guesthouse. Several bamboo bungalows spread behind a small terraced bar overlooking a lake. Beers in hand, we played *pétanque* in the sandy garden. Hens scratched around and pecked at the jack. Another monsoon deluge began after sunset, and we sat in the bar playing cards and drinking *lao-lao*. The owner excitedly darted to and fro, catching the thumb-sized crickets which appeared with the rains. He told us he would remove their wings and innards before frying them for his family to eat – a seasonal delicacy in Laos.

The card game stretched deep into the night with increasing hilarity, as the *lao-lao* gradually made fools of us all. When we finally slumped into bed, Clare told me it had been her happiest day in months. It had been my most content day in a while, too: an unexhausting ride through beautiful scenery, a dip in an enchanting creek, a small group of easy-going people that I liked, and someone beautiful to hold as I drifted off to sleep.

The next day, we stopped in another village for cold drinks mid-morning. A villager was strapping the shell of an unexploded bomb to the back of his scooter. It was two yards long and he had found it in the jungle. *U.S. ARMY* was still visible, stencilled along the outside. The man was pleased because it would fetch a good price as scrap metal.

After a lunch that strongly disagreed with my stomach, we joined a tarmac road and headed west. Clare tentatively took the handlebars for the first time. I sat behind her, happily holding her hips, and playing at being a 'biker chick'.

Morning rain had cleared the air, and the sun presided over an azure sky. Warm air caressed our bare arms and legs as we went. The road climbed into hills, rounding tight corners with crash barriers guarding steep drops. As we approached one of these corners, a lorry sped around the bend in the opposite direction. It kept to its lane but appeared so abruptly that Clare hesitated for an instant. She struggled to find the brake lever, accidentally twisting the throttle instead. We hit the crash barrier head on at about twenty miles an hour. Clare flew over the handlebars. Clearing her completely, I was catapulted a couple of yards further.

My face was the first thing to hit the stony ground. My sunglasses jammed hard into the bridge of my nose, and smashed. I ragdoll-rolled a yard or two and came to a halt on the edge of a drop. An adrenalin surge dragged me quickly to my feet and over to Clare. She was lying on her front, just past the barrier, her face in her hands. She was shaking and whimpering. Carefully removing her helmet, I saw her face was twisted with shock.

'I'm so sorry. I'm so sorry, Charlie. I'm so sorry. It's my fault. I'm so sorry.'

Loc and Ansie had arrived without me noticing, and were crouching by Clare's legs. Loc told me to keep her calm while he bandaged a cut on the back of her calf. I hadn't seen this, and still didn't as I focused on reassuring her. Loc said we needed to get to a hospital, and Jeff soon flagged down a pickup truck. We lifted Clare onto the back. She grimaced with pain and her eyes streamed. On the short journey to a nearby village clinic, Clare was writhing with agony. I began to realise that this wasn't just shock, and that she must be badly injured. She kept apologising, too. The guilt of hurting me added to her torment. I could feel my lip throbbing and my broken nose swelling, but I was not yet in pain.

As we drove, stacked clouds raced across a sky starting to splinter with vivid forks of lightning. The rain began just as I lifted Clare off the truck and carried her into the clinic. The crumbling concrete structure was almost entirely devoid of paint, and the metal roof was rusted to the point of flaking. A timid-looking man with a lazy eye led us inside. I put her down gently on a wooden bed which had dirty sheets strewn messily across it. With only one high, glassless window, the room was cell-like. Clare began crying again and meekly said she could wait until we reached a 'real' hospital. I told her that this was the best we could do for now, and that we would find a hospital as soon as possible.

Another man joined the first and asked me to remove the makeshift bandage from Clare's leg. She rolled onto her front and looked at me with pleading eyes. I carefully peeled back the reddened gauze, and was horrified to discover an angry, inch-deep rip running vertically for four inches down the top of her calf. Spilling from the gash was a mess of muscle, tendon, pooling blood and white globs of flesh. She must have caught her leg on a sharp corner of the metal crash barrier as she flew over it. It had literally torn her calf open.

'Is it bad? Charlie? How bad is it? Tell me!' She was on the verge of panicking again. A loud peal of thunder crashed through the clinic, and the noise of rain on the roof grew louder.

'It's not as bad as I thought,' I lied. I tried to sound confident. 'It'll be OK. Don't worry. Really, we'll have you right as rain in no time.' Clare gave a snort of amusement and tried to smile. Tears continued to roll down her cheeks. I crouched by her head and desperately tried to keep her attention on me, rather than her leg. Blood dripped from my face onto our clasped hands.

'Should I look at it?' she asked.

'Nah, I shouldn't bother.' I raised my voice over the increasing clatter of rain on the metal roof. 'It's in an awkward place for you to see anyway.'

My stomach started to rumble ominously. Lunch was still wreaking havoc within me, and I knew I would have to find a toilet imminently. The men began squirting iodine over the wound, and Clare began a low groaning. The clinic had no painkillers or anaesthetic.

'Listen, Clare. I'm really sorry. I have to run to the loo, urgently. I'll be really quick, but I have to go *right now*. I'll be back before you know it. Just stay calm and don't look at your leg. I'll be right with you.'

'Don't…'

I sprinted into the storm and round the side of the building as fast as I could. Another lightning flash strobed, illuminating the outhouse among a cluster of trees a couple of yards from the window behind which Clare lay. While I was squatting inside, a scream split the air. Clare had evidently looked. As soon as I decently could, I hurried back through the slanting rain to the front of the clinic. A crowd of small children had gathered in the doorway, blocking my path. They didn't hear me ask them to move over the rain drumming on the roof. I started to push through them. At that moment, a brilliant bolt of lightning silhouetted me. Just as the thunder clap boomed overhead, they turned, startled, to see a bloody-faced *falang* looming over them. Terror spread across their faces, and they fled screaming.

The man with the lazy eye had fetched a surgical needle

and was preparing to stitch the still-oozing wound. Clare screamed again.

'That man is not giving me stitches. He can't bloody see straight. Is he even a real doctor?' She asked as the other man gripped her leg, pinning it to the bed.

'Of course he is. He's got a stethoscope,' I replied foolishly.

After the needle was first pushed alarmingly deep into her flesh, Clare resigned herself and went quiet, sobbing while the nine stitches were sewn. She still had nothing to dull the pain, and clenched my hands tighter with each piercing. I had never felt so useless and unable to help someone.

The storm eased, and the others arrived on their scooters. Ansie was riding ours, which, amazingly, had suffered nothing but scratched paintwork and a small dent. I gave the two men some money and told the others to take the scooters ahead to Vieng Kham, a small junction town on the Route Nationale 13, where we had planned to spend the night.

We soon managed to flag a large tuktuk going the whole fifty miles to Vieng Kham. I lifted Clare in, and she lay across my lap on the floor of the back, much to the bemusement of the two other passengers. She was now calm and exhausted, shivering uncontrollably. Her shock had worn off, and the pain was worse than ever.

We checked into the guesthouse and I got hold of some powerful codeine to help Clare with the pain. I slept fitfully that night. My face swelled and throbbed. Clare was wide-awake every time I woke, watery-eyed and staring at the ceiling fan.

Getting back to Vientiane was a headache. Clare couldn't walk, and we had no crutches. I left her in the guesthouse, with Bev cleaning and redressing the wound. Scott, Loc, Ansie, and I rode a brisk hundred miles on the highway back to Thakhèk. I was relieved to use Clare's helmet, complete with a visor.

Before returning the scooter, I pushed the dent out, and cleaned it as well as I could. The scratches didn't look too bad and, surprisingly, the owner didn't charge any extra. He looked pensively at my scuffed, scabbing face, and seemed relieved that the scooter was in better condition.

I caught a local bus to Vientiane and asked the driver to pause when we passed through Vieng Kham. He didn't seem to fully understand so, when we reached the town, I sprinted to the guesthouse, slung Clare's backpack on my back, scooped her up, and ran back to the bus with her bouncing uncomfortably in my arms. With her bandaged leg and my plastered face, we entered the bus looking like battered newlyweds stepping across a threshold. The other passengers laughed at the unusual spectacle. Someone in the front row gave Clare a seat so she could raise her leg, and I perched on a plastic stool in the aisle. Five hours later we checked into the same Vientiane hotel and put ourselves to sleep with a bottle of wine.

'*Bof!* Zey can do stitches in the villages. Stitches zey can do,' shrugged the French doctor, noncommittally, while glancing briefly at the wound. 'What else do you expect me to do, uh? Is just a cut.'

He lent us a pair of crutches, but failed to foresee the vicious infection that would reveal itself a week later, or the fact that a nerve had been severed. Part of Clare's calf would never regain sensation. She also learned later that she had fractured her elbow in the accident.

I spent the last few days of my visa in the capital with Clare. We had grown extremely close and it felt like we had been together for a long time. On our last evening together, we bumped into Jeff and Bev and had dinner in the hotel bar.

'I was meaning to ask,' said Bev, 'how many years have

you two been together now?'

'Three weeks,' I replied with a sidelong glance at Clare. I later took Bev aside. 'Clare and I have to say goodbye to each other tomorrow. My visa is expiring, and I have to leave her. Please look after her as long as you're in the capital.' She nodded solemnly. I still felt awful.

TWENTY-THREE

SPRINTING

Travelling tends to magnify all human emotions.
- Peter Hoeg

14 May 2011

Evening fell as I raced through the city of Nakhon Ratchasima. Yet another vengeful storm was racing out of the north behind me. The last few days had been a confusing blur of heat, interminable hours on the bicycle, exhaustion, and a longing for Clare.

Upon entering Thailand, I had opted for a visa-free fortnight rather than pay for a three-month tourist visa. I knew I would visit the country again after Singapore, so decided to cycle the 1,300 miles to Malaysia nonstop in just two weeks.

As the rain began, I had already completed the ninety-five miles I needed to cover that day. It was time to camp, but Nakhon Ratchasima was large and I was still near the centre. I decided to throw myself on the mercy of religion. I pedalled towards one of the towering, gilded Buddhist *wats* that are ubiquitous across Thailand. The place seemed deserted. I wheeled Old Geoff into the vestibule and wandered off in search of someone to ask permission to sleep there. Finding nobody, I returned to my bicycle to wait, and began digging in my pannier for a book.

'Good evening.' I jumped. The soft voice spoke just behind my ear. I turned to see a monk of about fifty smiling with amusement. 'How may I help you?' His English was casual and flawless.

'Good evening, sir. I'm travelling across Asia on my bicycle. Usually I sleep in my tent, but the storm looks heavy tonight. Can I please sleep somewhere here? I have everything I need. I will be no trouble.' I blurted out my request, worried about being refused before I could finish. The monk smiled and led me to a deserted prayer hall. He fetched a mosquito net and said he would come again in the morning. I ate dinner and lay down to read. Within a page, I was asleep.

I woke to the sound of bare feet on tiled floor. It was dark except for a floating face illuminated by a taper that was drifting across the room. A small forest of candles came into the taper's halo, and it began to light them, slowly and methodically. The glowing hands on my wristwatch told me it was 3.30 a.m. The monk had returned rather earlier in the morning than anticipated.

I lay still, watching, enjoying the slight chill of the small hours. Another monk padded into the now candlelit hall. He crouched over a knee-high bronze pot brimming with sand and ash. He lit a fistful of incense sticks and prodded them into the pot, one at a time. The warm musk of sandalwood reached my nose as a line of monks entered in silent single file. They took their places, cross-legged, facing an altar with various statues of the Buddha.

A gong sounded, followed by the tinkling of chimes, and the sizzle of cymbals rubbed lightly together. The monks began their chant. It was similar to mantras I had heard in Tibet. They gradually gained volume, never drawing breath as a group. It was repetitive and hypnotic. Glad I had hung the mosquito net at the back of the hall, I lay on my back, listening to the chant, and staring up at a small hole in the netting. My blinks became heavy and my focus melted.

When I woke again it was light. I was alone but for a monk in his early teens sweeping at the far end of the hall. Before leaving, I was invited to sit for an interview with the chubby senior monk. He spoke no English, but happily grinned back at my stupid smile as we sat in silence for five minutes, cross-legged and face to face.

The weather was increasingly sticky, and the bouts of torrential rain were more regular. The land was largely flat, and I followed an immaculately paved dual carriageway. Tesco Lotus hypermarkets stood beside the highway, and 7-Elevens proliferated on street corners in the towns. Photos of Thailand's king and queen adorned walls, billboards, road signs, and factory gates.

With my visa race, I had little time to do anything but cycle. Eight to ten hours a day, through thunder and sunshine. The hours yawned while my legs plugged away at the pedals. I searched for avenues of distraction. No game to help pass time was too simple: counting dead snakes on the road; listing the names of villages I had passed through that morning; naming every country with a Russian border going anti-clockwise. I incorrectly recited *The Jabberwocky*, and other half-remembered poems or songs, over and over until forgotten lines resurfaced. *Are the 'lords a-leaping' on the tenth day of Christmas, or the ninth? And when are the 'geese a-laying?' Is it Azerbaijan, Georgia, Kazakhstan? No, wait! Isn't it Georgia, Azerbaijan, Kazakhstan?*

Sweat stung my eyes and left me squinting all day. The frequent service stations had self-service machines where I bought cheap buckets of shudderingly sweet soft drinks to fuel my flagging legs. One afternoon I bought a two-pint tub of ice cream and finished it in one sitting.

On the fifth day from Laos I neared Bangkok, and the road swelled to eight lanes. I had planned to bypass the capital, but the lure of a bed and some conversation for an evening was too strong. Southeast Asia already seemed to be softening my resolve.

I dumped my bags and showered in a hotel infested with bedbugs, before walking to the infamous Khao San Road in search of food. The short street used to be a rice market, but gradually it became a backpacker ghetto in the 1990s. It is now the primary tourist hub of all Southeast Asia.

I wandered down the main drag – a sea of gaudy neon lights and milling westerners in shorts and vests. It was just getting dark, and the hoards were drunk already. Couples ambled with little fingers linked – a token gesture in a climate too clammy for handholding. A small band of dreadlocked white men drifted past smelling of weed. Vendors tirelessly repeated their rhyming couplets to passers-by:

'T-shirt, CD, flip-flop.

Cheap cheap price in my *shop.'*

I overheard some European teenagers discussing which show to view that night:

'I heard that the live sex show is pretty crazy - literally just two people going at it on stage in lots of really ambitious positions - or there's the ping-pong show where girls shoot balls from their pussies and others catch them in their mouths'.

A couple of young Nordic girls were getting their hair braided into cornrows on street-side stools. Their expressions already smacked of regret as the hairdressers yanked each braid aggressively tight. Four middle-aged white men sat expectantly and apart from one another at tables outside one of the less grimy bars. They contemplated their tall glasses of beer in silence. Each had a vacant chair suggestively pulled up beside them, presumably waiting for an attractive young Thai to approach. I continued down the road, eyes agog, soaking up the seedy atmosphere.

I bought a kebab from a gap-toothed Turkish street vendor called Altan. I talked with him while eating the greasy snack. He came from Dogubeyazit ('Dog Biscuits') in conservative Eastern Turkey, near the Iranian border. It was the town where Leigh, Ash, and I were pelted with stones. Altan had worked on Khao San Road for three years. He told me he was still regularly shocked by the things he saw late at night, when business was at its best, with peckish drunks sloping back to hotels.

'They are shouting and showing their behinds, and putting hands in each other's underwear on the street.'

I sat in a bar, catching up on the last two days of diary writing. A friendly looking group sat down at the next table. I detected Kiwi, Dutch, and French accents. Wanting to open conversation, I eavesdropped for a while, waiting for an appropriate point to cut in. However, after a couple of minutes they hadn't stopped talking about how high they had all been at a recent full moon party on the beach. I walked back to the hotel and went to bed.

Waking in the night in need of the loo, I went down the corridor to the communal bathroom. On my way back, I passed an Italian woman in the next room. She was standing, topless, leaning against her doorframe. Moments later there was a knock on my door. I answered to find the Italian now wearing only a towel. She dropped it, and asked if she could come in. I was as tempted as she was modest, and hurriedly closed the door.

While clearing the outskirts of the city at first light, relieved to have escaped, a greying, chest-high Thai man pulled over in a 4x4 and asked me to join him for breakfast. I followed his car a few hundred yards to a roadside restaurant. Just as the food arrived, he began stroking my leg under the table, and asked me to come to his house. I hastily made an excuse and remounted my bike. He soon caught up, however, and cruised alongside for a couple of minutes shouting and pleading. 'I give you *many* dollar! Please! Hairy boy! I pay you *big* money!'

For a couple of nights I camped in rubber plantations, among the perfect lines of trees. Each tree had a spiral strip of bark peeled off, corkscrewing around the trunk. At the bottom of these strips, coconut shells collected the raw rubber latex that dribbled down. The mosquitos in these plantations were among the most aggressive I had encountered. They continued to hurl themselves against my tent long after I had zipped myself in. Workers came in the middle of the night, when it was coolest, to collect the rubber sap. They called and nattered quietly to each other. Their high yet cracked voices betrayed them as middle-aged women. They were gone when I woke in the mornings.

The long daily miles continued to exhaust. The road began loosely tracing the coast but never came within sight of it. Signposts pointed down side roads to my left, indicating beach resorts, both lavish and basic, that I knew I couldn't afford to visit.

I rode through Thailand's stretched-out south – the land bridge which the Malaysian peninsula dangles off. At one point, the strip of Thai territory separating Myanmar from the Gulf of Thailand was only seven miles wide.

One morning I watched my odometer clock up 12,450.75 miles. I smiled. I had cycled the equivalent distance of halfway around the world. I visualised a globe displaying my wiggling route so far, and imagined grabbing each end of the line and stretching it out, pulling it halfway around the planet. If one end was fixed in my parent's village, the other would land in the blue southeast of New Zealand's heel and a hundred miles from Antipodes Island.

As my visa expiry ticked closer, the Malaysian border grew nearer. On the last night in Thailand I stopped by a roadside house with a tidy garden surrounded by palm trees. A peaceful-looking old man was sitting in a woven chair, suspended from the verandah. I used sign language to ask if I could camp on his lawn. He smiled and led me a half a mile down a footpath in silence. The trees grew denser and denser until we came into a clearing. A tiny wooden *wat* stood, lopsided and empty, but for three monks eating bananas on a bench. The eldest welcomed me with almost incomprehensibly accented English.

The frail senior monk introduced himself as Aumnuay

and showed me to a cell where I could sleep. He swatted a mosquito as we went.

'How say daa insek? He asked.

'It's a mosquito,' I replied.

'*Mo-phi-pho*,' he repeated with a grin.

'No, no. Like this: moss-key-tow,' I corrected.

'*More-po-po*,' he countered.

'Moss-key-tow,' I said again, slower.

'*Poky-po-po?*'

'Yes! That's it. Mosquito,' I conceded. The deep lines in his face deepened further as he smiled at his new English word.

I was later amazed Aumnuay spoke any English at all. He told me he was sent by his family to be a monk at this all-but-forgotten *wat* when only five years old. Thai families who can't afford to feed all their children often commit one to the monastery. Now aged seventy-five, he had never left.

Physically at the end of my tether, I made it out of Thailand with only a few hours to spare. I vacantly endured the final ninety miles to George Town in Penang. The land was largely palm oil plantations and there were no more *wats*. Muezzins called the faithful to the village mosques. Roadside loungers greeted me with *salaam alaikum*, then addressed me in conversational English. A man frying noodles at a village stall told me Osama bin Laden had been killed that morning.

When cycling over the five-mile bridge to the island of Penang, I realised it was the first time I had seen the sea since I crossed the Bosporus in Istanbul, nine months earlier. The salty breeze invigorated my flagging body, and I freewheeled down the far side of the bridge in high spirits. I had earned a little rest.

TWENTY-FOUR

VALERIA

*'The traveller's life is one that includes much pain amidst its
enjoyments. His feelings are forever on the stretch and when he
begins to sink into repose he finds himself obliged to quit that on
which he rests in pleasure for something new which again engages
his attention and which also he forsakes for other novelties.'*
- Mary Shelley, *Frankenstein*

24 May 2011

Malaysia boasts an incredible fusion of cuisines. Over
the centuries, invaders and colonists came from
distant lands and settled on the peninsula, each bringing
their culinary traditions with them. The national cuisine
fittingly reflects the country's ethnically diverse population.
Indian and Arab traders arrived in the thirteenth century,
bringing curries and chapatti and Islam. The first wave of
Chinese migrated south two hundred years later, when
parts of Malaysia were tribute states to the Ming dynasty.
They introduced tofu and noodles and numerous styles of
cooking from the various provinces. Thais ventured across
the border, bearing lime and lemongrass and spicy seafood
soups. All the while, Indonesian traders and fishermen
plied the coast, leaving satay and *nasi goreng* (fried rice) in
their wake.

Then came the Europeans, building forts and churches
but adding little to the cuisine: first came the Portuguese in
the sixteenth century, on their Vatican-sanctioned
conquest of 'The East', then the Dutch drove them out
and clung to power for a few decades. Finally, the British
East India Company swept through, with Stamford Raffles
at their head.

On my first evening in George Town, I treated myself to a

feast with Robbie, a young German studying English. We trawled the Malay-Chinese night market, working our way through plate after plate of local specialties: *chai tow kuay* dumplings, *bak kut the* (pork rib broth), fish head curry, oyster omelette, and *mee goreng* (fried noodles) with tofu and lime.

Full-bellied, we sprawled across a sofa back in the guesthouse.

'I'm uncomfortably full,' said Robbie. 'But it feels great. I'm completely...replete. Is that the correct word? Replete?' Robbie's impressive English often had me on the back foot.

'Yes. Umm, but I think you shouldn't say "*completely* replete". Replete is correct by itself. At least I think so.' My hesitance brought out the student in him.

'Well, is there another word I can use for this?'

'Sure. You could say you're "stuffed", or that you're "sated".'

'Sated? I like it. I am completely *sated*,' he proclaimed, with a grandiose hand gesture and a mock English accent.

The receptionist bustled through the room carrying a backpack. In her wake flitted a graceful figure with a trail of shining brown hair and a flash of sparkling teeth. Long, tanned legs, crowned with frayed hotpants, disappeared up the stairs. Robbie and I looked at each other and giggled like a pair of lovestruck teens.

'English,' guessed Robbie.

'German,' I reckoned.

After a few minutes, the woman came down the stairs and introduced herself as Valeria from Frankfurt. When she spoke, her green eyes danced. There was always a half smile playing across her lips.

'I'm just on a six-week holiday,' she explained, 'then I go home to start a new job. I arrived from Thailand just now, and go to Bali after Malaysia. Hey! Let's go out for drinks. Where's fun here?'

'I'm not sure,' Robbie answered. 'But, we're too full for drinking. In fact, I'm replete with food.'

'Don't be lazy, Robbie,' I said, a little too eagerly. 'I saw some nice-looking bars just down the road. Let's go.'

For four days, Robbie, Valeria and I were inseparable. We went to the beach, played volleyball, visited museums, and ambled through the botanical gardens. In the evenings, we sat outside bars in the old British colonial quarter. When they closed, we bought bottles of beer from an all-night shop and lounged on chairs outside the guesthouse until daylight.

All the time we talked. We debated subjects that I might usually have thought pretentious. We discussed philosophy and charity and war and love. Valeria had met her boyfriend three years earlier. They lived together in a little apartment by the River Main. I admitted that I had never had a relationship spanning more than a few months.

Valeria told us about growing up in Soviet-ruled Moldova, and hating the borscht she had to eat every day. She moved to West Germany when the wall came down, and was thrust into a school, just eight years old and speaking no German. She worked hard and graduated from university with high honours in biomedicine. Now she was about to start work for a global medical research company.

Both Robbie and I were hopelessly smitten with Valeria. I was filled with a thrilling energy when near her and was never tired, despite how little we all slept. But she had a boyfriend, and I kept a careful distance.

At sunrise on the morning we were all due to go our separate ways, we were still sitting outside the guesthouse. The table groaned with beer bottles and an overflowing ashtray. Robbie went inside to pack, and Valeria slipped into the chair beside me. Her taxi to the port would arrive soon, and from there she would take a ferry to a cluster of islands called Langkawi, where there's little to do but laze on the beach.

'My taxi is in twenty minutes. I've really enjoyed this time together. Come with me to Langkawi.' She put her hand on my shoulder. 'Just for a few days.'

I exhaled deeply, desperate to accept. 'I would love to, but I can't really afford it, and I've already arranged to meet my friend Kuala Lumpur the day after tomorrow. It's two hundred and fifty miles away, so I should really get moving. But, you said you might go through Malacca before you fly to Bali. Maybe we'll meet there.' I hoped so.

That afternoon, I rode slowly through hot, fuggy air under a steamy sky. I had only slept for a couple of hours before packing my panniers and setting off. Although sapping, I had come to appreciate the peace and clarity that cycling with a hangover gave me. It was much easier to focus on just one thing, or even to attain the elusive blank state of mind that made the miles slip by unnoticed. Steering and watching the road for danger by reflex, the mind can climb inside itself and go to sleep.

An inexpert Laotian mechanic's weld, holding together a snap in my bicycle's frame, gave out in the afternoon. I pushed Old Geoff off the road and found a village metal workshop. A man with grease-smudged forearms neatly fixed and reinforced the frame. Within five minutes, Geoff was ready to ride, and we sat down for a cup of sweet tea. Omar refused payment for his services.

'I will not take anything, my friend. I am a Muslim. You are a traveller. My religion says I must help travellers in need. One day I will make the *Hajj* to Mecca, and I hope people will help me too. Besides, I learned how to weld when I lived in Manchester, so it is a pleasure to help a British.'

I camped in a bush on a traffic island that night, too tired to eat, and slept for twelve hours. Two policemen apologetically turfed me off the highway the following morning. Despite the safe refuge of a hard shoulder, bicycles were forbidden from using it, and I exited onto a narrow, potholed road through an old tin-mining district. Approaching the former tin-rush town of Kampar, a white hatchback pulled over, and the driver – a journalist – asked if he could interview me over lunch. We sat down to *mee goreng* in a basic restaurant, and Elween began asking questions.

'So, where have you come from and how long has it taken?'

'Well, I started in England eleven months ago, and have ridden about thirteen thousand miles. I'm now on my way to Singapore where I'll turn around and head for Chi–'

'Wow! That's great. Now tell me, how many girlfriends have you had on this journey?'

'I'm not sure how to answer that.'

'Come on. Don't be shy. Which country has the most beautiful women? And which nationality would you most like to marry?'

'Which newspaper did you say you write for?'

I reached William's house in the early afternoon. He and I had studied journalism together in London, and he had now returned to his native Malaysia to look for work. William spotted Elween's article in *The Star* newspaper, Malaysia's equivalent of *The Sun*. He laughed at the colourful embellishments of my coy answers about women. The article confirmed that, 'in the cyclist's expert, and widely travelled opinion, Malaysian women are the world's most beautiful'.

I left the city deep in another hangover, having celebrated William's birthday the night before. However, an email from Valeria that morning spurred me on. She would arrive at 'Sama Sama' guesthouse in Malacca the following day.

I found her in a café next to Sama Sama, a charmingly

ramshackle building in a Chinatown backstreet, with a courtyard of overgrown plants in cracked pots. Valeria jumped up when she saw me and I hugged her, perhaps a little too tightly. She let the embrace linger, and suggested we check in.

The dormitory had fifteen beds, peeling paint, and an odd smell. The young Nepali receptionist showing us around, innocently mentioned that doubles were the same price per person. I could have kissed him. We looked at a little white-walled room, with a nautical blue window frame, looking out over the river. There was a small double bed under a ceiling fan. We caught each other's eyes and nodded. Valeria said we would take the room.

Late that night, after drinks and dancing in a reggae bar, we lay in our underwear beneath the motionless fan. The power was down, and the night was warm. Valeria had music playing from mini speakers, and a candle burned on the table. The bed was just wide enough for two to lie on their backs, arms by sides, without touching.

To me, the room pulsed with energy, and my thoughts raced. *Is she thinking the same?* Our talk slowly petered out, until just the music remained: a twanging Malian guitar ballad.

After two minutes of charged silence, I took a deep breath, raised my hand, and laid it on hers. She twitched slightly at the contact. For a couple of seconds neither of us moved. Then she turned her hand the other way up, and clasped mine. The next five minutes were the most exciting of my life. We lay still and speechless, our hands stroking each other. My breath grew faster. The guitar strummed on and on, building to a crescendo. The song, the last of the album, came to an abrupt end and there was silence. A moment later, unable to bear the tension any longer, I rolled over and pulled Valeria towards me. Our lips locked. Within seconds, with a mixture of laughter and desperation, we peeled off each other's underwear and locked together in a frantic contortion of shapes.

As first light crept into the room, Valeria drifted off to sleep. I was impossibly awake. My hands were shaky, and I was trilling with excitement. I couldn't lie still, and I didn't want to wake her. I gently kissed Valeria's face, dressed, and tiptoed outside. The blue hour of pre-dawn morning was at its richest, and I trod lightly along the side of the canal. I didn't know where I was going, but I floated forward as red and golden yellow streaked across the sky. Sunbeams struck the tops of buildings and began crawling down walls.

That afternoon, Valeria went to an internet café and put her flight to Bali back by a week. We spent the days exploring colonial churches, cycling coastal paths, and walking countless miles, hand's clasped. We stopped at cluttered Old World cafés to sip coffee and gaze at one another. We were wholly engulfed in the haze of romance, the dreamlike state in which couples find transcendence in otherwise mundane things.

One night we took a bottle of wine to a small hill by the seafront. At the top stood the ruins of a church built by the Portuguese in 1521. The roof had gone, but the dense stone walls survived, crowned with tufts of grass. We sat on the grassy hillside, among the weathered gravestones of long-dead Portuguese noblemen, and handed the bottle back and forth. On the horizon, the navigation lights of passing container ships, bound for Singapore, blinked. Music from a nearby bar was carried to us on the breeze, and we lay back to look at the stars. The wine finished, we had just started back down the dark pathway when Sinatra's 'Fly Me to the Moon' started up in the bar. We danced slowly in the dark for a while, before laughing at our cheesiness and wandering back to Sama Sama.

On the last night we lay on our sides, staring at each other in the near darkness, both unable to speak. My heart thrashed audibly. Valeria laid her hand on my chest, finger tapping in time with my quickening pulse. I was scared. I was about to say something I had never said before, something that could spell the end of my journey. The words rose to my throat, and then stuck. I thought about it one last time. *Am I even sure what the word means? I didn't know before. But, yes, now I know. What else could this be?*

'Valeria, I love you.' Her finger stopped tapping, and a moment of silence hung cruelly in the air. She inhaled.

'I love you too.' Her voice was tremulous. 'I wasn't going to say it. We must say goodbye tomorrow, and it will be even harder now. But, fuck it! I love you! *Ich liebe dich!*' We kissed desperately, almost violently.

Valeria rolled onto me, placing my calloused hands on her hips. We moved in sync, burning in the warm night, clenched together in an exquisite mixture of urgency and sadness. Life ceased to exist beyond our mosquito net. We took flight together, then lightly touched down, remaining still, breathing quickly and deeply. Valeria leaned over my face, gazing intently.

'I feel dizziness, a good dizziness though,' she said, at last. 'Like a headrush. I can't see your face. But there are all these amazing patterns and colours swirling and mixing together in the darkness. Don't move, it's beautiful. I don't want it to stop.'

Outside, somewhere above the clouds, the full moon was burning red with the first total lunar eclipse in over a decade.

In the morning, we packed our bags in mournful silence. We hadn't spoken about so many important things. When would we meet again? And where? What were we willing to sacrifice for one another? My adventure? Her boyfriend? She had hardly spoken about him, except that she was surprised not to feel guilt. We felt too natural together for that.

Valeria's eyes watered as we faced each other beside her taxi. We kissed and then hugged with a gut-wrenching sense of finality. Returning to her native language, she whispered into my ear. '*Ya lyublyu tibya.*' I love you.

The taxi pulled away. I sat on the pavement and cried.

TWENTY-FIVE

DECISIONS

A man's mind stretched by new experience can never go back to its old dimensions.
- Oliver Wendell Holmes, Sr.

30 June 2011

Waves rolled in and flopped onto the sand, their white crests glowing in the night. The horizon was a flat line of anchored ships, queuing to offload their cargo. Above and below was inky sky and sea. Jamie, Tomo, and I sat on the beach, facing south and sipping from beer bottles. Our bicycles stood behind us, propped against a sign threatening fines for public consumption of alcohol. Nearby, another sign announced: *THE SOUTHERN MOST POINT OF CONTINENTAL ASIA.*

Exactly a year earlier, I had sat at the kitchen table with my family. We were enjoying a last supper, anxiously anticipating my departure the following morning. I reflected on the last year of my life. A year in which I had cycled over 13,000 miles through twenty-six countries. I had crossed three deserts and seven mountain ranges, patched fifty punctures, and endured the hottest and the coldest temperatures of my life.

How had I changed during that year? Was I wiser, stronger, braver? Kinder? I contemplated the prospect of three more like it. Three more years on the road, living in a tent, cooking simple meals, seeing weird and wonderful places, enjoying only fleeting personal relationships. I didn't know if I was relieved or disappointed that I would now be turning my back on all that.

'You've been back a day now, Charlie.' Jamie's voice broke in on my thoughts. 'Are you going to tell us what happened in Bali?' It was a good question.

* * *

17 June 2011

I arrived in Singapore two days after parting from Valeria. In ninety per cent humidity, I pedalled as hard and long as I could. I needed distraction from the gnawing pain of separation, burrowing deep in my stomach. The more desperately out of breath I became, the less I focused on the uncertainty of my future, of *our* future. But it was never far from my thoughts.

As the sky faded from a smoggy, lavender-orange sunset to a collection of dull greys, I crossed the causeway onto the island of Singapore and rode to the home of Yati and Abdullah, my uncle's sister-in-law and nephew. We had never met before, but they welcomed me with touching warmth and took me to a nearby restaurant for dinner. Yati asked me why was making this journey. At that moment, I was more confused about this than ever before. I didn't want to be on a cycling trip. I wanted to be with Valeria.

The next day I followed a friend's instructions to a bar. Jamie had arranged for me to meet his cousin. He told me via email that he had recently left Singapore, having completed a three-month internship, but thought I would get on well with his cousin, Ben. I was told Ben knew me from photos, so I simply needed to turn up on time. I self-consciously wandered around the bar, waiting for someone to recognise me. There was a tap on my shoulder and a familiar voice.

'Hello dickhead!' I turned to find Jamie, wearing a mischievous smile, chuffed that his ruse had worked. I was speechless; I hadn't seen him for eighteen months. A few yards behind him stood Tomo, an old family friend who now lived in Singapore. Ben arrived with his fiancé Asya, and we all sat in the sun drinking craft beers.

After a short while, they revealed that they had a surprise for me. That evening was Singapore's annual beer festival, and we had VIP tickets. In the vast marquee, Jamie and I tried to work our way through each of the open bar's thirty world beers. The Day Trippers, a show-stopping Beatles tribute band, performed on the stage in colourful Sergeant Pepper outfits, and the beer-fuelled crowd roared their approval.

I don't remember the night finishing, but woke up on the floor, still drunk, at Ben's flat. My head felt like it was ripping apart between my eyes. Ben and Jamie weren't faring much better. They dragged us onto a squash court where boozy sweat oozed from our pores.

At lunch, an email arrived from Valeria saying that Bali was beautiful but she couldn't enjoy it without me. I talked things over with Jamie that evening, telling him about Malacca. He said little, but coaxed me towards making my own decision.

Early the next morning, I booked a flight to Bali, emailed Valeria, and flew out that afternoon. I wandered out of Denpasar airport into the warm coastal air. Valeria had emailed to say a taxi would be waiting to drive me an hour inland to Ubud, where she was staying. The waiting crowd at arrivals was dense, and there must have been a hundred name signs, many scrawled in biro on scraps of cardboard.

After a while I spotted my name. The man holding it signalled to meet him at the end of the barrier. I walked around and shook the driver's hand. He grinned and his eyes darted over my shoulder. I turned and was hit by Valeria flinging herself at me, locking her arms around my neck. The wave of joy that coursed through me made me certain I had made the right decision.

We spent a week between Ubud and a small beach in the south, talking late into the nights and rising late in the mornings. By day we explored, but nothing seemed as interesting to each of us as the other. We cycled through villages of lime-green rice paddies and wandered around ancient Hindu temples. We spoke of the future. We made decisions and plans. Valeria would go home, leave her boyfriend, start her new job and find us a flat. I would continue to Beijing, sell my bicycle, and move to Frankfurt. I wouldn't have a job at first, but I was resourceful, and we would make it work. Maybe in a couple of years we could return to Asia and cycle on a tandem. I knew I was sacrificing what I had dreamed about and worked towards for a long time. I would never finish my bike ride. But it didn't matter because I had her now. Everything else paled into insignificance.

On our last evening together, we lay on the fine sand of Balangan Beach. Valeria taught me to count to ten in Russian. The last surfers of the day came ashore, walking out of the setting sun, droplets of gold scattering from their elbows and boards. Valeria turned to me with a slight frown. She looked serious.

'I want to ask you an important question,' she said.

'Of course, anything.'

'You know I am a little older than you?'

'I do. But it's only three years. Or *tree goda*!' I said proudly, in a Russian accent.

'Well, we've made our plans together and I couldn't be more excited.'

'Me too.'

'So, I have some other plans too,' she looked out at the waves. 'Plans that will fit with what we've talked about this week. Family plans.' Her eyes tentatively scanned mine.

'Carry on.'

'In three years, I will be thirty. At that time, I want to know that I can start thinking about children, and that I have *someone* with me who is happy to think about children too.'

We had already spoken about marriage and I had privately considered that this would probably be followed by children. It shocked me how calmly I was able to contemplate this at the age of only twenty-three.

'I am *that* someone,' I told her. 'I've already thought about it. Three years from now is a little sooner than I expected to have children, but that's fine with me. I love you and I'm excited. We have so much to look forward to.'

Arms around each other, we walked up to our room above a basic bamboo surf shack. It was a three-by-three-yard box, woven from palm fronds, and contained nothing but a bed and a glassless window to the sea. We didn't need or want anything else. It was the last night of the happiest week of my life. We had a taxi at 3 a.m. to the airport, where we would have to say goodbye again. But this time I knew I would be moving to Frankfurt in November, just four months away.

* * *

2 July 2011

'In summary, he's met this German girl and is hopelessly in love,' Jamie explained to Ben, in a Singapore bar.

'Oh God! That's a fucking disaster!' Ben seemed quite serious. 'Who is this girl? Show me a photo,' he demanded. I took out my camera and showed the last one I had taken of her in Bali. She was looking straight down the lens, unabashed, and wearing a carefree smile. 'Shit! She's beautiful too,' continued Ben. 'This really is a fucking disaster!'

'Why a disaster?' I asked.

'Because you're young, and your life just got a lot more difficult.'

I laughed off Ben's reservations and ordered another round of beers. Hedge would be arriving shortly, joining us directly from the airport. We had a year to catch up on, so the conversation would shift, thankfully.

I met Hedge in my first week at university. He was so named for his dense crop of curly hair. We had always got on well but we were never especially close, so I was surprised when he got in touch. He wanted to meet in Singapore and cycle up the east coast of Malaysia. My surprise was partly because his email was very out of the blue and partly because he was never the fittest of my friends, tipping the scales at over twenty stones. Hedge had never cycled more than five miles but was hoping to kick start a new era of personal fitness with a baptism of fire. Where better to begin, he reasoned, than a hundred miles from the equator, in the choking humidity of Singapore?

The taxi pulled up to the bar, right next to our table, and out stepped Hedge, the picture of English joviality. A baby pink polo shirt, navy Blue Harbour shorts, and a well-worn pair of brown docksides. 'Gin and tonic, anyone,' he offered with a grin.

We found a slick new bicycle for Hedge in the Chinese quarter the next day. It was made of aluminium and weighed a third of my old steel bike. I took it for a short test ride, and handed it back enviously. All twenty-one of its gears worked perfectly, and the brakes came into effect with startling immediacy. Sorry-looking Old Geoff was hideously heavy and unresponsive by contrast.

With our mismatched rides neatly loaded up, we crossed the causeway back into Malaysia, sweat instantly plastering the shirts to our backs.

TWENTY-SIX

BOASTS

Having seen the myriad varieties of life it is possible to live on this earth, I am amazed that so many people condemn themselves to an unfulfilling existence in dreary circumstances.
- Ted Simon

3 July 2011

On Hedge's first day, we cut across the southeast corner of Malaysia. After two weeks of inactivity, I relished the feeling of movement and set an unsympathetic pace. With only my one-man tent, camping was out of the question and we planned to find a hostel for the night in the river town of Kota Tinggi. It was only a thirty-mile stretch of softly swelling hills, but the fierce mid-afternoon heat proved a challenge for Hedge. He got through three times the water I did and moved at a fraction of the speed.

I waited at the bottom of hills, giving him a head start. After a year on the road, I was able to cycle throughout the day at a decent pace. My leg muscles were hard and grainy. I happily pumped away at the pedals, without thought, watching the shifting landscapes and village scenes I passed: two children playing a game with stones and a coconut husk; a man splitting palm fronds down their seams and his wife skillfully weaving them into matting; a young girl shelling prawns with a thin mongrel nibbling the discarded debris beside her; a white-robed imam leaning listlessly in the doorway of a pastel green mosque.

The long, gentle inclines we worked our way over were barely perceptible to me. Hedge arrived, breathless, at the top of one to find me sitting under a tree, speaking pidgin Russian along with a language lesson on my MP3 player. I wanted to surprise Valeria the next time I saw her. I paused the lesson as he slumped down beside me.

'Kota Tinggi, *eto nye dalecko!*' I said proudly, pointing down the road.

'What's that gibberish?' asked Hedge, between gulps of air. 'Speak English, dammit!'

'Kota Tinggi, it's not far *seichass.*' He rolled his eyes. '*Now!* It's not far *now!* Just a few more of these hills, and it'll be time for a cold beer.' I got to my feet and grabbled Old Geoff's handlebars. 'Let's go! *Davai!*'

Hedge weighed more than me, my bike, and my kit combined. He shot ahead on the downhill, hurtling to the bottom at speeds I could never match. Momentum carried him a little way up the next climb until his legs kicked into action, spinning in the lowest gear.

On the second day, we aimed to reach the port town of Mersing. There was a ferry to Pulau Tioman, an island in a marine conservation area. The port was sixty miles from Kota Tinggi, and we rode the first twenty through a thrilling electrical storm. The only available shelter was under trees or tin-roofed shacks on the roadside. We thought it safer to stay on the road. Forks of lightening slashed through the sheeting rain. We saw one strike a tree with startling violence. The tarmac became a seething sheet of water. Each thunderclap wrapped us in a deafening wall of noise. When the storm subsided, we continued on the empty road, speechless but invigorated.

The sun soon burned the sky clear, and within twenty minutes the tarmac was dry. Heat mounted, and the humidity closed in again. By the time we boarded the ferry in Mersing, Hedge was pink and lightheaded. He slumped across a bench, reviving himself with a sugary drink. I was amazed at his achievement that day. He had dragged himself through sixty miles in hostile weather and hadn't once complained. He had earned a rest, and so we gave ourselves two days to enjoy the island.

We shared a tiny, airless room with sagging foam mattresses and no fan. Outside the window was a narrow strip of sandy beach on which a five-foot monitor lizard basked each day. We hired snorkels and floated over a small reef, alive with fish of every colour. A blue-and-yellow banded octopus flapped its way over the serrated coral spines, and a smack of pink jellyfish floated past.

We spent the last evening in a beach bar with overpriced cans of beer and phosphorescence in the water. Far-off storms played across the horizon while we stood knee deep in the sea, looking out.

'There's something I've never asked you,' Hedge started. 'Why are you doing this? I mean, I know you set yourself this challenge, and you're following it through. But, really, what made you want to do this thing? How did it even occur to you?'

'It's simple really.' I replied, smirking. 'I didn't have the gumption to get myself a proper vasectomy. You know, just to be on the safe side. Sitting on a hard leather saddle for four years struck me as the next best option.'

'That's very funny, but I've already heard you say that to Ben back in Singapore.' He turned to face me. 'That little joke of yours? It stayed with me precisely because it avoided the actual question, like you are now. Why *are* you doing this trip?'

'You're right. It is a cop out. But I don't avoid answering because I don't *want* to. It's because I'm not really sure. I've been asking myself that question a lot recently, particularly during the difficult times. Every time I think about it, I arrive at a different answer. There's truth in all of them, but I'm yet to come up with something I feel really gets to the root of it.' I swished my leg through the water, stirring up the luminous algae. Swirls of light danced in the wake of my foot.

'An easier question then,' Hedge was also staring at the glowing water in front of me. 'What were you doing when you came up with the idea? And how come four years?'

'I'll give you the long version. Settle in!'

We walked back towards the bar, ordered a couple

more beers, and sat at a table, our wet feet coated in sand.

'You remember a few years ago I went to Nepal with Ed and Emma and the two Wills?'

'Yeah. You lot cycled, didn't you?'

'Only about three hundred miles. The rest was trekking. From Kathmandu we went to Mount Everest base camp and back, the whole way completely under our own steam. Before that trip, I had never considered cycling as a way of travelling. I was into backpacking in Africa. Taking endless cramped bus journeys to nowhere in particular, just to be 'off the beaten path'.

'One of the Wills brought a book to Nepal. It was about this bloke who set off on a bicycle and literally cycled around the world. It took him years, and he pedalled God knows how many thousands of miles. I had never considered that that was even possible. The whole thing only cost him a few grand.'

'I suppose it's obvious when you think about it.' Hedge mused. 'There are roads all over the place.'

'Exactly! Where there's a road there's a way. Anyway, as the next summer approached, I was looking for a new adventure. A girl I was infatuated with told me about a trip she had taken to China and Mongolia. She wasn't in the least interested in me. In fact, I think she thought I was a bit of a prick. You remember that kooky little theatre group I joined at uni?' Hedge nodded. 'She directed a Greek tragedy and I played the tyrant. I stomped around the stage, fuming and shouting and generally overacting. She wasn't much impressed. I decided on travelling to China and Mongolia, hoping that having a common talking point might bring us together.

'I didn't know a thing about either country. I simply had a flight into Beijing and a flight out of the Mongolian capital, whose name I couldn't pronounce. To get from one to the other, I would have to cross the Gobi. On a bit of a whim I decided to take my bike, the same one I have here, and ride across the desert.

'Ten days before flying to Beijing, I went to a twenty-first birthday in Surrey. I'm not sure how I did it, but I woke up mid-morning unable to walk. My right thigh was swollen and turgid: internal bleeding. A scan revealed I had snapped one of my quadriceps in two.' Hedge winced. 'The doctor game me crutches, and said I should start walking ASAP. Apparently, the two ends of the snapped muscle would "flap around like a couple of fishtails" for a while, before grafting uselessly to the femur.

'I left the crutches with my dad when he dropped me off at the airport. He watched with a worried expression as I limped through to the security check. He had failed to dissuade me from taking the bicycle. "*Just leave it here, old boy, and take the trains. No point making that leg worse.*"

'I stayed a couple weeks in Beijing, waiting for the leg to heal. A friend, Rupert, took me out on my first night. We went to a gaudy karaoke bar where Chinese businessmen bought us endless whiskies to impress the pretty hostesses. I drank too much and lost Rupert. The rest of the night is a bit of a blur, but I somehow managed to find my way back to his apartment at dawn. He opened the door to find me limply holding my broken right wrist with my left hand. Must have fallen somehow. My vest was torn, and I'd lost a flip-flop. Not a strong moment for me.'

Hedge drained his beer and waved at the barman, who wandered over with two more cans and an incense coil to keep the mosquitos off.

'When the leg healed enough to cycle, I hacksawed the plaster cast off my wrist, bandaged it up, and cycled towards the desert. The ride was only two weeks, about a thousand miles. It was pretty unenjoyable: miserable in fact. There was a foul headwind the whole way, and from the Mongolian border onwards there were no roads, just corrugated tracks wiggling off into the desert. The heat reached obscene levels, and I ran out of water at one point. My wrist and leg ached, and I had no suncream. I was really lonely, too.'

'It sounds horrendous,' Hedge said.

'Well, there were special moments, too. Nomadic families in the desert welcomed me in and fed me foul things. Month-old mutton and fermented horse milk, for example. There was the unimaginably good taste of a cold Coke after two of days on strictly rationed water. The joy of reaching tarmac after the desert, knowing that the sores behind my balls might finally heal. Also, the entire two weeks cost only fifteen quid. I camped every night, even in sand storms, and cooked my own food.

'When I reached Ulaan Baatar, some friends arrived from London in an old Ford Escort. Oli, Archie, and the twins, George and Arthur. They'd been on the Mongol Rally with a couple of hundred other student types in battered cars. The rallyists milled around the bar in oil-stained jeans, toasting their arrival.

'It got around that some bloke had come across the desert from Beijing, not in a car but by bicycle. Strangers bought me drinks, and there was this pretty Israeli girl who liked my stories. She dragged me into the dark stairwell of an old Soviet apartment block. The attention was intoxicating, and the rose-tinting set in. I began to remember the desert ride as a golden fortnight.

'My friends had tickets to Moscow on the Trans-Siberian railway. But their car was knackered, and the charity they had planned to donate it to wouldn't accept it. They now had to get the thing back to England or be stung with sky-high import taxes. In a moment of drunken bravado, I volunteered to drive it back, so they could take their train.

'A shoulder-high Cornish man with insomnia asked for a ride. His name was Chip and, conveniently, he was a mechanic. We stripped out the back seats, stuffed in my bicycle, and set off with only a seven-day transit visa to cross four thousand miles of Russia.

'At the border, we were stopped by a Russian official with a ludicrously big hat. "We have your friends," he said ominously, and led me to a room. Some visa problem had resulted in Archie and Arthur being pulled off the train. They were now free to go, and we squeezed four of us into the two-seat car.

'A couple of nights and several breakdowns later, we drove down a track into the birch forest to camp at midnight. A fire was lit, meat was roasted, and vodka emerged from backpacks.

'And so, Hedge, to cut a long story long, that was it. That was the night I decided to do this trip. The bottle of paint-stripping Chinggiz Khan vodka was fast disappearing and lulling me into a silly mood. "I think I'm going to do a longer bike ride," I said, to no one in particular. "You know, a big one." "Go for it," Archie replied, humouring me. "No mate! I mean *really* long. Like, all around the world or something…literally."

'It was the sort of drunken boast that unlikeable characters make in Homeric poems, and I could have left it there. Archie would have forgotten by morning, but I didn't. When I wasn't driving, I sat in the back, plotting my journey. I had felt a growing sense for a few years that I would one day make a long journey of some sort. An odyssey, if you will.

'There was a world map in the back of someone's guidebook; I stared at it for hours and slowly made my plan. I wasn't thinking clearly at the time – we were all permanently exhausted in that car. Recent memories of how much I'd suffered in the Gobi didn't feature in my reasoning. My backside still hurt from the bumpy desert tracks. But I was excited.

'As for the time estimate, I guessed it would take a month to cycle the width of my thumb on that little world map. So, I thumbed my way across the continents, and the forty-eighth thumb's breadth landed me back in England. A year later, with no *real* planning, I set off, and here we are!'

'You could have simply not gone through with it.'

Hedge said. 'You were sleep deprived and drunk when you made the plan.'

'Well, that night in Siberia, I said I'd do it. A couple of weeks later, I drove that knackered car off the ferry in Dover, and got it home to my parents. I told them my plan. I told my brother, my sisters, and my friends. I enjoyed how impressed they were, even if they thought me foolish. It would have been embarrassing to then not go through with it.'

'Wait!' Hedge was staring at me with disbelief. 'You're telling me you decided to do this thing while pissed. *And*, that you went through with it simply to avoid embarrassment?'

'When you put it like that, I suppose I am. Silly isn't it!' I raised my beer to Hedge, and tipped it down my throat.

TWENTY-SEVEN

NORTHWARD

Between longing and regret, there is a place called the present.
Like jugglers who ply their trade while standing on the neck
of a bottle, we should train ourselves to become balanced in the
sweet spot. The dogs manage it.
- Sylvain Tesson

7 July 2011

We continued north, with jungle to our left and the sea to our right. There were no villages between the sparse towns, and few cars on the road. The jungle began abruptly, a yard from the tarmac's edge. It was dense and riotous with twisting vines, barbed ferns, and the chatter of unseen monkeys. Wildflowers – pinks, oranges, blues, and purples – caught my eye amid the bank of green. On the other side of the tarmac was untouched beach, slanted over by a few coconut palms. When the afternoon heat broke our resolve, we would rest under a palm and wilt in the wind's fiery breath. We swam in the South China Sea a couple of times, but the water was so warm that we would emerge more salty and sweaty than before.

At the end of a seventy-mile push, we entered the small city of Pekan, and began searching for a place to sleep. It was mid-afternoon, and the bleached streets seared under the white sun. Hedge was understandably close to collapse, and I wasn't fairing much better. We had been spurring each other on for the final ten miles with talk of finding a hostel and throwing cold buckets of water over our heads.

To our surprise, every type of accommodation in the sleepy town was full. After two hours, the only option we had found was a windowless first-floor room with visibly flea-infested sleeping mats on the floor. Deflated, we rode out of the city in search of a mosque upon which to supplicate for the night. We still hadn't rested or found a cold drink.

After a short time, we passed a polo club with a poorly attended tournament in progress. Seeing the clubhouse tables neatly laden with drinks and ice buckets, we parked our bikes and sauntered in, attempting a veneer of belonging. Over a loudspeaker, an anglicised Malaysian accent commentated on a game that sounded much more exciting than the bumbling sport played before us.

We tried to blend in, chatting to the young Argentinian men imported to bolster the Malaysian teams. After a while I clocked a tall, thin Malay man walking towards us.

'Good afternoon!' He said. 'You are the gentlemen with those bicycles? How do you do?' It was the voice from the loudspeaker.

'Good afternoon, sir! We are those gentlemen. We do very well thank you,' Hedge said in his most jovial tone.

'Where might you be from?'

'We're British!' Hedge exclaimed. 'Here for a cycling holiday. You know, just pedalled up from Singapore. Charlie, here, he has cycled all the way from England!' I tried not to shrink.

'You're British? That's marvellous. But, cycling in this heat? You must be bonkers. And you,' to Hedge, 'a big fellow too! Well, "mad dogs and Englishmen" as they say.' He laughed.

'Yes, completely bonkers! And dying of thirst,' I said. 'I hope you don't mind us having a cold drink.' I wore my most pathetic smile.

'I'm sure the Boss won't mind. His son has spotted you by the way, the Boss's son. That's why I'm here. He sent me. He would be honoured to meet you.' Hedge and I looked at each other nonplussed. 'The Boss' sounded ominous.

'Excuse my ignorance. We've just arrived,' Hedge said, 'but who might 'the Boss' be?'

'The Boss? Why, the Boss is the Sultan, of course! This

is his party, and these are his lands.' He waved an arm expansively. 'His team are hosting this great tournament. Please follow me.' I shuffled along behind Hedge who strode confidently after the man. I noticed a long wall running alongside the field. It was crowned with coiled razor wire, and every few yards there was an insignia of crossed tusks and a spearhead on a laurel. Behind the wall was a canopy of treetops and, in the distance, the roofs of a palatial building.

Tengku Abdulla ibni Sultan Ahmad Shah, the Sultan's son, and Crown Prince of Pahang, was sitting on a high-backed wooden chair. He was a small man with short, grey hair and a wispy moustache. He wore jodhpurs and his team's red and black shirt. A man crouched behind his shoulder with a small fan, keeping flies off a plate of chicken satay on an ornate footstool. A soldier in tasselled uniform stood apart, watching us closely.

'Your Highness! These two gentlemen are cyclists from England,' began the commentator. 'One of them has travelled all the way from England by bicycle.'

'Pleased to meet you,' said the Crown Prince.

'It's our pleasure, sir,' said Hedge, not daring to reach out for a handshake.

'I schooled in England, of course. I also used to swing the mallet with Prince Charles. We still meet to churn the turf on occasion.' Hedge and I said nothing. 'Well, do help yourself to refreshments, and stay to enjoy the tournament. Oh, and do cheer for Royal Pahang, won't you. We've got Carlos from Buenos Aires on our team this year, so we're in with a good chance.'

We thanked him and walked quickly to the snack table, imbued with the confidence of the Prince's permission.

I later asked a team manager about Malaysia's monarchy. She explained that of the nation's thirteen states, nine have sultans. Every five years, the sultans convene, and the position of *Yang di-Pertuan Agong*, or king, is passed on in a forty-five-year rotation. If still alive, the

Crown Prince's father would become Malaysia's head of state in December 2016. If not, then Prince Charles' polo chum would assume the mantle instead.

A few days later, Hedge took a bus back to Kuala Lumpur and flew home. He would be re-installed in his London office the day after that. We had been an unusual pairing on the road, but we had complemented each other well. He had lost some weight since Singapore and was determined to keep exercising back in England. I was impressed by his resolve and sad to see him go. As with Ash, Leigh, and James, the intensity of travelling as a two had forged a closer friendship.

Ahead of me was a thousand-mile ride back to Bangkok. Four hundred of those, through Thailand's southern bottleneck, would be retracing the route I had taken south. Hugging the coast, I pushed hard on the pedals and traversed Malaysia's two most conservative states: Terengganu and Kelantan. Supermarkets had separate queues for men and women, muezzins were amplified louder, and burqas were common. The area was also rich in oil and gas; tall jets of flame danced atop refinery chimneys along the coast.

Crossing back into Thailand, I was surprised that Malaysia's frequent mosques were not immediately replaced by Buddhist *wats*. Narathiwat and Pattani are predominantly Malay Muslim states – two of only four in Thailand – where the positions of power are all held by the ethnically Thai Buddhist minority. On my first afternoon, a policeman pulled over, hopped out of his car, and flashed his badge. I wondered if I was in trouble.

'Sir, please no cycle this way.'

'Why?'

'Is not safe.'

'Why?

'These people Muslim. Bad people. Killing and stealing

you.'

'Why would they do that?'

'They no Buddhist. Bad people.'

'I am not Buddhist. Am I bad?'

'That different. You white man. These here simple people. Veeeeery dangerous.'

I thanked him for his concern and rode on. That night I was invited to sleep in the staff quarters of an Islamic summer camp. A hundred children excitedly ran around clutching their Korans before we all sat down to dinner together.

I forged on through unrelenting heat with gritted teeth. Violent downpours still punctuated the days. I managed to speak on Skype with Valeria in a village internet café one morning. She was in turmoil. Her friends and family didn't understand why she had thrown away the years she had spent with her ex-boyfriend in favour of some young English upstart currently cycling around Asia. Her mother, in particular, was trying to convince her that our relationship had been a blip, a holiday romance.

For two hours, I reassured her that everything would be fine. I would soon be moving to Germany and we would start our lives together. She calmed down and we talked of other things, but when we said goodbye I was worried. A seed had been planted in Valeria's mind. I feared it might grow if watered by those around her.

I cycled hard through the rest of that day, trying to wrench my mind from the unpleasant train of thought that had been set in motion. I didn't stop for lunch, but spun onwards through sunset and into the night, clocking up a hundred and ten miles. Panting heavily, I arrived uninvited at Wat Tham Tu Khao Tong monastery. Six frightening dogs bounded towards me, and it took a fearful minute of fending them off before I spotted a doorway faintly illuminated from within. I approached and, as my pupils swelled in the dark, sixty monks came into view, silently sitting in the lotus position facing a gold Buddha.

A figure, shaven-headed and androgynous with age, materialised in the doorway and took me by the wrist: on closer inspection it was a woman. I had never seen a Buddhist nun before. She led me to a floor space at the front of the silent room and indicated that I should sit and meditate along with the rest. It didn't seem like a request.

With difficulty, I bent my legs beneath me, feeling them swell with lactic acid. The quiet was unnerving. Three minutes earlier, I had been cycling at twenty miles per hour, and now I sat amid orange-robed tranquillity. Sweat beaded my forehead, and my heart thumped high in my chest. Nobody moved: I couldn't even hear breathing from the monks. A couple of yards in front of me, ranged around the Buddha's legs, was a collection of smaller statues. The guttering of a candle among them was the only sound in the room.

It wasn't long before I grew uncomfortable and restless. My busy mind began darting around, leap-frogging over itself. I fretted about the people telling Valeria to forget me, while I sat, helpless, in a Thai temple. I pictured the faceless ex-boyfriend, encouraged by Valeria's mother, turning up on the doorstep. He would promise that things would be different, that things would be better. She would invite him inside to talk and they would drink wine. They would remember the better times...

No! I couldn't allow myself to think like that. I decided to count down from three hundred, one count with each exhalation. When my countdown reached zero, I would have humoured the nun long enough, and could feel justified in creeping out.

Three hundred, two hundred and ninety-nine, two hundred and ninety-eight, two hundred and ninety-seven... I stared impatiently at the swaying candle flame. *Two hundred and seventy-four, two hundred and seventy-three, two hundred and seventy-two...* My breath steadied and the count slowed. *Two hundred and thirty-seven, two hundred and thirty-six...* The candle swelled, filling my periphery. My eyes began to glaze, and the crawling count required all my concentration.

I don't remember reaching two hundred. The next thing I knew, a hand settled on my shoulder. I looked up into the lined face of the nun. She was smiling knowingly. I looked around. The monks were stretching out behind me, talking quietly. I had been awake, with my back bolt upright and my eyes open, when the nun roused me. But my mind was without thoughts. I had been happy. I checked the time. Almost an hour had passed. Through social pressure, it seemed I had successfully meditated. I was shown to the bathroom to wash, then handed a large plate of plain white rice and a glass of thick mango juice. I slept soundly on the prayer hall floor.

TWENTY-EIGHT

RUINS

If history repeats itself, and the unexpected always happens,
how incapable must Man be of learning from experience.
- George Bernard Shaw

7 August 2011

My uncle arranged for me to stay with a friend of his in Bangkok. I used the promise of clean sheets, a hot shower, and air-conditioning to pull me along scorching roads I had already ridden two months earlier.

John welcomed me, noticed my sorry state, and insisted on taking me to the buffet dinner at the Marriott Hotel. The choice of food was overwhelming. Long rows of heated brass pots and shining platters held a dizzying array of dishes. I made a scouting lap to take it all in and devise a strategy; I didn't want to start with the wrong dish and realise later that I had missed a trick elsewhere but was too full to take advantage.

A plate of sushi and a glass of champagne left my palette clear for a follow up of neatly parcelled dim sum, dunked in dark vinegar stirred through with an oily paste of chilli flakes. An Australian sauvignon blanc accompanied half a dozen oysters and some piping hot satay chicken skewers. I limited myself to one roll of the tempting seeded bread with rich, ochre butter – it would only take up precious space in my stomach. John watched with amusement as I repeatedly returned to the table with heaped plates, explaining my game plan between courses.

Before my first main course, I attacked a bowl of *tom yum* spicy seafood soup and an aggressively piquant *kung po* chicken on a bed of soused cabbage. The heat of the chicken had me waving over the wine waiter twice more.

There was a beautiful display of colourful Indian

curries to choose from, so I had a little of each ladled over a minimal mound of rice. Beginning to sweat, but sensing space for one more course, I decided to challenge myself. I ordered a merlot and heaped one final plate with beef wellington, pan-fried vegetables and roast potatoes. It took some time to work my way through that seventh plateful, but I got there in the end and leaned back in my chair, breathless but beaming.

'I hope you left room for some dessert,' said John, as he indicated our empty glasses to a wine waiter.

'There's always room for a little something sweet,' I lied, hauling myself into an upright position.

A bowlful of rum and raisin ice cream, drizzled with butterscotch source and chocolate truffles, somehow revived me. John and I then joined forces for one final assault: the cheeseboard. A selection of imported world cheeses on the thinnest of wafers. I tried a knob of each one.

Eventually, I laid a napkin across my plate and slumped low in the chair, grasping a tumbler of single malt on my chest. It was undoubtedly the best and largest meal of my life.

When we got back to John's flat, we flicked on BBC World News to discover that London was burning. Protests against the police shooting of an unarmed man had escalated into rioting, arson, and looting. For over a year I had received emails worrying about how I was surviving in 'dangerous' or 'lawless' countries. I now watched as familiar shops at home lay in ruins and cars burned in the streets.

I stayed a week in Bangkok. I needed the rest and only ventured out of John's flat for a few hours a day to collect visas and visit some tourist attractions.

Weighing a few extra pounds, I left Bangkok and took rutted, quiet back roads to Cambodia. The border was congested with a long queue, and several coachloads of tourists slowly sweated their way through the immigration office. A four-foot-wide tree grew through the floor of the building and disappeared out an opening in the roof.

I was stamped through and pedalled into a country very visibly poorer than its neighbour. The tarmac was loose, and the lines faded. Unkempt verges and overgrown fields lined the way, and I wondered if unexploded landmines from the 1970s civil war still lay there. I made a mental note to be careful when camping.

Villagers waved more enthusiastically than in Thailand. Men wobbled by on motorbikes with four or five live pigs stretched out in wicker racks behind them. The hogs were silent but for brief outbursts of indignant squealing.

I passed the first night in a *wat* at the end of a flooded track. While cooking my dinner, I watched a seven-year-old monk casually drawing on a cigarette and blowing artful smoke rings. In the morning, a palm-sized tarantula sidled out of my shorts lying on the floor. I showed one of the monks, who fried it with sugar, salt, and crushed garlic. We ate four crispy legs each.

I pulled into Siem Reap in the late afternoon and found a cupboard room under a staircase for £2 a night, in which I couldn't stand up straight. The light bulb was dead, so I switched it with one from the corridor, and I mopped a thick layer of dust off the surfaces with a wet rag. I knew I would be there a few nights – the temples around Siem Reap are not to be rushed past.

In the morning, I bought a three-day pass for the temples and cycled the few miles to the entrance. On the way, I met a young French student called Charles on a rented bike. Together we crossed a moat on a broad flagstone walkway and entered the West Gate of Angkor Wat's two-mile outer wall. It was early, and we had beaten the crowds. The temple pulls in two million visitors a year, and at least five thousand tourists could be expected to wander through the gate that morning.

I had seen countless photos of Angkor Wat and heard about it from numerous friends who had visited. Yet I knew next to nothing about it, and was equipped with only a scrunched handful of pages torn from an old guidebook. They informed me that the temple, the largest religious structure in the world, was built in the early twelfth century by the Khmer Empire as a monument to Vishnu. Not long after, the Khmers were conquered by the Cham kingdom. The Khmers felt let down by their gods after being sacked by a fellow Hindu kingdom and so began paying protection to a new divine power. The state religion changed to Buddhism, and Angkor Wat was abandoned.

Charles and I approached the central temple. Its five steeply tapering spires represent the mythical five-peaked Mount Meru. The outer gallery has a bas-relief frieze running its entire length, with eleven thousand figures enacting the battles between gods and men from the Hindu epics of Ramayana and Mahabharata.

Before climbing the steep stone staircase into the central temple, I stuffed the guidebook pages in my back pocket, preferring simply to wander around with my eyes open. The size, detail, and age of Angkor Wat were overwhelming. The amount of labour and wealth it must have required to build were also sobering considerations. In the nine centuries since it was built, almost every surface has acquired a thin covering of lichen and shimmers emerald in the sunlight.

As the morning wore on, the tourist hoards began to sluice through the gates, swilling around every nook and breathlessly congesting the stairways. The tour groups were largely East Asian. Groups of fifty or more, in matching t-shirts and baseball caps, clogged every walkway. Many bore cameras with foot-long lenses. Charles' mother was Japanese, and he spoke the language fluently. We enjoyed loitering near tour groups and eavesdropping on the guides instructions, given as if to a school class, and the tourists' conversations about who hadn't yet been photographed next to a particular architectural feature.

Leaving the temple to the crowds, we re-crossed the moat and wandered down some footpaths into the surrounding jungle. Just a few hundred yards from the freshly paved road was a different world: bamboo villages, forgotten chunks of ancient brickwork drowning in long grass, a woman fondly scratching the head of a buffalo calf, a lusty cockerel scattering a distraught clutch of hens, and barefoot boys playing football with a coconut shell. The small children seemed genuinely surprised by the novelty of a foreigner in their village, despite living a five-minute walk from one of the world's most-visited tourist attractions.

Next, we strolled among the thousands of unplaced blocks scattered around the Baphuon. The towering temple was falling in on itself by the 1960s and was taken apart piece by piece for restoration. The location of each stone was noted and catalogued. However, the plans were lost during the civil war, leaving 'the world's largest jigsaw puzzle' of three hundred thousand pieces. The completed puzzle had been formally opened the previous month, but many blocks couldn't be crowbarred into anywhere appropriate and still lay around the place.

In the late afternoon we pedalled on to a temple even more picturesque than Angkor Wat. Built initially as a Buddhist university monastery, Ta Prohm is very literally being swallowed by the jungle. Mighty trees straddle nine-centuries-old crumbling buildings. Swelling roots work their way slowly through colossal walls, casually edging aside one-tonne blocks of masonry. The site was busy at first, but soon cleared as the groups filed out, recalled to their coaches for the pre-ordered dinners awaiting them.

Charles and I climbed a stack of stones and perched on

a tilting wall that was built during the crusades. Ta Prohm is one of the few major temples left exactly as it was found, its slanting walls in a breathless state of near collapse. I could imagine the sense of wonder French explorer Henri Mahout must have felt when he arrived in 1860, the first European to document the ruins in detail. He assumed them to be as much as two thousand years old, the leavings of a disappeared people.

Quiet fell. The sun dipped and the shifting collage of greens intensified in the mottled light. The whole crumbling, glowing scene was achingly beautiful. Peaceful and melancholic.

I explored alone for two more days, studiously avoiding the crowds. While cycling between temples, I often came across anonymous stacks of stone or brick that had survived a millennium or more. The temples, great and small, are scattered everywhere. Most are unmarked and unremembered – the story of human civilisation. Monuments painstakingly built to deities and worshipped for a time: an empire falls, and the favoured gods fall with it. Some of the most ambitious architectural achievements the world has ever seen are left to the jungle, while another transient empire is founded with the vow to out-glory the achievements of the past. The pyramids, the Acropolis, the Taj Mahal, the Potala Palace, the Forbidden City, Versailles, Buckingham Palace. These are the games and occupations of kings and priests. Meanwhile, ordinary people go about their lives under whichever power or faith happens to inhabit a self-aggrandising stone pile in a far-off place.

* * *

13 August 2011

'Hello meester! Buyee postcar?' The waist-high urchin looked at me over a raised handful of postcard books. His large almond eyes were glazed and pleading.

'No, thank you. Not today.'

'Buyee postcar!'

'Not for me, thank you.'

'OK! No postcar. Buyee book?'

'Which book?'

He produced a battered copy of *First They Killed My Father,* an account of a girl's experiences during Cambodia's genocide in the 1970s. I had picked it up in a shop that morning. 'I'm sorry. I already have it.'

'You buyee book! Buyee book!

'No thank you. I don't want to buy the book.'

'Come on! Don be stinkee guy!'

'I've just showered.' I said

He eyed me closely. 'You! Wha country? Fran? Isray? Englan?'

'I am from Eng-land. I am Eng-lish' He scowled at my over pronunciation.

'Englan,' he began. 'Countree in Unite Kingdom. Pryminster is Davee Cameron. Before dat Gordon Brow. Before dat Dony Blur. Before dat John Madge. Before dat Maragre Datchee. Before dat Jam-es Calleehan. Before dat Harol Weelson. Before dat Edwar Heet…'

I stopped him when he reached 'Davee Loy Jodge', and gave a dollar for some postcards. He shook me by the hand in a business-like manner, nodded curtly, and moved on to a different table. I soon heard the opening strains of another impressive recital.

'Germanee. Countree in Europe. Chancer An-glar Merky. Before dat Gerhars Road. Before dat…'

Perhaps unsurprisingly, he was stopped, and he made his sale before reaching the counterpart of 'Weenston Charch-heel'. He was an enterprising little boy.

I was sitting outside a bar on the main tourist strip. It was late in the evening on my twenty-fourth birthday, and I was scribbling about nothing in particular in my diary, passing the time until a pre-arranged Skype call with

Valeria at midnight. I finished my drink, flicked my journal shut, and wandered through the crowds of travellers milling in and out of bars.

In the internet café, I logged in on a sticky keyboard and replied to a couple of emails until Valeria came online. When her face appeared, I felt once again the rush of excitement ricocheting around my stomach. However, the connection was ropey, and I struggled to hear her.

'…hallo…hi…hear me? Can y…' The video feed alternately froze and jumped, locking her face in strange mid-sentence expressions.

'Valeria? Hi! Can you hear me? Can you see me? I'm so happy to see you. I've missed you! Valeria? Can you hear me?'

'Hello meester! Buyee postcar?' The voice came from my side. It was the same little boy.

'Not now. I am talking to someone. Please.' I tried to keep calm.

'Buyee postcar?'

'Just go away, will you.'

'Buyee postcar? Meester?'

'Ch…Charlie…hear   me?   Not   possible…talk now…really…eally sorry…thing's come up…soon.' And she was gone. The video went blank. She hadn't even wished me happy birthday. Or had she? It had been so hard to hear anything.

'Meester! Buyee postcar?' His tone had turned imperative.

'Bugger off! I don't want any more fucking postcards, OK? I've already bought postcards from you. An hour ago. David Lloyd George, remember? I was trying to have a private conversation here and you interrupted. Why?'

'I'm just leetle boy. No problem.' He wandered over to the man in charge, paid a dollar, and logged onto the neighbouring computer without catching my eye.

While he watched hidden-camera comedy clips on YouTube, I sat looking at photographs of friends on

Facebook. They were all enjoying summer parties, weddings, and holidays in Europe. Tears rolled down my cheeks. It had only been a combination of weak internet, bad timing, and the distracting boy, but, somehow, Valeria was slipping away and I had to do something about it.

The next morning, I woke to a message from her: 'Charlie, I am sorry. I need time.'

TWENTY-NINE

FRANKFURT

There is the heat of love, the pulsing rush of longing, the lover's
whisper, irresistible — magic to make the sanest man go mad.
- Homer, *The Iliad*

25 August 2011

The plane began its descent towards Frankfurt. I felt physically sick with nerves. She didn't know I was coming, and this was make or break. As requested, I had given Valeria time. But ten days had passed, and I'd heard nothing. Ten days in which I managed only an hour or so of fitful sleep each night, even after long days in the saddle.

On my second morning in Phnom Penn, Cambodia's capital, I rose from my sweaty, sleepless bed, and booked a ticket to Germany, departing that afternoon. After visiting a barbershop to remove my beard, a market to buy a clean shirt, and a jewellery shop to buy a silver necklace, I packed a small bag, locked Old Geoff to a railing, and hailed a tuktuk to the airport.

During a seven-hour transit in Seoul, I paced the airport lounge in the quiet, fluorescent nighttime. Disoriented travellers slept, curled under coats on reclining leather chairs. On the flight to Frankfurt I watched no films, but stared anxiously at the world map with the little plane moving imperceptibly across it.

It was a brilliant 35°C afternoon when I reached Frankfurt and took the train to the city centre. I estimated that Valeria would arrive home from work at around six o'clock. With time to kill, I took a walk along the River Main. It was one of those rare summer days when strangers smile and look at one another unabashed as they pass. Young couples ambled hand in hand and sprawled on lush grass in the parks. The air smelled of summer, and fluffy seeds floated on warm breezes. The city centre was small and old and beautiful. The cathedral's Gothic spire rose over a square of steeply gabled buildings, and handsome iron bridges spanned the river.

I quickly felt at home in Frankfurt. I could happily live there, I decided. I *would* live there, and happily, too. I started to know that I had done the right thing by coming. I felt at peace with the idea of moving there permanently. More than at peace: excited. I cast my mind over the impossible happiness I had experienced with Valeria in Malacca and Bali. The fresh wave of joy that swept over me on waking every morning and seeing her beside me. The ability to simply pass time together and be blissfully happy doing nothing in particular. The world became a more fascinating place when in her company.

When the time was right, I made my way to Valeria's flat. I waited across the street for almost an hour, picturing the forthcoming scene in my head. She would walk around the corner, stop at the door, and delve in her bag for keys. I would step into the empty road and say her name. Valeria would turn and run into my arms, just like at the airport in Bali.

When she finally appeared, I approached and said her name. She turned, saw me, and froze. We stood in silence for a beat before I managed 'I had to see you'. She walked forward but, instead of flinging her arms around my neck and kissing me, she hugged me limply. She led me not inside, but to a nearby bar. The warmth and radiance I knew her for was gone. She seemed hardened, sitting rigidly in her chair. I tried to smile but couldn't. My heart fidgeted in my chest and a lump swelled in my throat. My stomach ached. She opened her mouth a few times but said nothing. When she finally spoke, I knew what was coming.

'Ten days ago, I got really lonely and went to see my

ex-boyfriend.' She looked me in the eyes for an instant. 'I think I still love him.'

'And *us*?' I croaked.

'I am in the impossible situation of loving two people at once.'

'You do love me though?'

'You are too late, Charlie. He and I are together again. I am so sorry. I don't know what else to say.'

I was silent for a full minute, in agony, thinking.

'It doesn't matter,' I said. 'You've made a mistake, but I don't mind. I understand. I know how tough loneliness can be. We can still make this work. I am going to move to Frankfurt, and we'll be happy.'

Hearing my medley of clichés, and seeing how she looked at me, I knew it was over. My eyes watered, but I refused to break down in front of her. She invited me inside for dinner and said I should stay. Guilt. She couldn't bring herself to send me away. I knew it would be easier if I left. But still I didn't go.

We cooked pasta, but I had no appetite. I sat on her sofa, watching her eating and trying to make small talk. I couldn't focus on what she said. It all felt so distant, like I had slipped away from the world and was watching a muffled dream at the far end of a dark tunnel. It was the saddest dream I ever had.

'What will you do, Charlie?' She said it twice before it registered.

'I don't know. What can I do? I'll probably go to England to see my family. Then I'll go back to Cambodia, and get on my bicycle, hating myself for loving you. You can go to bed. I'll sleep on the sofa, and leave in the morning. I know you've made your decision, but please think things over once more tonight.'

I lay awake in the dark, staring for hours at the orange shapes cast on the ceiling by a streetlight shining through the window. Long after midnight, Valeria's door creaked open and she tiptoed towards me.

'Are you awake?' she whispered.

'Yes.'

She took my hand and led me to her bed. It was at first faintly hopeful, then mournful, and finally tearful. It was her offering of closure but, ultimately, it felt like charity. We didn't talk.

After she fell asleep I laced my fingers through hers. I gave a gentle squeeze. There was a slight reciprocal pressure, but I knew that she was asleep and that it meant nothing. It broke my heart even more.

I booked a flight to London while she showered and dressed for work. Standing in the window, I watched as she stepped onto the tram, casting a quick upwards glance at me before dropping her head and disappearing from my life forever.

Before leaving the flat, I placed the necklace on her pillow with a note. I had chosen it for her and wanted her to have it, regardless. I knew she would never wear it.

I walked through light rain in no particular direction, listless and lost. My flight left early the next morning. The resplendent city of the previous day had wilted; it was now sombre, grey and ugly. I had no sweatshirt and grew cold. Sitting on a damp bench under a tree, crying, I wondered what to do. If I completed my journey, Valeria would likely be married and a mother by the time I returned to Europe. I would be little more to her than a road bump in the rearview mirror, a holiday romance that got out of hand. The prospect of cycling made me shudder. It seemed pointless now.

However, the thought of moving back to England horrified me. The pain and embarrassment would be too much. All that sympathy. The tilted heads and pitiful tone people would adopt when talking to me. No. I should deal with my pain alone. Life back on the road would be miserable, but at least it would be private.

Hugging my knees on the cold airport floor that night, I poured my broken heart into the dog-eared pages of my diary: "*she is both the best and the worst thing that's happened to me. But 'happened' is sorely accurate...past tense.*"

More tears hit the page, and the ink began to run.

London was greyer and wetter than Frankfurt. I made my way to the flat of my friend Ben, and told him what had happened. He opened two beers and simply toasted our reunion. I hadn't seen him for almost two years.

'At least you tried. You won't go through life wondering,' he said. 'And look on the bright side. You might write a book about your adventure one day. Every book needs a villain, right?'

That night I met my brother, my sister, and several friends. They bought me too many drinks and laughed politely when I made awkward jokes about my lovesickness. One friend was leaving for Afghanistan with his regiment in three weeks' time. He was off to war, and I was merely heartbroken. I was ashamed at my self-pity. I kept drinking, and it wasn't long before I was unable to speak at all. I did, at least, snatch several hours of unconsciousness.

I surprised my parents by turning up unexpectedly at their home. They thought I was somewhere in Cambodia. My mother phoned ahead when I went to see my grandmother for fear that she might suffer a heart attack if I showed up unannounced. For a few days, I hid from the world in my childhood village, reflecting, walking the dog, and struggling to sleep. I often felt physically sick.

After a week in England, my father drove me to the airport and I boarded the first of three flights taking me back to Phnom Penh. I had decided to finish the ride to Beijing, to recover alone, and escape the pity. From Beijing, I would fly home, find a job, and slip quietly back into English life.

It was over. Now there was only the road.

THIRTY

HORROR

The unbearable burden of recall placed on survivors of a conventional holocaust would be a relief to the survivors of a self-inflicted genocide. With no one to blame but themselves, Cambodians seem still to teeter on the edge of a pre-dug grave…Seeing the country as other than the site of a holocaust proves nigh impossible.
- John Keay

5 September 2011

'In this room the prisoners would be locked up at night, one in each cell, sometimes two when the prison was overcrowded. They were shackled to the floor and had no mat, blanket, or mosquito net. If they were caught talking, or even moving too much, they would be taken to one of the interrogation rooms for punishment. Normally lashes or electric shocks, sometimes lashes *with* an electrified wire…'

The guide, in his crisp, white shirt, had an uncanny knack of catching each member of the group's eye, one after another, as he spoke. His expression was grave, but he had become immune to the horror from giving the tour every day. As immune as it is possible to be, when telling such a shocking story.

I looked around the room as he spoke. It had been a classroom once, but crude, head-high brick walls had been hurriedly erected inside. These dividing walls formed cells of roughly one by two yards. There were no ceilings to the cells but, as the inmates were chained to the floor, they were intended more for separation and isolation than as actual cages. The rough bricks had gobs of cement protruding from them, and many of these had blood smears, blackened with age. One cell had the ghost of a bloodstain on the floor in its corner, a stain that hadn't been scrubbed hard enough: the print of a short, wide, bare foot.

'...of course,' the guide continued, 'not all of the inmates were put in cells like this. There were far too many of them, as many as one thousand five hundred at times. Most prisoners were lined up on the floor in the larger classrooms. All would have their ankles locked to metal bars running the length of the room. They were packed in so tight that they wouldn't be able to move or turn over. And nobody could get up to visit the toilet...'

The brutality was incomprehensible. We hadn't even reached the interrogation rooms yet. I had joined a ragtag group on a guided tour around Tuol Sleng Prison in Phnom Penn. This infamous prison is where suspected traitors were taken to be held and questioned by the Khmer Rouge.

Cambodia's capital was evacuated on 17 April 1975. The Khmer Rouge had just defeated the government forces, putting an end to a five-year civil war. The city's entire population was relocated to rural areas across the country and set to work: a slave class to the existing villagers. Educated or urban citizens were to be 're-educated' to a rural, communist way of life. It was 'Year Zero' in what the Khmer Rouge intended to be a pure, agrarian society – an aggressive take on Marxism with no currency, cities, or meddling foreigners.

The whole nation was put to work in the rice fields or on forced labour projects. Every citizen wore obligatory black trousers and shirts and was supposedly provided with food and shelter by the ruling Communist Party of Kampuchea (CPK, or simply 'Angkar', meaning base). As so often happens, the planned utopian peace required weapons to enforce it. Guns were bought from China, paid for with precious rice produced by the already starving population.

Peace also required soldiers to enforce it. Those soldiers were largely uneducated, indoctrinated village boys. Peace also required the arrest, interrogation, torture, and eventual execution of anyone suspected of being bourgeois. Having fair skin or soft hands, speaking a foreign language, or even wearing spectacles could be used as proof that someone had not spent a life toiling in the fields for the greater good of the people and was therefore eligible for a fractured skull and a shallow mass grave.

In 1975, before the genocide, Cambodia's population was 8 million. Estimates of the death toll during the Khmer Rouge's four-year regime range from 1.5 million to 3.3 million. To put that in context, fewer than 900,000 British and Americans, combined, died in the whole of World War II.

Mass graves in Cambodia are still being unearthed today, adding to the twenty thousand already discovered. Only three of the Khmer Rouge's leading cadre have been tried and sentenced. Pol Pot, the mysterious orchestrator and longtime party leader, died in 1998 aged seventy-three. He had served only one year under house arrest and was due to be handed over to an international tribunal when he conveniently passed.

'...and this is the largest of the interrogation rooms, or torture chambers, if you prefer.' The guide stood by the door in the corridor and ushered us through. He seemed unwilling to enter the room if he could avoid it and continued his spiel from the doorway. 'On the walls, you will see the thousands of prisoner pictures of the inmates. They were all photographed and catalogued on arrival. It was surprisingly well organised...'

I walked along beside the wall. There was a grid of hundreds upon hundreds of black and white four- by six-inch portrait photographs. Each showed someone who had been brought into the prison, questioned, tortured, and executed. They all had prisoner numbers pinned to their clothes. Some had battered and bloodied faces from beatings during arrest. Men, some bent with age, women, teenage boys and girls, even a few elderly women. Only twelve survivors were found in Tuol Sleng after the Khmer Rouge abandoned the city to the advancing Vietnamese troops.

'…on the far wall is a photo taken of this room when the prison was first discovered…'

I looked at the enlarged sepia print over the heads of two silent Australian girls. We were all silent. In the photo was the bare room with a metal bedframe at its centre. A lifeless shape was twisted across it. Dark, silhouetted almost, but with patches of light revealing the contours of a naked body.

'…the man on the bed was killed by the guards before they fled. He had been tortured for some time and, as you can see, is covered with blood…'

When the Vietnamese liberated the city in January 1979, they found the prison quickly. The blood smothering the body in the photo still looked wet. The prisoner was on his front, with his legs chained to a metal bar, and his wrists cuffed behind his back. The floor below the bed bore a large bloodstain, pooled in the centre and spattered towards the outside.

'…he had been tortured using burning irons, nail pulling and, judging by marks on his neck, short stints of hanging…'

I turned around and looked at the sinister old bed frame in the centre of the room: cleaned up, with no corpse, still in the same spot, and with the leg irons positioned as they had been found. The pool of blood had been removed, but the dried grouting between the tiles was darker below the bed than elsewhere.

'…this man was one of fourteen final victims found in the torture chambers, left as they died. Some of the other methods used included waterboarding, sleep deprivation, suffocation with plastic bags, and even skinning alive. Anything possible to force a confession of guilt. The interrogators always insisted on gaining a confession, and preferably a list of other perpetrators – friends, family, colleagues – before condemning the accused to death. We believe most people would eventually admit to any charges, simply to end the torture and hasten their execution...'

The perversity of forcing a confession, when everyone involved knew the charges were spurious or absurd, struck me as little more than an outlet for sadism. Even the guards lived in fear of being betrayed to the authorities, and yet they did terrible things to people in a situation they could easily imagine themselves in. Most of the several hundred guards were uneducated village boys. Rows of their photographs were also displayed in the torture rooms.

'...the torturers encouraged their victims to provide one hundred names of other traitors. At that time, many people wouldn't know a hundred people, so they would finally say the names of their brothers, sisters, parents...their children. Those named would then be found and brought in for questioning...'

Before the Khmer Rouge took over, the building had been a high school where some of the victims would once have played with their school friends and gained the knowledge that would later have them classified as bourgeoisie and enemies of the state. In four years, 14,000 people were interrogated and tortured in Tuol Sleng before being transported outside the city for execution.

I was relieved when the tour ended and the guide slid away to marshal another group. The small museum exhibition gave more facts, and showed plenty of photographs, but was hopelessly unable to explain *why* such things had been able to happen. It gave no indication as to what rot had set into the heart of Cambodian society, in order to enable normal people to commit such atrocities upon fellow humans.

The following day I hailed a tuktuk to take me to the other

end of Tuol Sleng's operation. The condemned prisoners were taken ten miles outside the city to Choeng Ek for execution and burial in mass graves. With the country in financial meltdown, ammunition was in short supply. Executioners (once again, village boys) killed with blows to the head with farming implements, or by cutting throats. Sometimes, when no blades were available, they used the jagged edge of a palm branch to decapitate their victims.

When one grave was exhumed, the bodies of eighty small children were found. Each had been held by the feet and swung, head-first, against a nearby tree. Choeng Ek 'killing field' is an area of only two hundred yards squared. Around eighty of one hundred and twenty-six identified graves have been exhumed, and 15,000 of an estimated 19,000 bodies have been found.

It had rained the night before I visited and, as I traced the uncomfortably narrow paths between the exhumed pits, I spotted teeth that had washed to the surface, both in the graves and on the path. Short shards of bone jutted from the sandy earth, and a small sign beside the path read 'Please keep off the mass graves'.

It is hard to describe the chilling atmosphere of the place, but I noted that no visitors spoke as they wandered around, reading the bluntly informative information boards. I thought their silence was more from a feeling of horror than from respect for the unfathomable number of dead.

An unusual, upright building stood beside the killing fields, with the steep roof of a Buddhist *wat*. The Genocide Centre museum contained a glass cabinet, fifteen yards high, with seventeen shelves displaying a few thousand skulls. Many had fractures where victims had been beaten to death with blunt objects. As at the prison, the museum stated facts (few and oft repeated) but still offered no real explanation as to *why*. How could such brutality lurk in once-ordinary people? One of the great difficulties the country faced after the genocide was the naked truth that the killers and victims were all Cambodian citizens. As in Rwanda, people had to learn to live side by side with those who had murdered their friends and relatives.

Feeling profoundly disquieted, I returned to the city as the sun was setting. Stepping off the tuktuk in the colonial quarter, I walked along the banks of the Tonlé Sap River before turning down an unlit street towards the hostel. As a motorbike passed me carrying three men, a figure leaped out of the shadows beside me and pulled the hindmost passenger roughly to the ground. There was a shout and the motorbike sped off. The floored man struggled to get up, but was punched in the jaw before he could stand. As he got up and started to run, twenty or so figures emerged from the shadows and gave chase. Most looked to be teenagers. One who ran close by me was wielding a wooden table leg with a long nail driven through it. He caught my eye and his severe expression broke just long enough for him to smile and say 'hello' before straightening his face and charging off. Within thirty seconds everything was silent again, and I continued my walk. Had those youths lived thirty-five years ago, they would likely have been drafted to the Khmer Rouge as revolutionary guards.

Back in the hostel, as on every Tuesday night, the staff put on the 1984 film *The Killing Fields* about a Cambodian journalist, Dith Pran, who was arrested by the Khmer Rouge and forced to undergo 're-education' between bouts of hard labour on a collectivised farm. Pran feigned that he was a simple-minded peasant and eventually escaped to Thailand. For the final half hour of the film, I sat in a dark corner at the back of the room, weeping. It was a relief to be crying for a reason other than Valeria, as I had done every night since Frankfurt.

The guesthouse staff were teenage boys, brothers I guessed, born long after the genocide ended. They had evidently seen the film countless times, and were disinterested in it. They quietly joked with each other behind the bar. With the passing of generations, Cambodia as a whole has tried hard to move on, and many now see the past more as a horror story than a history. A gruesome thing of fiction from which hopefully some lessons can be learned.

VIETNAM

Travel makes a wise man better, and a fool worse.
- Thomas Fuller

9 September 2011

The sense of despair from the genocide sites stayed with me as I crossed into Vietnam. With temperatures of 30°C by 7.30 a.m., it was really too hot to linger on such horrors, but I was still coming to terms with heartbreak and chose to dwell on the misery.

The time in England had eaten into the fixed dates of my one-month Vietnamese visa, and I now had three weeks to cover 1,300 miles to the Chinese border.

I entered Ho Chi Minh City (formerly Saigon) at midday. The thick smog created by the city's three million motorbikes could be tasted in the mouth, and I focused on breathing through my nose. After a few hours lost on the labyrinthine roads, I finally reached the intersection of Pham Ngu Lão Street and Đê Thám Street, which serves as the backpacker district. The area was a clutter of signage, both neon and printed, offering meals, drinks, massages, happy hours, happy endings, pirated DVDs, visa services, passport photos, group tours, laundry, and shuttle buses to touristic hotspots.

I hauled Old Geoff up three flights of stairs to an airless £2 room and peered into the tiny, cracked mirror. My face was blackened with exhaust fumes, streaked where sweat had beaded down to my tangled beard. I blew my nose and looked at the spatter of black gobbets on the toilet paper. Stepping into the showerless bathroom, I repeatedly filled a cup to sluice away the plastered grime covering my body – a paste of sweat and dust and exhaust soot. Deciding I wasn't yet ready to mix with the crowds, I set an alarm for early morning departure.

Over the next week, I sullenly slogged seven hundred miles. I followed the busy National Route 1A. This arterial road describes a 1,430-mile 'S', largely along the coast, from the Chinese border in the north, via Hanoi and Ho Chi Minh, to the tip of the Cà Mau peninsula in the south.

Each day saw a couple of short but tumultuous tropical storms which would briefly blanket the road with a couple of inches of water. After the rain, the land would audibly sizzle. The heat between rains was excruciating, and I was inevitably exposed to the sun. Suncream sweated off in minutes, and my skin entered a cycle of burning, bubbling, blistering, peeling, and burning anew.

Villagers lay inert in roadside hammocks, while their goods (rice, wheat, husks, seafood shells, seaweed) lay drying on the tarmac's edge. Red national flags hung everywhere, and the communist hammer and sickle adorned many walls. Along with Laos, Vietnam is among the last remaining self-proclaimed communist countries. The other three are China, Cuba, and North Korea. The Buddhist *wats* I had seen so often in Laos, Cambodia, and Thailand were nowhere to be found. Years of suppressive atheist rule had left their mark on the country.

The road was lined with a string of villages, never quite petering out, but bleeding into one another. Finding camping sites was tough, as the land on either side of the road was usually waterlogged. The only raised land tended to be little clusters of trees, each with a few ancient-looking graves among them. Thankfully, most Vietnamese only visit their ancestors once a year on the ceremonial 'tomb-sweeping day, shortly after the spring equinox. I would pitch my tent in half-light, taking care not to disturb the pots of sand intended for holding incense offerings.

The nights were still painful. When I closed my eyes, the ghosts of pleasures past danced and flickered mockingly before me. I tried to console myself. I would reach Beijing in less than three months, and I could then fly home and draw a line under this misery tour. I was no longer pursuing a dream, but merely fleeing from humiliation.

One afternoon, as I rested in the shade of a tree on a rice paddy, I saw an odd sight. A small, dark-skinned boy approached across the flooded paddy. He was naked, and mounted on a large, brown cow with short, blunt horns. The cow had no reins or saddle, or even a nose ring. Her hooves flicked the water with each step. It seemed she knew where they were going. I guessed the child to be no more than four. I watched as he rolled his hips unthinkingly, keeping his balance. He had the casual ease and impassive face of a cowboy riding down a dusty strip of wood-fronted buildings in the Wild West.

As they drew closer, the boy noticed my prostrate form. I waved. His eyes swelled with surprise, and his brow furrowed. The cow trod onward, unconcerned with the white devil, but the boy kept staring. When the cow had passed, the boy thrust his legs up and neatly swivelled on the cow's spine, until he was facing backwards and could continue staring in disbelief. Despite having just seen a naked boy riding a cow on autopilot, I realised that on that day, in that Vietnamese rice paddy, I was the oddity.

With the punishing weather, and heartache still effervescing within me, I receded into my mind. I rarely engaged with the country, culture, and people around me. I fixed upon China for a fresh start: a rebirth in the cool autumn weather I would find there. I had been in Southeast Asia almost five months, and its heat and humidity had worn me thin. The part of the world where I had expected my journey to be easiest and most fun had been my unravelling. I had lost my sense of wonder – the inquisitiveness so vital to learning from experience.

In this disconnected state, I sensed increasing amounts of hostility directed towards me. The waves, laughs, and cheers that had come as I rolled through villages in other countries became mocking jeers in Vietnam. When I bought food I had to haggle vehemently, first for the correct price, and then once again to extract the correct change.

One afternoon a van slowed alongside me. The driver honked and swerved dangerously close on the otherwise empty road, threatening to force me off the tarmac. Later, I spotted the van again, pulled over with the driver and passenger (both young men) standing on the roadside. They were laughing at me. One of them moved quickly as I passed. Before I knew what had happened, I was struggling to regain balance, having been punched hard in the face. I rode on, not wanting to confront the men. They soon overtook again, this time nudging my pannier and sending me careering into a bush. My temper boiled over. I shouted furiously, but the car had sped off and I was left embarrassed at my impotence.

I contemplated why I was experiencing such antagonism. I still met as many friendly and helpful people as in any other country, but several passing encounters with young Vietnamese men had unprecedented aggression. Perhaps, as I was willfully dislocating from my surroundings, people sensed my closed-mindedness, which is, of course, a negative and threatening trait.

It was also likely that some Vietnamese nurture a resentment of Americans for prolonging such a gruesome and costly civil war in their country. To those feeling that resentment, any white person could easily be mistaken for an American. A twenty-year war can certainly engender a lasting atmosphere of easy violence.

I looked at the landscape and imagined it in its former, embattled state. Where have bombs fallen? Where have people died? Where *hasn't* someone died? The country is sadly synonymous in the western mind with war and horror and tragedy. My mind's eye played through a montage of gruesome films where normal men were pushed to the extremes of murder and inhumanity.

I also considered that this attitude could be a by-product of Vietnam's recent tourism boom. Australian budget airlines had been offering cut-price flights to Vietnam for a few years, and the influx of late-teenagers on three-week benders was evident. As I traced the coast I rushed past beach resorts where I knew thousands would be lazing on the sand by day and drinking into the small hours each night. I glimpsed snapshots of these tourists' sleeping faces as coaches ferried them, hungover, from one beach to the next. I tried to look down on them, but I knew that, truth be told, I envied them. Not the partying, but the company.

During occasional periods of unpleasant self-realisation, I would see myself: a hurt, self-pitying little boy, pelting through a poor country, convinced everyone is out to get him and dwelling pathetically on himself. I needed to address this problem.

The old harbour town of Hoi An seemed a good place to force myself to reset. After I arrived and showered, I sat down outside the hostel with a coffee and a book. A motorbike roared up the road, pulled onto the pavement, and jolted to a halt a yard from my chair. The young western rider wore shorts, vest, and flip-flops. His rounded helmet was a military green with a slightly turned out rim. It reminded me of smartly uniformed German soldiers in World War II films.

'Hef you seen a Schottisch und a Velsisch mens?' he shouted over his still-running engine.

'Turn off your engine!' I shouted back.

'Vot?'

I pointed at his Honda and ran a finger across my throat.

'Ach! Sorry.' He killed the engine. 'The Schottisch? Hef you seen him? I am meeting him here now.'

'No. I'm sorry. I don't know him.'

'Hahhh,' he sighed. 'I am late. I must hef missed him. Why don't you come?'

'Come where?'

'A bar, The Sleepy Gecko, und there ist a party there tonight, a small one, because the bar girl is leaving. Englisch girl, I think. It will be all we can eat und drink, und only acht dollars!'

I drained my coffee, stood up, and swung a leg over the pillion.

'Gut man!' he said, and stamped the engine back to life. My upper body jerked backwards as we accelerated onto the road. He reached a hand over his shoulder and I briefly shook it, wishing he would keep both hands on the bike.

'Mein name ist Michi,' he yelled. 'I'm from Bawaria.'

Michi from Bavaria had spent the past two weeks in the mountains on his motorbike. Twenty years old, he had recently finished school and was due to fly home in a couple of weeks. I liked him. He had a bold, no-nonsense approach to life. In him, I recognised the positivity and excitement of a younger me, first setting out from home. Mine had faded noticeably.

Michi was abrupt and unapologetic, untarnished by sadness, and fun to be around. People thought him rude when they first met, but soon saw he simply had no false politeness to his conversation. He simply said what he thought.

We sat with ever-replenished beers and heaped plates of barbecued food in the pokey bar on an island in the Thu Bôn River. It was a small gathering of Vietnamese and expats, and it was cheap due to the largesse of the owner – a rotund, hairy-shouldered Englishman, who later began drunkenly wielding a tattoo gun.

Michi told me about his girlfriend waiting in Bavaria,

and how Germany's unusual education system meant he had to attend a college after leaving school to obtain sufficient grades for university acceptance. I told him about my journey across Asia and the final ride ahead to Beijing.

The night grew long, the music loud, and the company rowdy. It was roughly 4 a.m. when Michi, dancing next to me on a pool table to the 'Hippy Hippy Shake', shouted over the din.

'Charlie! I think I will sell my motorbike. Then I will buy a bicycle, and coming with you to Peking.'

THIRTY-TWO

REBIRTH

Must in death your daylight finish?
My sun sets to rise again.
 - Robert Browning

I left Hoi An alone again, but it was different to before. Michi went ahead to Hanoi to apply for a Chinese visa, and I would meet him there. I now had the prospect of a couple of months in good company to pull me onwards.

As I skirted past Da Nang, and with a menacing cloudbank approaching, a young Vietnamese man came alongside me on his motorbike.

'My friend! Where are you going?'

'I am going to Hanoi,' I replied.

'Wow! That is great! You are strong man!'

'Oh, not really. I just go a little distance each day and then it's possible.'

'There is a storm coming now. It will be my honour to buy you some lunch?'

We ducked into a restaurant as the first drops fell. Duong asked questions about England and my family while we ate *pho* soup. The waitress cleared away our bowls and brought two cups of syrupy black coffee. Duong placed his hand on my thigh under the table, and suggested we go to a hotel together. I gently removed his hand and told him I was not gay. Embarrassed, he apologised politely and began to tell me how hard it is to be gay in Vietnam.

'There are many men who will attack me if they find out,' he whispered, 'and my parents are forcing me to marry a woman. They know, because my father caught me kissing a man. They are worried that people will discover this, and they will become outsiders because of me. They say I will be cured if I marry and have a baby. But I just want a boyfriend, and to be happy.'

We spoke for over an hour before I thanked him for lunch and got up to leave.

'Wait!' he said. 'I see you have a very hairy chest. It will be my honour to shave it for you.'

'But why would I shave it?'

'I want the hair,' he replied, 'to remember you by.'

After six days of almost continuous rain, I reached the capital and found Michi in a cavernous backpackers' hostel. It was in the heart of Hanoi's Old Quarter, a warren of narrow streets where merchants used to trade goods. Restaurants and souvenir shops now inhabit the fading colonial buildings, and tourists amble down the roads, ignoring the beeps of motorbikes trying to pass. Tangled webs of power lines are slung all along the space above the roads.

Michi and I sat at a street stall eating beef noodle soup and drinking generous measures of rice liquor, served by a small, grinning fat lady. A tall, attractive woman approached, roughly my age, and asked in a soft German accent if she could join us. Dani had a freckled face, a pile of dark brown hair, and searching blue eyes. She wore no bra, and her nipples showed conspicuously through her thin top. Michi, hearing the accent, opened conversation in German. I watched them speak for a while, until Michi suddenly switched to English.

'...so, you're actually American?'

'Yes.'

'But I neffer meet Americans who can truly speak German like you.'

'I moved to Germany to study, and now I live there, working as a dance choreographer. People do say I have a German accent in my English now, but I can't hear it.'

We sat drinking the rice liquor until the old lady packed up, shooing us off the little stools and onto a concrete doorstep. Michi disappeared for a couple of minutes and returned with a bottle of rum.

I woke, sprawled, face down across the bed in a boxy hotel room. There was no other furniture. I rolled over and a harsh beam of sunlight struck my face. My head screeched with a violent hangover. I was naked, and the door was wide open. A man walked past in the corridor and stopped, aghast, when he saw me. I reached out a leg and kicked the door shut. Struggling to my feet, I looked around for clothes. My shorts and vest were thrown to opposite corners of the room. *How did I get here?* I dressed, and looked for shoes. There was a single flip-flop, but it wasn't mine. Just as I was leaving, I noticed a small square of paper on the pillow. The writing on it was neat and feminine:

I ask myself how a boy who has seen so much and travelled so far can still question every passing moment. We were having fun, Charlie. It would have been lovely to be with just you. But your 'Valeria' was in the room with us. C'est la vie! Dani xx

Out on the street, one-shoed and stumbling, I traipsed through the early morning Old Quarter, looking for a familiar landmark with which to find my way. The vendors were setting up their stands and opening their shops. An old man spotted me and laughed at my bare foot. He offered me coffee and a cigarette, then happily jabbered away while I sipped and puffed.

Back in the hostel, Michi said his China visa application had been denied. Apparently, it was a common quirk of the Chinese embassy in Hanoi, but it would be easy in Bangkok. He already had a flight to Bangkok in two days to connect with his flight to Germany. He decided to take it. He would get his visa, fly to Hong Kong, and take a train or bus to meet me in southern China. I was impressed by his commitment to the idea of cycling across

China with me – an idea born of whimsy when dancing drunkenly on a pool table.

I set off for China with 110 miles of hills to the border. Only a day and a half remained on my Vietnamese visa. There was heavy rain and I soon grew tired. Visibility dropped as the road wound upwards. I had seen on the news that a typhoon had just torn through the Philippines and was now careering towards northern Vietnam.

Late in the afternoon, with seventy miles behind me, my front tyre punctured. I stopped at a village workshop. The owner was squatting over an engine part, welding gun in one hand and shard of tinted glass held before his eyes in the other. He smiled when he looked up and saw me, shivering and dripping, in his doorway. I asked with sign language to shelter while I made the repair.

The man approached me, took my hand, and led me to a wooden chair. He poured me a cup of green tea and put a towel around my shoulders. I said nothing but smiled gratefully. He pointed at mud splashes on my legs, and tutted. As soon as the cup was drained, I was marched through a door into his family's home. There was a cubicle built onto the back with a little hosepipe attached to the wall at shoulder height. He pointed at a bar of soap, and left me to shower.

When I returned, clean and in dry clothes, the man was just pumping up my tyre, having patched the puncture. He stood up, tapped his chest with a knobbly finger, and said simply 'Trung.' I pointed at my chest and said 'Charlie'. We shook hands. The rising wind rattled the door loudly in its frame, and he signed that I should sleep in his home.

Trung's wife and two daughters arrived on a scooter shortly afterwards and changed into dry clothes. The older girl, perhaps twelve, had some basic English, and practised her short vocabulary while we sat around a floor mat feasting on roast duck, fried pork fat, rice, and buttery Chinese cabbage. The typhoon started to really rage outside, and I helped Trung nail a wooden bar across the door. The wind flexed and unflexed the aluminium roof with a sickening sound, and we heard the screech of nails being slowly pulled from the rafters.

The family seemed happy, and Trung and I toasted each other incomprehensibly with little porcelain cup after little porcelain cup of rice liquor from a twenty-litre jerry can. Once sweetened with honey and flavoured with lemon, it became just about bearable. It made little difference that we couldn't understand each other's toasts, as it was near impossible to hear over the din of the storm, anyway. Trung's youngest daughter, roughly five, spotted my klaxon and delightedly ran around the room, honking it every few seconds and collapsing into fits of giggles.

Trung showed me through to a small room and pointed at a bed. I knew it was the bed he and his wife slept in, and I caught sight of him unrolling mats and blankets in the kitchen/living room, but protesting would have offended him. I slept deeply under a pile of blankets while the tempest blew past and petered out over the hills to the west.

In the chilly morning we ate noodles outside, while two hens squabbled over a fat earthworm. Trung shook my hand with a laugh when I rose to leave, and I bowed my thanks to his wife. I left the klaxon with the girl. She had found more joy in it in one evening than I had had in a year. I was indebted to the family for helping me dispel the negative perception of the Vietnamese that had crept into my mind in the south. I was also indebted, as I had planned to spend the night in my tent.

It was raining lightly as I neared the border town of Dang Dong. Swathes of mist slumped between hills, and the smell of wet earth hung heavy. Limestone karsts pillared from the land, disappearing into cloud, their feet ringed by fields of freshly flattened sugar cane.

I left the country with two hours remaining on my visa.

Crossing the border was a breath of fresh air. I sensed I could lay to rest the demons I had developed over my unexpectedly trying journey through Southeast Asia. I was back in the moment, and life felt good again. China was a land of opportunity, and I was freshly arrived.

Small back roads bore me northeast through cloud-pressed farming villages. It was the first day of China's 'Golden Week' national holiday. The villagers were relaxing, playing cards, watching television, eating, and drinking. The workers get precious little holiday each year, and they tend to do as little as possible on those days.

Glad to sit out of the rain for a while, I stopped for a 20-pence bowl of noodles in Ningming railway station. It was the only place open in the town. I sat shovelling the strands into my mouth with chopsticks, while a crop-topped boy stood opposite, slurping noisily from an outsized bowl. He gazed at me, wide-eyed and unabashed. An old man, with a semi-collapsed umbrella and white rubber boots, drove a water buffalo past the window, down the main street. He jockeyed his beast nonchalantly with a radio aerial.

People smiled and waved politely as I passed their homes. There was none of the boisterous shouting I had become accustomed to. Perhaps the Chinese have a sense of modesty towards strangers more akin to the British. Or perhaps they were simply warier of *gwai lo* (foreign devil or, literally, 'ghost person') than the Vietnamese.

I reached Guanxi Province's capital, Nanning, and dried out myself and my kit. I stayed in a small, fully booked hostel where the manager allowed me to sleep on a sofa for £1 a night. When I used the computer, the following email arrived from Michi:

I arrived in Bangkok and was told I cannot get the visa for a whole week…there is some gold holiday apparently. I was not sure if I should wait or just take my flight home tomorrow. So,

REBIRTH

last night I flicked a coin. Heads I am coming to China. Tails I go to Germany. It was heads! The gods decided I go to China. So, let's go China! There is an empty seat flying to Germany tomorrow!

When I have my visa, I will take the train to meet you. And we can find me a bicycle. I have found a tent for €3!

Ah! I nearly forgot. After I flicked the coin, I discovered that it was a head on both sides! It was actually the king and the prime minister of Thailand who decided I will go to China! See you soon.

THIRTY-THREE

FRIENDSHIP

A journey is best measured in friends, rather than miles.
                                        - Tim Cahill

Michi joined me in Yangshuo, the jewel in the crown of Guanxi Province. Karsts with lush skins of greenery stand sentry over the Li River, and a carpet of flat farmland connects the karsts, glowing emerald in the late-afternoon light. The harvest had just finished, and tidy little sheaves leaned together in freshly cropped fields, awaiting collection. The scenery features on China's twenty-*yuan* banknote, and lures droves of tourists, who shuffle through the town's small cobblestone streets, herded by flag-waving guides.

We easily bought a bicycle for Michi. It had an ugly white basket and was in poor condition, and after an hour of picking dry cakes of oil and dust from the chain and gear cogs, Michi dubbed him 'Furious Otto'. We fixed Otto up as best we could and cycled out of town on a minor road.

Pedalling side by side, chatting away the miles on fresh autumn mornings, in the warm afternoons we cooked large lunches with fresh produce and took luxurious siestas. Michi had never travelled this way before, and his slowly emerging joy at its simplicity rekindled my love of cycle touring.

Companions in incomprehension, Michi and I navigated the quirks of China together, finding amusement in the smallest things: a woman twigging that we couldn't *speak* Chinese and so *writing* what she wanted to say in Chinese characters for us to read; the stern-faced policemen who stopped to demand our passports with suspicion in their tone, but who soon regressed to giggling schoolboys and asked to take photos with us; an old man diligently working his way through a vast bowl of peanuts using chopsticks; an indifferent chef, smoking, hawking, and spitting, while frying tripe and cabbage in oil and chilli.

One afternoon we spotted a cast-iron water pump, like something from a Victorian London street scene, in front of village house. Grimy after two days riding through a smoggy coal-mining district, we decided to wash. Seeing no adults around to ask for permission, I fished a bar of soap from my pannier and handed it to Michi who quickly wet, soaped and rinsed himself.

The long handle needed several cranks before the water flowed, and the flow would last only a second after pumping ceased. Stripped down to my pants, I tried pumping a few strokes, and darting forward to thrust my knotted hair under the rush of water just as it stopped. I attempted pumping with my arm awkwardly outstretched, my head hovering expectantly under the nozzle. However, from that angle, I couldn't pump with enough force to pull the water up. Michi, who had somehow managed by himself, lay a few yards away, drying happily in the sun. A couple of tiny village girls stood by him, hands clapped over mouths in pantomime titters.

While I flitted around the pump, trying and failing, a door squeaked open. A squat old matron, forehead concertinaed by many turbulent decades of Chinese history, shuffled towards me with a plastic jug. She wore a padded blue smock and a black felt cap, from which a plait of silvery hair ran over her collar. She smiled, pointed me towards the nozzle, and began pumping. I wet my body, and began working the soap into a lather, focusing on my hair, beard and armpits. The woman let go of the handle and watched with a gap-toothed grin, emitting occasional phlegmy chuckles.

When I moved towards the pump again, she stopped

me with some wordless exclamations. I looked confused and she pointed at my crotch. Bashfully, I thrust the bar of soap into my pants, and hurriedly wriggled it around. Michi now also held his hand over his mouth, his body convulsing with laughter. The little woman called one of the girls to the pump. Resigned, I sat on the concrete, damp, soapy, and in my pants. The girl pumped, and the woman repeatedly filled the jug, pouring it over my head, until I was rinsed. I felt like I had undergone a strange sort of baptism.

Late each afternoon, we stopped in a village to buy ingredients for dinner. Rural Chinese markets were always fun. They are the domain of women, and are as friendly a place as can be. Being head and shoulders taller than all present made us somewhat of an eyesore, and friendly laughter followed us as we browsed. Small crowds formed, following us through the rows of concrete slabs that act as counters, asking question after question in Chinese.

We spoke almost no Chinese, but the questions were predictable, and we soon learned our replies.

'*Qù nǎlǐ?*' Where are you going?

'Beijing!' we chanted, vaguely pointing in whichever direction felt most like north.

'*Shénme guójiā?*' Which country are you from?

'*Yīngguó!*' I would say, enjoying the extended, croaking cadence at the end of the word. '*Déguó!*' Michi would chip in, pointing at himself and matching my croak.

When we were asked our age – '*Duō shào nián?*' – we would answer in turn, '*èrshí nián*' and '*èrshí-sì nián*', and receive incredulous expressions. Most guessed Michi to be in his thirties and with my bushy beard, a rarity in China, I was placed anywhere between forty and fifty-five.

The phrase *bù yáo* ('I don't want') proved useful. Vendors had a habit of thrusting foul-smelling duck eggs, or unidentifiable cuts of meat, in our faces. One ruddy-faced woman triumphantly produced two kilos of garlic (*dàsuàn*) when I asked for rice (*mǐ*). When I said I didn't want it, she slipped a couple of bulbs inside my bag with a mischievous wink.

I soon learned the Chinese for egg (*dàn*). They were usually easily to spot in their stacked cardboard crates. However, I preferred to ask with a charade that I had perfected in countless village shops over the last year. I would bring my fists to my armpits, and flap my elbows like chicken wings, clucking as I did so. The clucking would grow gradually more fraught, until I put one hand behind my bottom, and made a popping sound with the little finger of the other hand inside my cheek. The first hand would then reappear from behind my back with the thumb and forefinger touching to form an egg-shaped ring.

'*Ahhhhh! Dàn! Dàn! Lǎowài tā yào jīdàn!*' The old foreigner wants eggs! The crowd would roar delightedly, and the children would start sucking on their fingers and blowing out their cheeks, trying to make the popping sound.

With £1 we could buy everything we needed to prepare a feast. The vendors were scrupulously honest, and we happily left our bikes unlocked and unattended at the entrance to the market. Petty theft is almost non-existent in China.

By the time we returned to Old Geoff and Furious Otto, our tail of curious followers would have absorbed every child present. They jostled one another to get closer, but with caution. None wanted to get too close to the tall, unpredictable *lǎowài*. I could rarely resist the opportunity to scatter the crowd. I would suddenly turn, and emit a furious roar, wringing my hands either side of a snarled face. They would flee for their lives for few short seconds before laughing again, returning, and trying to yank the hair that grows on *lǎowài* chests – an odd and disgusting feature to Chinese eyes.

Camping spaces were easy to find, and we enjoyed peaceful nights. With its socialist ethos, China's rural land is often perceived as common, regardless of who is cultivating it. When people chanced across us, they usually gaped for a second, smiled, waved, and wandered on. We ate dinner bent over one vast pan, the crowns of our heads bumping together as we greedily slurped up noodles and smacked our chops, both racing to eat more than our share. Stretched out on the ground to digest, fireflies hovering above us in the gloaming, we talked until it grew chilly and then retired to our tents for nine hours' sleep.

We slept in a variety of places: a mandarin farm (where we picked fruit to add to our breakfast porridge); abandoned building sites; a quarry; and on ping-pong tables in a half-built apartment block. I woke in the morning, just as my table collapsed. One night we camped on a hillock of wasteland in the suburbs of a relatively small city – just shy of one million people – called Yongzhou. In the morning, our mount was climbed by a parade of elderly individuals practising an array of unusual exercises. Some swung their arms in great arcs with each step, while others repeatedly clapped their hands or slapped their chests. A few progressed with an odd stumbling jog that was somehow slower than a walk. A few gave out a strained 'huhhgh' with each exhalation, as if they had been punched in the stomach. All was done with a look of intense concentration. One of our visitors stopped a few yards from us, and launched into a series of odd yodels that pierced the still morning.

The areas we passed through offered opposite extremes. There were idyllic landscapes of rice terraces, bamboo forests, tea plantations, and fruit orchards. However, dotted between the beauty spots were the results of China's sprint towards industrialisation. Hulking power stations belched thick blackness from towering chimneys; ragged vagrants, with meagre bundles of possessions dangling from sticks, sifted through piles of rubbish; run-down coal yards wallowed in clouds of pollution; and swollen towns sprawled outwards with ghostly, uninhabited suburbs of unfinished apartment blocks, built in preparation for the increasing migration to urban areas.

China is home to twenty of the world's thirty most-polluted urban areas. It has 150 cities with over a million people, and the demand for resources and energy is bottomless. Five new coal-fired power stations opened each week during our visit.

We left Guanxi Province and entered Hunan: China's communist heartland. In 1893, in the unassuming village of Shaoshan, Mao Zedong was born. His parents were simple peasants – a term used in China to describe farmers to this day. The Chinese Communist Party (CCP) was formed in 1921 and based its operations in the provincial capital, Changsha.

In the aftermath of World War II, the communists won a long-running civil war, and took power, with Chairman Mao at the helm. The number of deaths resulting from the purges and famines of Mao's subsequent Great Leap Forward and Cultural Revolution are uncertain, but estimates are counted in the tens of millions.

After Mao died in 1976, Deng Xiaoping, successor to The Great Helmsman, said that Mao had been seventy per cent right and thirty per cent wrong. This line has stuck, and it is trotted out every time a foreigner criticises Mao.

Today Changsha is a modern city of two million people. It has a clean, neatly laid-out grid of roads and parks, and a steel-and-glass central business district. However, as with many modern Chinese cities, it felt soulless: a once-sleepy provincial capital, robbed of its character when catapulted into the twenty-first century. The result is a place where I saw a mother stop outside a fifty-storey glass bank. She held her three-year-old son off the floor at arm's length while he emptied his bowels onto the pavement. Donkey-drawn carts plied roads on the outskirts, while waxed Volkswagens with tinted windows cruised the centre. Moneyed professionals in business suits strode smartly past alleyways where the inhabitants still wore the thin, navy-blue worker's tunic of last century's revolution.

We spent a day in a hostel, sitting out the rain and avoiding an over-friendly male nurse who, in his own words, 'taught masturbation in a sperm bank'. I also met Julian, an Irish cyclist bound for home after three years riding the roads of Africa, the Americas, Japan, and Korea. I recognised in him a familiar weariness, but we spoke long into the night over a bottle of *báijiŭ* (rice liquor), and I sensed a contentment. He had evidently pushed himself far beyond what he considered his limit, and yet he was still going, still smiling, and happily rattling off tails of derring-do and cultural quirks from the roads of Africa.

Beyond Changsha, our route took us via Heng Shan, the southernmost and smallest of China's five sacred Taoist mountains. Emperors and pilgrims once journeyed here to hunt and make sacrifices to their vast pantheon of gods. We passed the 1,290-metre peak – little more than a steep, rocky hill – during the first International Taoist Forum, which had drawn thousands of visitors from around the globe. It's a three-hour devotional walk to the temple at the top, but most pilgrims opted for either the minibus or the cable car, both of which ran to the summit.

The next big city was Wuhan, the capital of Hubei province, a vast metropolis, with almost ten million inhabitants. The mile-wide Yangtze ran through the centre, its waters having descended from the Three Gorges Dam, some four hundred miles up-river.

We took a rest day and went for a ride around the city. After an hour happily lost on quaint streets in an art district, we strayed onto a fast-moving motorway. The surging traffic drew us up the incline of a suspension bridge. While cruising, side by side, down the other side at about 25 mph, our handle bars caught. Michi was the first down. He collided hard with the tarmac that raced backwards beneath him. His falling bike knocked the back of mine, and down I went too, my toppled bike kicking up sparks as it scraped to a halt. Thankfully, no speeding bus or car ran us down from behind, and we staggered onto the pavement to assess the damage. Neither of us owned helmets, but we were relatively unscathed: only cuts, bruises, and two broken cameras.

Our bikes were only superficially damaged, and the traffic continued to rush by, as did the pedestrians on the pavement. Not a single person stopped to offer help after our very visible and spectacular accident. In our shaken state, this upset, but didn't entirely surprise, us. Only two weeks earlier, the international press had exploded with the story of a toddler called Yue Yue.

The little girl stumbled into the alleyway outside a market in Guangdong Province and was hit by a slow-moving van, the front wheel running over her two-year-old body. The driver stopped, but quickly drove on, running over her with his back wheel, too. Two minutes later a second vehicle approached and halted. Yue Yue's mangled body was blocking the way. The driver slowly drove over her protruding leg with front and back wheels. Seven minutes after the initial accident, a female street sweeper gathered her up and took her to hospital. The event was captured on a traffic camera. Eighteen passers-by had ignored her bleeding body during the seven minutes she lay there. Yue Yue died eight days later in hospital.

Apparently, there is an obscure feature of Chinese law which deduces that any person helping someone after an accident is somehow responsible and could be liable for damages or medical fees. Assisting someone is seen as an admission of guilt, and there are many stories of bystanders impassively watching preventable tragedies unfold.

The days ran shorter and the nights colder as we progressed north, moving deeper into autumn. The trees combusted into numberless reds, oranges, and yellows, and next year's rice crop was sown: immaculate lines of delicate seedlings, stretching away to the horizon, waiting for the winter freeze. As the temperature dropped, I started wearing socks and zipping up my sleeping bag for the first time in months. We upped the pace and set our sights on Beijing. The fiery hues of autumn sank over the horizon behind us, and we were soon in a land of brown and grey, shot through with China's red flag, which flapped from most roadside buildings.

Rain began again, and Michi's tent collected a puddle each night. His sleeping bag wouldn't fully dry, and neither would his clothes. He remained stoic for a few days before I suggested he take a train to the capital.

'Yes, I was thinking that. But I didn't want to leave you cycling alone.' His consideration warmed me. We waved down a passing bus that would take him to Zhengzhou, where he could catch a train. The driver loaded the bike onto the bus, and Michi hugged me.

'I'll see you in Beijing. There will be girls and beers and I don't know what else waiting for you when you arrive,' he said with a smirk. The bus pulled away.

I put my head down and pedalled hard for the final leg, bypassing cities and pulling hundred-mile days. A ten-mile bridge hoisted me through the mist, high above the enormity of the Yellow River.

On a rainy evening, in a ghost town of unfinished apartment blocks, I hauled my bike off the flooded road and up some flights of stairs. There seemed to be no workers around. On the third floor of a building, as yet without walls, I hung a line for my dripping tent and clothes. There were enough scraps of wood and paper to make a small fire, and I cleared a bed-sized patch in the rubble. I woke in the morning with a few workers gathered around me who were wondering what to do. I said a simple hello and brewed them some green tea before leaving.

The rain stopped. The further north I went, the drier the atmosphere became. Despite the creeping cold, I was enjoying being alone again. With no one to talk to, I had more time to think. Over-thinking had made life hard earlier in the year, but now it seemed a luxury.

What should I do when I reach Beijing? I asked myself, repeatedly. *Should I go home? Do I actually* want *to go home? Deep down, what do I* really *want to do?*

Almost subconsciously, during the time I had spent with Michi, I had begun to feel that my journey was still in its infancy. His upbeat attitude had shown me how to be interested again.

There was so much still to see: Mongolia (*Perhaps I can buy a horse when I reach the grasslands*); the mountains and deserts of the 'stans' in Central Asia; Uzbekistan's fabled city of Samarkand; another visit to Iran (*Maybe I'll see Monireh again*). And Africa: the pyramids; the game-filled savannahs; the ancient Ethiopian churches; the friend's I might make. My mind trilled with an endless string of possibilities. I knew then that I would continue. I had to. The trip was far from over.

I smiled for hours when I realised. I said it aloud to myself while pedalling. 'It's not over! This is just the beginning!'

The years ahead would be challenging, and they would be joyful. At times, they would be tough and lonely. Above all else, they would be interesting, and they would be varied beyond imagination.

And *why* was I doing it? That nagging question. I still didn't have a definitive answer. But it didn't seem to matter anymore. There were hundreds of small reasons:

the savage beauty of Tibet, the boundless space of the Kavir desert, the sweet-smelling Boreal forest, the sunrises, the incomparable highs, Luc and Bruce, thumbless Derek, the Romanian plum farmers, Ash and Leigh, Jarved and Assad, Monireh, the Lissanevitches, Erik the Uighur, my saviour family in Tibet, Clare, Aumnuay, Duong, Trung, and Michi.

I restarted the Russian audio lessons with a view to the former Soviet republics ahead of me. I remembered the excitement of starting those lessons in Malaysia. I had wanted to please her, Valeria, and I had been hurt worse than I thought possible. However, when I thought of her now there was no longer pain. Just a sense of sadness, and of waste.

I would not be moving to Frankfurt. But I *was* free to roam, to do, and to learn. Free to continue following a foolish dream, drunkenly conceived in a Siberian birch forest.

EPILOGUE

On a cold, clear morning, I entered Beijing. I crossed each of the six ring roads and threaded my way through rush-hour traffic to Tiananmen Square. Dressed in new clothes, a grinning, freshly shaven Michi met me under the portrait of Chairman Mao. Crowds of Chinese tourists swelled around us, excited to be visiting the heart of their nation.

I wore socks with my sandals, fingerless gloves, secondhand clothes, and a red handkerchief to keep unruly hair from eyes. I hadn't shaved since Cambodia, and my face was dirty. 18,000 miles of road lay in my wake.

'Welcome to Beijing, Charlie!' Michi said, giving me a hug.

'Thanks! It's good to be here. You look well.'

'I am! You know, I never saw this when we were cycling, but you look absolutely ridiculous!'

Twenty million people went about their lives around us and, at Michi's request, I went about finding a hot shower.

ACKNOWLEDGEMENTS

Firstly, I'd like to thank my parents for their unwavering support and encouragement over the years. You always took an interest, and never doubted me. Likewise to Emily, Harry, Amelia and Johnny. Sadly, my father will never read this book, but it's dedicated to him with all my love.

When embarking on the adventure of writing, I received invaluable guidance from Selina Walker, Jim Holland, and Mark Lucas, for which I'm very grateful. Thank you to Callie Morgigno for reading the first draft, and to Ben Evans for hosting me in Nairobi while I wrote it. Thanks to Denise Cowle for fast and thorough proofreading, and to Anthony Pelly at Rural Maps for the maps.

Countless people looked after me and hosted me during this journey. You are too many to mention, and most of you will never know this book exists, but I remember you all and am deeply grateful.

Wondering what happened next?

The remaining two and a half years of the adventure is now available in the sequel: *On Roads That Echo*

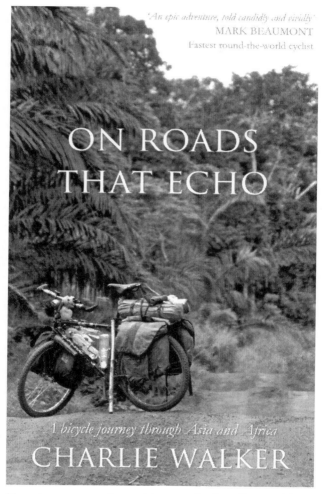

To get your copy, please visit www.charliewalker.org/shop

NOTE FROM THE AUTHOR

If you've enjoyed this book, it would be really helpful and much appreciated if you could leave a review on Amazon.

If you're a fan of audiobooks and would like to *hear* the story as read by the author, both *Through Sand & Snow* and *On Roads That Echo* are now also available on www.audible.com

Through Sand & Snow   *On Roads That Echo*

To find out more about my past and upcoming adventures, please visit www.charliewalker.org

You can also follow me on Instagram and Twitter: @cwexplore

Printed in Great Britain
by Amazon